HOW TO OVERCOME THE BULLY IN YOUR BRAIN

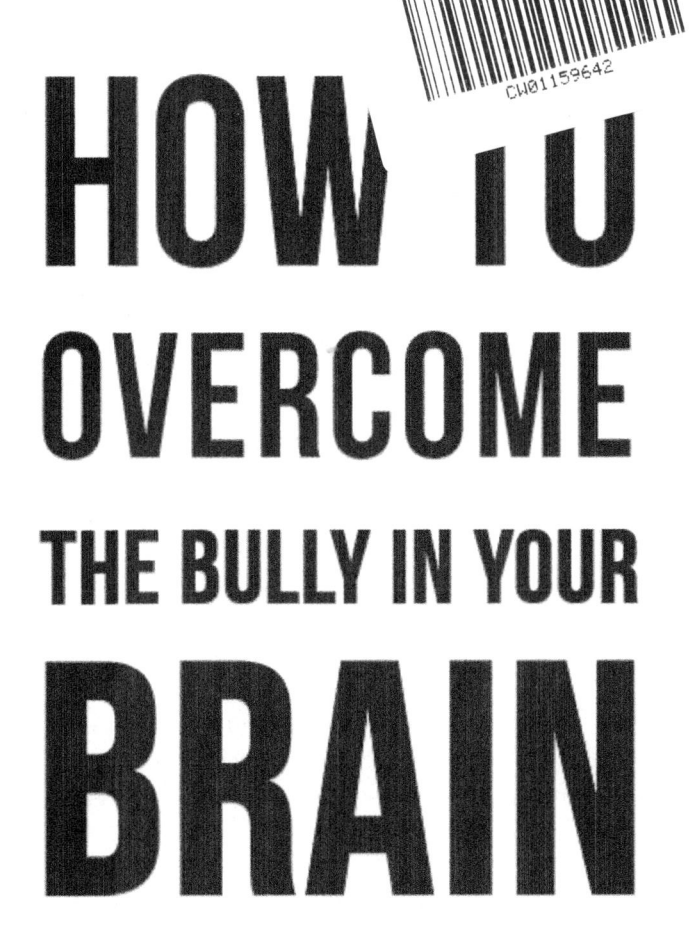

AND ACHIEVE THE LIFE
YOU WANT AND DESERVE

JAMES L. HOLMES

HOW TO OVERCOME THE BULLY IN YOUR BRAIN
*How to Reduce the Symptoms of Depression and Anxiety
and Achieve the Life you Want and Deserve*

James L. Holmes

© 2022– James Holmes and Sue Peckham

Email us at: hello@bullyinyourbrain.co.uk

All rights reserved.
No part of this book may be reproduced or distributed in any form without prior written permission from the author, with the exception of non-commercial uses permitted by copyright law.

No part of this book may be reproduced or transmitted by any means, except as permitted by UK copyright law or the author. For licensing requests, please contact the author at hello@bullyinyourbrain.co.uk.

All rights reserved.
No portion of this book may be reproduced, copied, distributed or adapted in any way, with the exception of certain activities permitted by applicable copyright laws, such as brief quotations in the context of a review or academic work. For permission to publish, distribute or otherwise reproduce this work, *please contact the author at hello@bullyinyourbrain.co.uk.*

References

*You're not what you think you are,
but what you think, you are!*
– William James –

*I wouldn't have seen it if
I hadn't believed it.*
– Marshall McLuhan –

CONTENTS

FORWARD	6
ACKNOWLEDGEMENTS	8
PREFACE	9
STAGE ONE: QUESTION	**12**
1: Introduction	13
2: I'm A Believer	26
3: Belief Comes Easily; Doubt Takes Effort	40
4: What You See Is All We Believe There Is	55
5: Beyond Belief	74
6: Close Encounters Of The Herd Kind	90
7: Just An Illusion	95
8: We Become What We Think About Most Of The Time	103
9: Quit The 'Bs-Bs'	119
10: It's The Thought That Counts	126
11: The Alfred Technique	139
STAGE TWO: AWARENESS	**149**
12: If You Eat Any More, You'll End Up Looking Like One!	150
13: The Bully In The Brain	155
14: Origins Of Change	170
15: I Fought The Law, And The Law Won	180
16: Perceptions And Beliefs	190
17: Time To Take A 'Circuit Breaker'	202
STAGE THREE: INSIGHT	**208**
18: Looking For What We Want To Believe	209
19: A Word To The Wise	224
20: Developing A Growth Mindset – Growth Negligence	238

21: Self-Esteem, Social Anxiety And Self-Sabotage	244
22: The Sky Is Falling	261
23: Fate, Luck And Chance	271
24: Control And Resilience	281
25: If Only Bananas Were Longer!	290
26: Trauma – Hurt People, Hurt People	306
STAGE FOUR: MASTERY	**318**
27: What Are The Chances?	319
28: Don't Worry, Be Happy	329
29: The Elusive Butterfly	343
30: It's About Time!	349
31: Don't Stop Believin'	363
32: The Most Important Question	383
References	393

FORWARD

The fact that you have picked up this book to see if you would like to buy it, or even you may have already bought it, means that you are most probably like me, fascinated by the title, and maybe, like me, a bit of a 'self-help book junkie'. I also suspect, again like me, your bookshelves are full of books of similar genre that you had bought over years in the hope that they would reveal something new to you or give you a perspective on things that was different; I guess always looking for a new 'Road Less Travelled, by M Scott Peck, that you bought many years ago. I also imagine that many of those books sit on your bookshelf only part read; they have been interesting, but in general have only served to reinforce the themes of the great classics and once you realise that they haven't said anything new, you move on the next one.

James Holmes', " How to overcome the bully in your brain and achieve the life you want and deserve', definitely does not fall into this category, it breaks new ground in our understanding of 'who we are and 'why'. At times it makes for uncomfortable reading because it forces us to challenge the very basis of our belief systems, how they were formed and how they can hold you back from leading the life you want live and being the person, you want to be.

In writing the book, James Holmes pulls upon his many years of experience as a psychotherapist at his Hampshire Hypnotherapy and Counselling Centre in the UK. However, in addition to that, the book is extremely well-researched with many references to the fundamental research behind the points he makes, which gives the credibility; making it must read not only, by the ordinary reader, but also by students and practitioners of counselling and psychotherapy.

Every point that James Holmes makes in his book is accompanied by a story, some very personal, making it extremely easy to read and one that is hard to put down.

How to overcome the bully in your brain and achieve the life you want and deserve' will become a classic; not only will it help you understand the problem of the bully in your brain, which we all have to some extent, but it also provides practical techniques we can use to overcome that bully, and, as it says on the cover, achieve the life you want and deserve. I am sure you will enjoy reading the book and could have a big impact on your life.

Geoff Baker MSc CEng FIMechE FIET

ACKNOWLEDGEMENTS

Dedicated to Geoff Baker for his idea and inspiration.

With thanks to Sue, Lara, Natasha, George, Florence, Alan, Josh, Paul, Adam, Mick, Max and all the lovely clients that inspired the writing of this book. Also, not forgetting Bilko – the dog I share with Sue. His unending persistence and resilience in trying to sit between me and my open laptop whilst I was attempting to write this book never failed to astonish me.

PREFACE

*The outer conditions of a person's life will
always be found to reflect their inner beliefs.*
– JAMES ALLEN

THE CONSCIOUS COMPETENCE LADDER

In psychology, there is a concept known as the *four stages of competence*, or the 'conscious competence' learning model. This model relates to the psychological states involved in the process of progressing from incompetence to competence in a skill. Indeed, when we acquire a new skill, we can often experience different emotions at different stages of the learning process.

As we work through the stages of understanding and begin to challenge our limiting beliefs, we will be moving through different levels. As this book is about challenging beliefs and building self-esteem, I have chosen not to opt for the original titles given to the first stage of the learning model, as being called a 'Conscious Incompetent' is not good for anyone's self-worth! Besides, we've just met, and it seems a little rude to call anyone incompetent on their first meeting!

Here then are the new stages of competence used in this book. Each of the four levels relates to an awakening in the understanding and challenging of our beliefs and belief systems.

- **STAGE ONE – QUESTION**
- **STAGE TWO – AWARENESS**
- **STAGE THREE – INSIGHT**
- **STAGE FOUR – MASTERY**

As you work your way through the book you will note that I have used several different analogies for beliefs and belief systems.

The reason for this is quite simply that sometimes one analogy resonates with one individual, where another may not.

Finally, at the beginning of his live seminars, American author and motivational speaker T. Harv Eker introduces his audience to what he calls 'the three most dangerous words in the English language'. What are those three words? They are perhaps the three most limiting words in the English language. They are, of course: 'I know that'. As you work through this book, please be mindful of not falling into the trap of thinking those three most hazardous words. Keep an open mind and embrace the possibility that is before you.

If challenging a belief makes you feel uncomfortable, then perhaps take a moment to recognise and examine where those feelings are coming from. Maybe even ask yourself why challenging a particular belief makes you feel those emotions.

In essence, if you are not living the life you want and deserve, then chances are those three little words may have held you back at some stage. I know I myself have fallen foul of them on occasions in my life. As William Shakespeare once famously wrote, 'The fool doth think he is wise, but the wise man knows himself to be a fool'.

Finally, with regard to teaching others what you have learnt and put into action yourself to change your beliefs, always endeavour to think of yourself as the 'guide and not the guru'. Few of us are the guru; most of us, me included, are still trying to figure it all out for ourselves. Incidentally, it's nice to have you along for the journey – it's going to be quite a ride.

As you work your way through this book you will notice that I have used song titles for the various subheadings. I have opted to stick to more well-known songs rather than some obscure track from a band that you and I have probably never heard of, even when the title fits the topic area perfectly. This book is a work in progress, so I would welcome your song title ideas for the subheadings. You can reach out to me at hello@bullyinyourbrain.co.uk I look forward to hearing your suggestions.

References

Welcome to a new exciting way of thinking and feeling. It's time to overcome the bully in your brain.

James L. Holmes

STAGE ONE

QUESTION

References

CHAPTER ONE

INTRODUCTION

We suffer more in imagination than in reality.
— SENECA

WE ARE OUR BELIEFS!

The poet Edgar Albert Guest once wrote the following beautiful verse:

> *Think happy thoughts! Think sunshine all the day;*
> *Refuse to let the trifling worries stay,*
> *Crowd them with thoughts of laughter from your mind.*
> *Think of the good, forget the bad you find,*

Edgar Albert Guest is right absolutely right, of course. If only it were that easy! If you have had a lifetime of thinking that way, then you won't need what's in this book. If you have struggled, like most of us, then this is the book for you. Welcome on board, put on your seatbelt and let's get started...

If you were to walk down any street in the world and have a conversation with yourself out loud, would passers-by stare at you oddly? Other pedestrians may glance at you in passing with an envious eye, believing perhaps you are the proud owner of some cool new invisible Bluetooth headset. Others maybe would see that there are in fact no headphones in sight, and those passers-by may indeed give you a wide berth. Strange as it may seem at this point, talking to yourself like that can be a good thing! Einstein did it! Children do it often and find it a really useful thing to do. But more on that later in the book.

The paradox of the above situation is that just about everyone talks to themselves all day long, every day. Most of us just don't verbalise this inner dialogue, so it isn't overheard by others. The habitual banter takes place in our conscious thought. You are the sole originator and eavesdropper to it. The problem, though, is how much of that internal dialogue is positive and empowering, and how much is negative, self-deprecating, and limiting in what we think is possible for us? As the Roman Stoic philosopher Seneca once said, 'We suffer more in imagination than in reality'.

Learning how to listen to those thoughts, and to effectively manage them, is at the core of what this book is about. That frustrating self-chatter that many of us have recurrently playing in our heads – perhaps even as you are reading this right now you are thinking or planning what you're having to eat later. Or perhaps you weren't thinking about that, but now you are!

Or, more likely, you may be preoccupied with thoughts such as, 'I wonder if M&S has a sale on yet? I need to get my cousin something for her birthday next week. I don't want to miss it like I did last year; that felt really awkward. I usually never forget birthdays. What is up with me these days?! It must have been the lockdown! I've got lockdown brain! Should I tell her she's put weight on, or will she think I'm being mean? She's really changed since she met Mark; he's not as nice as Tom. Tom was really sweet to her, but she treated him so badly. Oh, I must catch the *I'm a Celebrity* catch-up later. Blimey, I'm tired today! Must have an early night tonight! Gosh, I have so much on this week! I never seem to have enough time, I'm always so busy, no one understands how much I have to do every day!' ... and so on...

You get the gist of what I am saying: *that* voice! The one that never seems to cease and is with you every moment of every day. The one that will be with you until the day you bite the big one! Wouldn't it be nice to finally be the Master of It, rather than it dictating to you what it thinks? After all, if a friend said to you some of the hurtful and negative things that you have allowed it to say to you, well, you wouldn't hang round that friend very much. In fact, if they 'FaceTimed' you, you'd probably pretend you were just about to go onto an urgent Zoom call.

References

Sometimes that voice turns on the music player and will repeatedly play a song or a theme from an advert. It can appear that no matter how much you try to get that 'catchy' jingle out of your head, you just can't. On occasions it can feel like the voice and the music player are working in cahoots in a bid to control your mind. Fortunately, there are proven techniques to manage the meddling music player as well – more about this in the final chapter of this book.

Take a moment now to ask yourself how you hear your inner discourse? Indeed, try the following. Quietly say to yourself in your head the following words, 'You become what you think about most of the time'. Now say those exact same words but shout them out in your head. How did they change? Of course, we can't control the volume of our internal voice. It's always at the same level. But did the shouted version sound more stressed, or more strained perhaps?

Ask yourself, is the voice you hear your voice as you hear it when you talk? Is the tone and timbre the same as yours? When you think of others, do you hear their voice or your own? Is the voice in your head that of a supportive friend, an ambivalent parent, a jealous rival? Or perhaps the voice is that of a helpless child? Do different voices materialise in your head depending on the situation? When you think of others, do you hear their voice or your own? Indeed, have you ever given much thought to the voice in your head before, other than wondering how to manage it better?

Interestingly there seem to be five ways we can categorise our inner experiences:

1. Inner speaking – our inner narrating voice.
2. Inner seeing – images of things you've seen in real life or imaginary visuals.
3. Feelings – such as happiness or anger.
4. Sensory awareness – like being aware of the feeling of water under your feet.

5. Unsymbolised thinking – in essence, a thought that doesn't manifest as words or images but is undoubtedly present in your mind.

PURE IMAGINATION

Interestingly, we don't all have the capacity to picture images in our minds. Take a moment now to close your eyes and picture the front door of your house. Now imagine placing your hand on the door handle, opening the door, and then walking through it. On the other side you are greeted by a beautiful, sandy beach. Now imagine walking on that beach while gazing at the sunset. Now open your eyes and ask yourself the following: How clear is the image that you saw in your mind? What colour was your front door? What type of sand was on the beach? What was the water like? Did you visualise the door and the beach, or did you just know that is what they look like? Similarly, do you know what a car or a bike looks like without having to actually picture it in your head?

Most people can readily conjure images inside their head – what we think of as our mind's eye. Amazingly, it is estimated that 1 in 50 of us has a different way of seeing things in our minds. This particular way of seeing is known as aphantasia – essentially not being able to picture something in one's mind. Individuals with aphantasia are often also unable to recall sounds, smells or sensations of touch. Some also report experiencing prosopagnosia, the inability to recognise faces. Having aphantasia can often mean not being able to recall images of familiar objects or people. Perhaps surprisingly, people with aphantasia appear not to have any impaired creativity. In fact, many 'aphantasics' are successful in creative professions and have ways to compensate for their lack of a mind's eye.

It is believed that approximately 60–65% of us are regarded as 'visual thinkers' (also called visual/spatial learners or picture thinkers). Visual thinkers often describe what they see in their mind's eye as a series of pictures. Similarly, visual thinkers also have the ability to see words as a series of pictures.

Great visual thinkers throughout history include Nikola Tesla, Thomas Edison, Albert Einstein, and the chess grandmaster Bobbie Fischer. Fischer claimed that he could see all of the pieces on the chess board even when it wasn't in front of him. Equally impressive was the fact he was able to recall every move in a chess game after the match had ended. Albert Einstein often said words failed him when trying to describe the images in his head. Here lies the dilemma for many visual thinkers: how do you get those amazing creative visual images out of your head and into the minds of others?

Are you a visual thinker? Do you sometimes find that you can recall people's faces but can't easily remember their names? Perhaps when you think of the past the images in your mind's eye are incredibly clear. Are you able to picture perfectly how much space you have in the back of your car so that you can fill it without a spare inch of room? If so, then you may be more of a visual thinker.

Finally, when it comes to determining what type of thinker you are, imagine for a moment that you are in the street, attempting to find an address. You stop a passer-by and ask for directions. How do you prefer to have the location explained to you? Do you prefer the verbal explanation, do you prefer it written on a piece of paper or do you prefer to be shown it on a map?

WHERE IS MY MIND?

It is estimated that we have a staggering 60–80,000 thoughts a day. So, in simple terms, the issue around what and how we think is this: we create our reality from our mental chatter, and our mental chatter is created predominantly from our belief systems. But here's the rub: 95% of the thoughts we have every day are exactly the same as we have had the day before, and the day before that, and so on. Is it any wonder that we sometimes hold the belief that bringing about a change in our lives is hard? If we change our beliefs, we change our thinking. If we change our thinking, we change those thoughts, and in doing so we are not limited by the repetitive 95% paradigm.

Think about a time when you have strolled into a restaurant, florist or perhaps a coffee shop, and the strong aroma you experienced was almost overpowering to your senses. In no time at all, it can appear as if there is no distinctive smell at all. The powerful aroma that greets can soon feel like it has dissipated. It is still there, but we have swiftly become accustomed to it, and it no longer has an effect on our sense of smell. This phenomenon is known as sensory adaptation. It occurs when our bodies' sensory receptors are exposed to a particular stimulus such as loud noise, high temperatures or strong scents for a long enough period that the receptors decrease their sensitivity to the stimuli, making them less noticeable. In some ways, this is what can happen with our thoughts. Day after day, we become accustomed to having the same types of thought patterns – many of them mirroring the same habits and the same beliefs we hold. Like the ambrosial restaurant odour, it is not until we exit the establishment to go out to get something from our car that we once again enjoy the redolent aroma upon our return through the door. In many ways, that is what this book will be teaching you to do with your thoughts: to step outside of yourself and be the observer of the repeated pattern of thoughts that most of us have been having for perhaps the majority of our adult lives.

Of course, this inner self-dialogue is influenced greatly by our powerful, habitual subconscious minds. It reveals our innermost thoughts, doubts, questions, ideas and our biases. Self-talk, naturally, can be both positive and negative. It can be encouraging, creative and exciting, but it can also be annoying, limiting and upsetting. Much of our self-talk is dependent on our belief systems – particularly damaging are our self-limiting beliefs. This inner voice is also the culprit that informs us that we aren't good enough or we can't do or be something. Who are we to think we could ever do that thing or be that person? Put it out of your mind, someone like me could never achieve something like that!

VOICES IN MY HEAD

Throughout history, assured individuals have believed that this inner voice was something mystical, akin to a divine spirit or oracle. The Greek philosopher Socrates, for example, gave the voice in his head a special name. He called it his *daimon* or *daemon*. He believed that this voice warned and prevented him from doing something wrong or harmful to himself.

It appears that the majority of the time, this *daimon* would warn Socrates not to act on something. Some sources suggest it also sometimes prompted him to positive action. Socrates felt it took the form of an inner voice or non-vocal nudge. The guide never told Socrates what to do. It only indicated when Socrates was *not* to do something. Over time, Socrates learnt to listen to this inner divine voice. He acted in service to it. Today we would think of this *daimon* as much like our powerful subconscious mind. Perhaps then, like Socrates, we should pay more heed to what it is nudging us in the direction of.

Psychologists have long believed that there are two independent and permanently switched on facets to our brain. One part is the emotional side; the other is the rational side. New York University psychologist Jonathan Haidt uses an insightful analogy to explain both. He describes the emotional side as being like an elephant, and the rational side as the rider on the magnificent animal. Outwardly the rider of the elephant looks like he or she is in charge, but when there's a disagreement between the elephant and the rider, the elephant generally wins the day. Essentially, when you manage and regulate your emotions well, you will feel very much more in control of your own elephant.

This book will show you how to not only change your inner dialogue but have it working to your advantage, controlling and indeed directing our proverbial elephant so to speak. It will demonstrate to you how to question what you believe to the extent that you will question many of the choices and decisions you make every day. The majority of the time, we are completely unaware of the beliefs we hold, particularly the self-limiting ones. They seem to be just part of who we are, as if they have always been there. This book will help you to bring them to the surface, challenge them and possibly eliminate them for good.

For some it will be like stepping out of a mental prison – a psychological penned enclosure that others unwittingly placed us into. You can choose to remain there, or you can take the brave step to open the lock and see what great things await you on the other side. Welcome to a new alternative reality! A reality that you can begin to bend to suit your wishes and desires.

LITTLE LIES

It's a fortuitous coincidence that in the English language the word 'belief' has, at its heart, the word 'lie'. This book will assist in challenging these 'belief' systems and patterns of thinking, and in doing so we ultimately free ourselves from some faulty subconscious programming. By the end of this book, my hope is that you will come to realise that many of the unconscious beliefs you have held for so long have not been serving you. That potentially they are, in fact, misrepresentations of reality. I am of course not implying that they have been maliciously taught to you, but that by the nature of how beliefs are handed from generation to generation, they have continued unquestioned and unhampered. I sincerely hope that by the time you complete this book, you can be the individual who breaks the cycle and challenges those unsupportive and limiting beliefs. Think of life as a relay race in which we pass the baton to our offspring, as the baton has been passed to you. It's time to decide if you want to pass the baton on in its present form.

Indeed, how important are our beliefs? Do you believe you react to the world as it actually is? Or to the world as you perceive it to be? Whilst we generally trust our beliefs, and they usually serve us well, they can sometimes be very susceptible to inaccuracy and distortions. To understand why this is so, it is important to examine how they are formed in the first place. And, in doing so, discover how we can shift them. Also, how we can, over time, even overwrite them with new and more empowering programmes. Together we will gradually place those limiting beliefs under a microscope. We will question their origin and scrutinise their validity, and we will begin to challenge the ones that are holding us back, preventing us from achieving the life we truly want and deserve.

GENTLE ON MY MIND

In psychology, a belief is typically defined as an internal mental state otherwise known as a mental model. The term belief has become somewhat muddied over the years, and perhaps even overused. Often we can default to religious, political, philosophical, cultural and even superstitious beliefs when we think of the concept of beliefs. For this reason, I have chosen to continue to use the term beliefs in this book, but request the reader associates it more with the concept of a cognitive concept of mental models, rather than the more familiar associations that many of us have.

Belief systems (*mental models*) are the foundations of how we view and experience our world. We all have thousands of beliefs that strongly affect our world view. Things such as personal experiences, genes and environment, personal reflections, the kinds of cultural influences we are subjected to and a lot of other aspects play roles in and affect our world view, so people in India have a different world view to people in Sweden. But, interestingly according to research carried out in this field, individuals with the same cultural background have shown definite differences in personalities and world views. This suggests just how important our individual beliefs are in shaping our distinct and individualised personalities.

I would hazard a guess that if you were to give some time over to thinking about some of the limiting beliefs you have, you might only be able to bring to mind a handful. Or more accurately – the conscious ones, the limiting beliefs that perhaps you hold onto willingly as you feel they have served you well up to now. Sometimes it can feel uncomfortable to be shifted too far away from who we believe we are, and the constituent parts of our personality and self-identity as they are so much a part of who we are, we are virtually blind to their presence. Just like the choice of clothes we wear and the music we enjoy listening to, they are part of who we are as individuals. It is as if they have always been there. In reality, they have either been learnt through repetition, or by the powerful suggestion of a loved one or even an authority figure. Naturally anything that has been learnt, even though it may be unconscious, can be unlearnt through the same method. Like the Christmas tree lights that many of us take down from our loft annually and find ourselves having to untangle, the roots of our self-limiting beliefs can also be unravelled. As author Marianne Williamson writes, 'Nothing binds you except your thoughts; nothing limits you except your fear; and nothing controls you except your beliefs'.

This book is concerned with beliefs and belief systems and how they form the building blocks of our day-to-day thoughts and actions, both consciously and subconsciously. When a belief is subconscious, it has very much become a habit, i.e. very much out of our conscious awareness and therefore our perceived control.

How many times have you tried to change some area of your life and failed and then thought and perhaps even vocalised such beliefs as, 'I have no willpower, I'm so weak willed, I always let myself down', and so on? Well, the cold hard truth is quite simply this: whenever you have tried to change something in life and failed, it's not about you personally, it's about your habits. More specifically, it's about the reptilian part of your incredible brain. This portion of your brain is the specific part that is involved with our primitive drives – things such as thirst, hunger, sexuality and territoriality. Our habits are also linked to our reptilian brains, as is our Procedural Brain, the part of our brain where we have our motor skills, our long-term memory and the part that 'just knows how to do things'. So, when you've tried to change before and failed, it has nothing to do with weakness, it simply has to do with knowing how to work with your brain. In essence, in life we don't get what we want, we get our habits, and the habits originate from the reptilian part of our brains.

The reason we create habits, or rather the reptilian part of the brain creates habits, is ingenious. Just imagine that every time you wanted to drive your car or clean your teeth you had to learn how to do it from scratch. How inefficient and exhausting would that be in our day-to-day lives?

The astonishing thing is that just about everything you have in your life is a result of your habits. If you have good health, for the most part, that is a habit. If you have poor health, for the most part, that is a habit as well, and so on and so forth for other areas of your life.

IN MY HEAD

Perhaps unsurprisingly, the beliefs you have about yourself can drive your long-term behaviour. If you have moderate to high self-esteem, then you are more likely to persist in the face of difficulties. You are more likely to link your actions to your self-identity, and by focusing on small actions that you can carry out every day, you move towards your aspirations and form new habits. Identity-based habits can be incredibly powerful things, and of course your identity and your self-esteem are underpinned by the beliefs you have about yourself and your world.

You can force yourself into eating healthily or exercising two or three times a week for a little while, but if you don't shift your underlying identity, then it's hard to stick to any long-term changes.

Most of us start by focusing on appearance- or performance-based goals such as 'I want to lose 10 pounds' or 'I want to start my own business'. But these can be surface-level changes. At the core of behaviour change and building better habits is your identity. So, when you change your beliefs, you change your identity; for example, the type of person that you believe that you are, and what you deserve. When you do this, it's easier to change your actions. Again, often in life we don't get what we want, we get our habits, and our habits are formed from our subconscious beliefs about who we are. Change our beliefs and we change our identity.

Often, we will passionately fight to maintain our beliefs, even in the light of contradictory evidence – a phenomenon known as 'belief perseverance'. Belief perseverance typically occurs when we base our beliefs on information that we find logical, compelling or attractive in some way. Therefore, even when beliefs are seemingly disconfirmed by new evidence, the foundation for what we believe may still exist and can be reignited at any time. Sometimes, not only do we want to believe something, we *need* to believe it, as not holding on to a particular belief can make us uncomfortable. For example, if we believe we are not musical, but are forced through peer pressure to sing at a party or at karaoke, holding on to this belief allows us to confidently announce after the performance 'I told you I couldn't sing!' – almost to protect our self-esteem and our self-identity. Perhaps your inner self-talk is saying something like 'I know I am not musical; I don't have a musical bone in my body, it runs in my family, none of us are musical – other than my great granddad, he played the organ in church, he was musical! But not me, I couldn't rub two crotchets together musically' ... and so on! This type of rationale is beautifully described by author Elizabeth Wurtzel in her book *Prozac Nation*: 'The voices in my head, which I used to think were just passing through, seem to have taken up residence'.

Often, even without even realising it, we continue to seek out evidence that supports our beliefs. There is more about belief perseverance later in this book, where we will also examine the concept of cognitive dissonance; in essence the uncomfortable feeling we get when we try to maintain two opposing beliefs.

SUMMARY

This chapter is an introduction to the book itself. It discusses the internal voice that we all have and asks us, 'How empowering is this voice?'. We spend such a large portion of our lives narrating to ourselves and if this speech is not as positive as we would like it to be, or is in fact negative and self-deprecating, it can have a large impact on our thoughts and beliefs. The core lesson from this book is to learn how to listen to and manage the thoughts that we tell ourselves. The chapter looks at what style of thinker you are – visual or not – and how this can influence your beliefs. As 95% of our thoughts are a repeat of thoughts we have had on previous days, it is easy to see how our belief systems become engrained in our heads. This in turn shows us that if we change our thoughts, we can change our beliefs. We will come to learn how these beliefs that we hold, and may have held for a number of years, may not be beneficial to us anymore and how they are just a force of habit. These beliefs make up our personal identity and form all of our day-to-day thoughts and actions. This book will encourage you to step outside these habits and to view yourself as an outsider, as an observer of your repeated thought patterns.

CHAPTER TWO

I'M A BELIEVER

Your attitude is like a box of crayons that colour your world. Constantly colour your picture grey, and your picture will always be bleak. Try adding some bright colours to the picture by including humour, and your picture begins to lighten up.
– ALLEN KLEIN

Our beliefs can be divided into two distinct types. Core beliefs are beliefs that we have actively thought about, which form the foundations of our thinking. The other beliefs are what I like to think of as 'brick beliefs'. These are the beliefs we have 'picked up' as we have journeyed through life and often have not given that much thought to.

Brick beliefs

We tend not to interrogate these beliefs too much. These brick beliefs can greatly influence our behaviours and actions, often without us really knowing why they are being influenced. I see them as being akin to the bricks in a wall. The cement in this wall is the need to believe them. Brick beliefs are more often than not bound together to form a stronger overall wall of beliefs, a belief structure or system if you will. Imagine a young boy who believes he's not good at art. To him, that limiting belief links pretty much everything to do with art. It encompasses drawing, painting, sculpture or just doing a painting by numbers – he believes he has no ability. Art is just something he's not skilled at and will never be good at. It's not that he doesn't like looking at a work of art, it's just that people like him will never be good at it. Art is for other people. Using the brick analogy, I am pretty sure there would be other bricks linked to his 'art' brick, such as making things with your hands, perhaps woodwork, design and textiles, or even using the computer for media and for editing photos. Certainly, anything linked to the potentially uncomfortable feelings he has felt whilst doing art in school.

As another example, if you hold fast to the belief that you could never start your own business, then chances are you hold other linked 'brick beliefs' such as 'bad things always happen to me, if I start my own business it almost certainly will fail'. You may also hold associated beliefs such as 'I'm no good at speaking to people' and 'I'd never make a good leader'. Self-Limiting beliefs are simply assumptions we make about our reality. These assumptions come from our perceptions and our life experiences. They are aligned with our very identities.

The good news, however, is that when you start to knock a few bricks down, the others can begin to tumble quite easily. Picture a child who has the following thought: 'Wow, I can play the drums! I got a great reaction from it in class today, and that made me feel good. People seem to like what I do, perhaps I can read aloud in class after all, then, and maybe join the drama club!' All of a sudden, the bricks start to tumble. Of course, as an adult we have more defences around our belief systems and as a result they can take more cajoling to break down, particularly when they are core beliefs.

Core beliefs are more like boulders with reinforced concrete and a machine gun nest – just in case anyone dares to threaten them. This book is primarily concerned with the brick beliefs – those beliefs that are there which we have never questioned, we feel we just know what they embody. Only when we have weakened the brick wall and chiselled away at some of the cement can we begin to tackle the more resilient and troublesome core beliefs.

More often than not, there is a feeling of 'rightness' about our beliefs. It is as if our beliefs are on a spectrum, some we can let go of rather easily, whilst others we will fight for, and we can go to great lengths to reject something that contradicts what we 'know' we are right to believe. In many ways, it can seem as if we don't get to choose our beliefs, but one day we discover we have them – to the extent that we can wonder what the genesis was of a particular belief, or group of beliefs. Beliefs, or perhaps more accurately belief systems, provide us the 'mental scaffolding' for appraising our environments. They help us to explain new observations and construct a shared meaning of the world. Beliefs can apply to present and future events, as well as the past.

YOU'RE A HARD HABIT TO BREAK

One thing is for sure: our habits are more related to beliefs than the action itself. Our beliefs are part of who we are. They are part of our motivation for doing specific activities and tasks. For example, a personal trainer doesn't have to get up the motivation to exercise because it's part of who he or she is. A vegetarian doesn't have to remind themselves not to eat meat, it is just part of their identity. Similarly, a parent doesn't have to keep reminding themselves to be a parent and look after their offspring, it's just who they are. When we take on a new identity, our belief systems can adapt to that new identity.

At its core, this book is not about challenging a belief that you are consciously aware of; it is about revealing the beliefs that underpin many of the other beliefs you have. Using our brick analogy, these would be the bricks located nearer the bottom of the wall. In many ways, the beliefs we readily recognise are seldom the ones that are creating the greatest problem for us – it's often the beliefs that we have taken for granted, the ones that just run almost as lines of code in the background. These are the devilish troublemakers, and they need to be rooted out.

References

How much time do you spend thinking about events from the past? If you are devoting the majority of your thought time to past experiences and this is reflected in your inner self-talk, then your thoughts are reflecting your beliefs from the past, not your present reality. This programme will assist you in living more in the present and, in doing so, will allow you to find a calmer, more resilient and more optimistic mindset.

As a therapist who works often with clients wishing to lose weight or quit smoking, the beliefs around our habits frequently come into conversation. Often clients believe that they are unable to form new habits, or at least not as quickly as they would like to be able to. There are many myths around 'habit changing' that have propagated for many years, often stemming from leaders in the field of personal development. Perhaps the most famous belief around habit change comes from the brilliant Maxwell Maltz, who claimed it took 21 days to change a habit. Maltz was a world-renowned, pioneering plastic surgeon, spending most of his adult life in New York, where he established a reconstructive cosmetic surgery practice. During his time there, he wrote many books including *New Faces, New Futures* (1936) and the seminal *Psycho Cybernetics* (*1960*), a book that focused on using visualisation to achieve one's goals. Maltz believed that self-image is the cornerstone of all the changes that take place in an individual. He maintained that if one's self-image is unhealthy or faulty, all of a person's efforts will end in failure.

Fascinatingly, what Maltz began to observe in his plastic surgery patients was a distinctive pattern. He noticed that it took on average about 21 days before the recipient of the plastic surgery began to get used to seeing their new face. Similarly, when a patient had to have a limb amputated, Maltz found that the patient would sense a phantom limb for about 21 days. These observations prompted Maltz to re-evaluate his own adjustment period to changes and new behaviours, and he noticed that he also took about 21 days to form a new habit. In the decades that followed, Maltz's work influenced a whole swathe of 'self-help' professionals. The original claim by Maltz that new habits take a minimum of 21 days to form was lost in favour of the much better sounding 'It takes 21 days to form a new habit' model.

Over the years as a therapist, I have heard the 21-day rule quoted by clients I have been working with many hundreds of times. Indeed, hearing it quoted often reminds me how, if enough people quote something enough times, everyone else starts to believe it. In fact, it's remarkable how often the 21-day model is quoted as if it is a statistical, well-researched fact. It makes perfect sense why the '21 days' myth would seep into pop psychology. It's easy to understand, and the time frame appears achievable to most of us. Who wouldn't like the idea of changing your life in just 3 weeks?

So, the question is, how long does it take to form a habit? And perhaps more importantly, how long does it take to break the bad habits we have? Researcher Phillippa Lally and her colleagues from University College London wanted to better understand this question. They examined how long it took, on average, for a group of people to form a new habit in their life, such as going for a daily run or eating a piece of fruit every day. According to the study of 96 people over a 12-week period, it took at least 2 months, or about 66 days, on average to create new habit. Each person chose one new habit for the 12 weeks and reported each day on whether or not they carried out the behaviour and how automatic the behaviour felt. One of the most useful and positive observations the researchers unearthed was that that missing one opportunity to perform the new habit behaviour did not materially affect the habit formation process. In other words, it was possible to skip or forget a day and still successfully build that new habit.

Another fascinating aspect of the study was a marked variation in how long habits took to form for individuals. It took anywhere from 18 days to 254 days to form a new habit for those who took part in this study. The researchers also noted that one subgroup took much longer than the others to form their habits, perhaps suggesting some people are 'habit-resistant'. They also observed, perhaps quite obviously, some types of habits may well take much longer to develop. As you'd imagine, drinking a daily glass of water became automatic very quickly, whereas the habit of running for 15 minutes before dinner required significantly more time and dedication to build.

So, after 66 days had passed, a simple habit might be an autopilot subconscious behaviour, but as the research showed, it could take as long as 8 and a half months for more difficult habits to take hold. The upshot from this research is that for some of us habits take time to form, but this mustn't dissuade you from trying to retain a new habit. Whilst it can take at least 3 months to form a habit, perhaps the most important lesson from this is what Maxwell Maltz asserted about habits. Again, Maltz believed that self-image is in fact the cornerstone of all the changes that can potentially take place. The success we enjoy in our lives, or conversely the lack thereof, is directly related to the nature of our habits. Habits which themselves are a product of our beliefs. It stands to reason that to enjoy permanent, positive change in our life, you must challenge and change your negative beliefs. In fact, changing beliefs is at the very core of habit change. Again, if one's self-image is not healthy and resilient, then regardless of how much effort and willpower is expended on behaviour change, one's efforts will most likely end in failure. Use what we examine in this book to confront your belief systems and improve your self-image and self-esteem – doing so will make the creation of new habits even easier.

When it comes to bringing about a change in your life, try not to berate yourself if a habit has not stuck as quickly as you would have hoped. Doing so can understandably impact on your self-esteem. Remember that none of us is perfect and, as Lally's research showed, making a mistake once or twice has no measurable impact on your long-term habits. Give yourself permission to make mistakes and develop strategies for getting back on track again quickly. Try not to think of it as starting from the beginning again. Know that life isn't a race to the finish – it's the journey through life where the most fun is to be had. Embracing longer timelines can help us realise that habits are a process and not events in themselves. Understanding this from the beginning makes it easier to manage our expectations and commit to making those small but powerful incremental daily improvements.

The brain adapts and changes shape according to a very simple rule: neurons that fire together, wire together. These changes are down to neuroplasticity, a term used to describe the brain's malleability – its ability to change and adapt as a result of our experiences. So, if you repeatedly do one activity followed by another, then those two experiences become linked over time in your brain. Each time you do those things together, you further reinforce and strengthen that link. The connections become myelinated, meaning that the tendrils are insulated, and the signals travel down them faster.

ONE WAY OR ANOTHER

Small changes can make a huge difference over a long period of time. Each day, you're either getting better or conversely getting worse. You don't have to make huge changes today to see massive progress over the next year. You only have to focus on getting a little bit better every day. This simple technique is known as the 1% Rule.

In simple terms, if we focus on making something 1% better every day for a year, then by the end of the year we will be 37 times better at that thing. In sports, for example, the 1% Rule states that over time the majority of recognition in a given sport will accumulate to the people and teams that maintain a 1% advantage over the competition. The good news is that you don't need to be twice as good to get twice the results. You just need to be slightly better.

In 1998, the underachieving men's eight British rowing team led by Ben Hunt-Davis set themselves the goal of winning an Olympic Gold Medal in just 2 years. Ben and his team maintained a beautifully simple mantra when it came to achieving this goal. They developed a whole new way of working and began challenging everything they did with the question: 'will it make the boat go faster?' As a result of this approach, Ben Hunt-Davis and his crew won a gold medal at the Sydney Olympics in 2000.

References

Many of us are familiar with *Pareto's Principle*, perhaps better known as the 80/20 rule, which states that 20% of any effort will usually provide 80% of the results. In 1906, Italian economist Vilfredo Pareto noted that 80% of Italy's land was owned by 20% of the people and discovered that this 80/20 principle can be seen in just about all areas of our lives. For example:

- 80% of stress is caused by 20% of stressors.
- 80% of sleep quality occurs in 20% of sleep.
- 80% of grief is caused by 20% of people in your life.
- 20% of foods cause 80% of the weight gain. The list goes on…

Noteworthy with regard to delivering change in our lives is that it appears that 80% of success is due to our thinking, our mindset, our beliefs, and our emotions. The remaining 20% is actually down to the strategies used to bring about those changes. In other words, working on your mindset and your beliefs will have a considerably more positive effect on change than the strategies you utilise. Reinforcing once again what Maxwell Maltz claimed.

THE HEAT IS ON

In his book *How Will You Measure Your Life?*, Harvard Business School professor Clayton Christensen makes this powerful statement: 'It's easier to hold your principles 100 percent of the time than it is to hold them 98 percent of the time'. Similarly, author and motivational speaker Jack Canfield proclaims '99% is a Bitch: 100% is a Breeze'.

For example, if you're only 95% committed to losing weight or getting fit, in every future situation you're in, you have to ask yourself, 'Is this one of those days when I am trying to lose weight and eat healthily?'. The very fact you had to ask yourself this question means that losing weight and getting fit is not part of your self-identity yet. If this is the case, then you can very easily experience some cognitive dissonance in the heat of the moment. In other words, you cannot hold two opposing beliefs at the same time. Your internal dialogue is in conflict, and you go back and forth in your mind about what you're going to do. Is today a healthy eating day, for example? This 'push-and-pull' decision-making process can lead to decision fatigue and a weakening of willpower. In many cases, more often than not, you probably end up giving in to any temptation, particularly if you are influenced by a cajoling friend or partner. Indeed, the influence of the social situations in which we find ourselves can often be more powerful than our internal desires, particularly if our self-identity is not 100% aligned with that of a person who is getting fit and healthy.

As you begin to challenge your belief systems and your thinking, it is important to remember to commit to it 100%. There is strong evidence to show that committing to something and making it part of your identity makes it so much easier to follow. Indeed, when we are 100% committed to something, it becomes part of who we are – it's part of our identity. As a result, it can then be significantly easier to commit to something than if you were only 95% committed to it. You rarely have to make any decisions about whether you will pursue it or not. You just do, it's who you are.

For example, if you're a vegetarian or vegan you don't have to think too much about it. It's not as if you get home from a shopping trip and accidentally discover bacon in your basket. If you're an animal lover and see an animal injured on the side of the road, how much dedication and commitment does it take to stop and help the poor helpless creature? None of course, it's part of who you are.

Imagine for a moment that you are required to take an important exam on a certain date. You recognise that in order to do so you need to study for a certain amount of time, and you decide to study at least several hours each day. This becomes your 100% commitment. Let's imagine for a moment then that you are suddenly tempted to do something else, such as go to out with friends, see a show or go to a sporting event. Do you stick with your study commitment, or do something else? If you are truly 100% committed, then there is no temptation at all. Indeed, you don't see failure as an option. You briefly evaluate the options, recognise your commitment and stick to it. As Michael Jordan

References

brilliantly puts it, 'Once I made a decision, I never thought about it again'.

The difference between 99% and 100% might on the surface seem small, but as you pursue any worthwhile goal, it can mean the difference between success and failure. Imagine if the airline was committed to only a 99.9% safety record for their fleet – how safe would you feel flying? That 0.1%, as small as it may seem, can create conflict in your thinking. If it is left to dominate it will steal your drive, energy and enthusiasm. A 100% commitment on the other hand will make all of your decisions easy. In many scenarios, a 100% commitment is a breeze.

Stick to what we examine in this book with that 100% resolve, make it part of who you are, and the results will speak for themselves. In fact, in doing so you will be rewiring your brain. Thanks to neuroplasticity, the person you are today will not be the person you are in just a few short months. Remember, neurons that fire together, wire together.

Take a moment to picture many years from now, when you have become the person you want to be. You will have a new personality, a new way of thinking and, in many ways, a new brain ... literally! You will be wired differently, wired for success, wired to look for opportunities, wired to be happier in your day-to-day life.

Similar to the 1% Rule is the Japanese philosophy known as Kaizen. The translation of Kaizen is 'change for the better'. It is a philosophy that focuses on the processes of continual improvement. Kaizen sees improvement in productivity as a gradual and methodical process, with small changes to see long-term results. Originally pertaining to the practices of car manufacturer Toyota, the strategy has been successfully adapted to the business world, and more recently the self-improvement field. In the book *The Toyota Way* by Jeffrey Liker, Liker explains the use of Kaizen in productivity, focusing on 'baby steps', the small changes that add up to big long-term changes. Remember to adopt this Kaizen philosophy when challenging yoir thinking, to bring about the changes you want in your life.

BAD DECISIONS

When it comes to making decisions as individuals, we are all pretty poor at making good ones. One study established that we will make an incredible 773,618 decisions over a lifetime, and that we will come to regret a staggering one-fifth of them. Often, we tend to agonise over our choices and, once we've made up our minds, we're often not happy with our final decision. In addition, we often can spend up to 9 minutes considering every outcome before we commit ourselves to one choice. Interestingly, whilst 54% of the people surveyed stated that they considered themselves to be relatively decisive, 39% of that number claimed that their confidence in their decision started to waiver as they progressed throughout their day. In addition, some 55% of the people surveyed said that they would actually prefer it if someone else made their decisions for them.

Our fear of failure can prevent us from taking chances, trying something new and thinking outside of the box. We are often fearful of making a wrong decision, believing that failure is simply not an option. When we examine fast and slow thinking systems in the next chapter of this book, we will hopefully begin to learn to make better decisions based on our new paradigms and belief systems.

JUST AN ILLUSION

Before we fully dive in, let's take a few moments to have a look at the image below. Now consider the following: is the colour of block with the A on the same or different to the block below it with B on written on it?

References

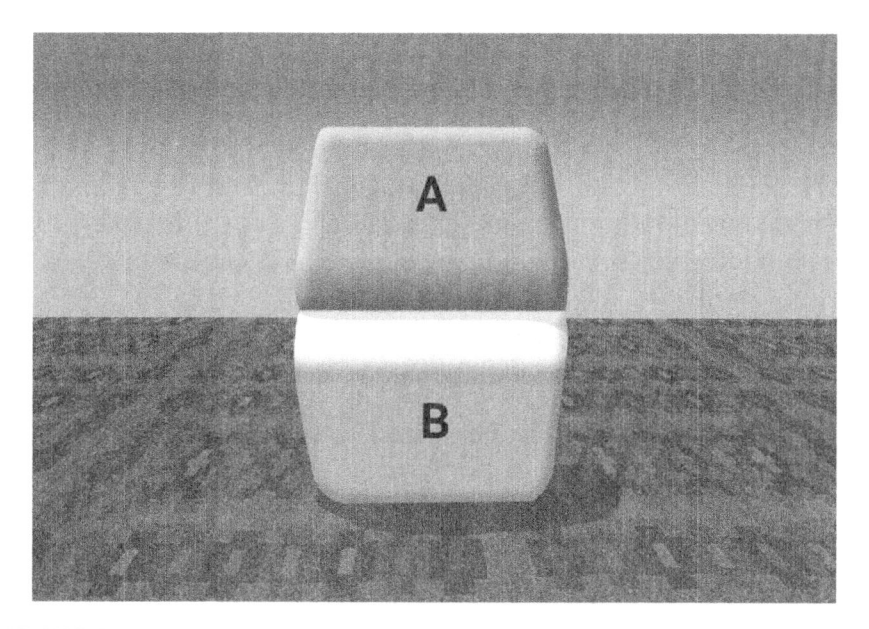

FIGURE A.

Most people would answer (unless they had seen the illusion before of course) that the colours of A and B are clearly different. The perhaps surprising answer is that A and B are in actual fact exactly the same colour. If you don't believe me, then you are most certainly not alone – understandably the vast majority of people when presented with this image would swear that they are indeed different colours. Have a look at the image at the end of this book to see how your brain has been tricked by the shading in the image.

So, what does a surprising optical illusion have to do with beliefs and belief systems? Well, it's very much about our perceptions. Our brain cannot process the millions of pieces of information we receive every second of every day, so it has to make judgements based on previous experiences, to make sense of what we are experiencing. In the optical illusion above, the shading between the two blocks has tricked your brain into thinking these are two distinct colours when, in fact, they are exactly the same. How often then do we accept something without applying some critical thinking to consider if a belief is based in truth, or do we maintain a belief because it suits us at that particular moment in time? As Wilfred Trotter once brilliantly averred, 'If we watch ourselves honestly, we shall often find that we have begun to argue against a new idea even before it has been completely stated'.

How free is our will? Is conscious choice just an illusion? Remarkably, it appears that our subconscious mind has made a decision on something a full 7 seconds before our conscious mind has, but of course your subconscious knew that already ... 7 seconds ago!

Our beliefs are like safety nets that we feel we need to hold onto – almost to the extent that if we changed them, or even shifted them slightly, the very foundation of our individualised world view would be brought into question. As if you had found out that you were living a life similar to the character Truman Burbank, who actor Jim Carrey brilliantly plays in the movie *The Truman Show*.

Imagine then how we can similarly form beliefs based upon what we think we are seeing and experiencing, from what our loved ones have taught us and shown us, and from what we have learnt during our years of education. Remember when your teacher said to you that you need to learn mental maths because you won't always have a calculator with you? Well, they were right! Incredibly, only about 4% of the Western world doesn't have a calculator with them all of the time. Fortunately, the other 96% of us do, in the shape of our much-loved smartphones!

Finally, on the subject of questioning what you are thinking, a fascinating insight came from Swedish-born writer, speaker and former Buddhist monk Björn Lindeblad when he was asked by a reporter, 'From 18 years as a monk with hours of meditation, every single day and no distractions, what's the one key insight that you took with you home?' To this question Lindeblad replied with the simple yet powerful declaration, 'I no longer believe in everything I think'.

In modest terms, this concept is at the heart of this book: you should question as many of your thoughts as you can, to determine how much they are based in reality, and how much they are based on the beliefs unwittingly programmed there by others such as your caregivers, who themselves received the majority of their beliefs from their caregivers. Together, let's start to disrupt the cycle of belief propagation and, to that end, hopefully bring about an exciting new way of thinking and looking at the world around us.

Welcome to the exhilarating new world of a new way of thinking. Welcome to creating your own new paradigm. It's time to wave goodbye to those old, outdated, limiting beliefs, time to put on your dancing shoes, buckle up your seat belt and get ready to upgrade your life using this book. It's going to be quite a ride!

SUMMARY

This chapter looks at our beliefs and split them into two types: core beliefs and brick beliefs. Our brick beliefs are those we have learnt and use to form a strong wall – our belief systems. We look at weakening these brick beliefs and, in turn, having a few tumble down from our wall. This book concentrates on the beliefs we have learnt, what other beliefs underpin them and how our belief systems adapt to an identity which we take on. The chapter also looks into our habits, and how these can either empower us or be detrimental to us. Our habits are a product of our beliefs, and our success a product of our habits. Therefore, to enjoy more success and positive change, we must first challenge our beliefs. Also explored in this section is the notion of 'Will it make the boat go faster?'. How does a small amount of progress daily lead to the large, dramatic changes we all wish to see within our lives? The 1% Rule states that we only need to be 1% better at a task a day to see a 37-times improvement within a year, meaning change may be easier than we thought. This book is very much about to questioning our thoughts; to find out what thoughts are true and based in reality, and what thoughts have been programmed there throughout our lives by other people.

CHAPTER THREE

BELIEF COMES EASILY; DOUBT TAKES EFFORT

The closer you come to knowing that you alone create the world of your experience, the more vital it becomes for you to discover just who is doing the creating.
– ERIC MICHA'EL LEVENTHAL

Consider for a moment the following question: are you more likely to be killed by a falling aeroplane part or by an attacking shark? I'll put you out of your misery in a few minutes.

In a fascinating experiment carried out by Sam Harris and his team at the University of California, individuals were placed into a brain scanner and asked whether they believed in various written statements. Some of these statements were simple factual assertions, such as 'California is larger than Rhode Island'; others were more related to personal beliefs, such as 'There is probably no God'. Harris discovered that the statements people believed to be true produced little characteristic brain activity – just a few brief flickers in regions associated with reasoning and emotional reward. In contrast to this, the statements the subjects didn't hold beliefs for produced longer and stronger activation in regions associated with consideration and decision making. This implies that the brain had to work harder to reach a state of disbelief. Statements the volunteers did not believe also activated regions associated with emotion – in most cases feelings associated with pain and disgust.

Harris's results perhaps demonstrated that the default state of the human brain is to accept beliefs. Seemingly, belief comes easily; doubt takes effort. While this doesn't outwardly appear like a smart strategy for navigating our world, it makes perfect sense in the light of evolution. This is a great rule when it comes to sensory perception, as our senses usually provide reliable information. However, the flip side is that it has perhaps saddled us with a non-optimal system for assessing more abstract stimuli, such as new ideas and concepts. If we hear, see or experience something new, we try to fit it in with our current beliefs. Rarely, if ever, do we attempt to fit it into something we have little or no experience of understanding, as doing so could potentially create what is known as cognitive dissonance. The mental discomfort caused by cognitive dissonance occurs when we endeavour to hold two opposing and conflicting beliefs, values or attitudes.

As we have discussed previously in this book, the average person has between 60,000 and 80,000 thoughts a day. Imagine if every thought about ourselves and our world was new – how would we even process that amount of information? Therefore, viewing these thoughts through a set of predetermined beliefs in many ways is reassuring, and possibly familiar. The result of this is that we don't need to continually question the validity of the things we experience every day, as they are experienced through our pre-existing lens or 'Belief Goggles' as I like to think of them.

Okay, here's a quick question for you. Ready? Answer it as quickly as you can.

How many of each animal did Moses take with him on the ark?
Quick now!

So, if you replied 'Two, of course', then you are perfectly normal. You are wrong, though, as of course the answer is that it wasn't Moses who built the ark, it was Noah! Okay, I tricked you somewhat, or rather tricked what has come to be known as the 'fast-thinking' part of your brain – the part of your brain that leads you to pull a door that says 'Push' on it. Naturally, when this happens you then have to pretend that there was something wrong with the door in the first place, so you don't feel too socially judged. If you said Noah, then you are the sort of person who will never ever pull a door that says 'Push' on it!

This crafty question has been given the name 'the Moses Illusion' by psychologists. On the surface it appears almost painfully easy. The context seems right, Moses and Noah fit together nicely in the part of our brain that groups things together. If I had asked 'How many of each animal did Donald Trump take with him on the ark?', then you would immediately have sensed something as being a little off.

Interestingly, when researchers pose the Moses question in hard-to-read cursive writing, far fewer people fall prey to the illusion, as doing so seems to circumvent the fast-thinking part of our thinking. Similarly, when people are asked to furrow their brows while answering questions like this one, they proceed with more caution.

MOSES SUPPOSES

In the ground-breaking book *Thinking, Fast and Slow* by psychologist and Nobel Prize winner Daniel Kahneman, Kahneman highlights his research, which shows that our brains have two operating systems. He refers to these parts as System 1 and System 2.

Here are the key features of the two systems:

- System 1 or cognitive ease is fast, unconscious, automatic, effortless, lacking self-awareness with little or no effort and no sense of voluntary control. Its role is to assesses situations. System 1 is responsible for 98% of all our thinking.

- System 1 or cognitive strain is slow, deliberate, conscious and effortful. It controls mental processes and rational thinking. It allocates attention to the mental activities that demand it, including complex computations. It seeks new/missing information and makes decisions. System 2 makes up the remaining 2% of all our thinking.

In many ways System 2 is a slave to System 1. System 1 sends suggestions to system 2, which then turns them into unconscious beliefs.

Think of System 1 as a group of busy reporters, writing stories and then passing them to System 2, the editor. The editor doesn't have the time to verify all of the stories and publishes them regardless. When a story is then found to be 'fake news' the System 2 editor will defend the story (belief) regardless, attempting to keep our fragile egos intact.

So why do most people fall for the Moses Illusion? That's because our brains perform a form of constant triage in approaching different tasks: some are assigned to the quick-thinking System 1 part of our brain that boils down easy questions to their essentials for faster processing; others go to System 2, the slower-thinking system that ponders each element of a more arduous problem more carefully. As part of its assessment process, the brain looks for cues that will help sort easy tasks from difficult ones. Sometimes the cues are deceptive: practically everything about the Moses question signals that you can breeze right through it, that's why it falls into the hands of the System 1 area of the brain first. We can perhaps see then why System 1 (the busy reporters) can pass information to the slower System 2 (editor) that can go unchecked and unverified, creating beliefs that will potentially be hard to challenge and change.

It is important to note that beliefs need not be conscious or spoken of to have meaning. It is likely that the majority of beliefs remain unconscious or outside of our immediate awareness. The majority of our beliefs are relatively mundane in their content. For example, if we go to open a door, we have beliefs about how we will open that door and what potentially lies beyond the door. We have beliefs about how a door works, and that we are capable of using it. Furthermore, without the goal of pursuing something beyond the door, the act of opening the door would probably not take place.

We all have many thousands of decisions to make each day, like opening a door. These differ in difficulty and importance. It could be you taking a step to your left or right when talking, or deciding to take the stairs or the lift. We are bombarded daily by decisions that have to be made. If you had to consciously process all these decisions your brain would most certainly become overloaded quite quickly. Essentially, our more automatic System 1 lightens the load on System 2. First of all, it takes care of our more familiar tasks by turning them into autopilot routines, in essence, our habits. But, what your System 1 is primarily doing is rapidly examining information and ideas without you even being aware of it, prioritising whatever seems relevant and filtering out the rest by taking shortcuts.

To process information and make decisions quickly, we use what are called heuristics. These heuristics are like mental shortcuts that help us make decisions and judgements quickly and, more often than not, effectively. They save us time and energy and they can help us create stereotypes. They can be fast and efficient. Indeed, imagine an average day in your life, where you are faced with the magnitude of decisions that you are normally faced with. Imagine then if you have to evaluate each one from scratch? It would take you 2 hours just to get out of bed in the morning!

People love certainty. Knowing what is going to happen puts us at cognitive ease. To that end, the single best, most cost-effective change that London Underground made in terms of improving the satisfaction of their passengers surprisingly wasn't faster and more frequent trains. No, it was putting simple, dot matrix display boards on the platform informing commuters how long they would have to wait for their next train. Similarly, if you ever had the misfortune to spend time in an accident and emergency department, you may have found that once the triage nurse has seen you and you have been sent through the doors into a new waiting area, you feel like you have made some progress. In this new waiting area, you don't seem to mind too much how long it takes before you are seen again. If, however you are sent back to the original waiting area, you feel somewhat deflated and as if you haven't made any progress in your search for assistance, even if the time you spend there is equal to the time you would have spent in the new waiting area. We hate uncertainty.

THE KING OF WISHFUL THINKING

So, did the shark get you, or the aeroplane part falling from the sky? Well, if you're like most people, you would probably say that a shark attack is the more likely way to die. But, in actual fact, you are approximately 30 times more likely to be killed by a falling aeroplane part. Similarly, you are twice as likely to be killed by a falling coconut at the beach than by the same poor old shark. Perhaps sharks need to have better PR – they get blamed for everything!

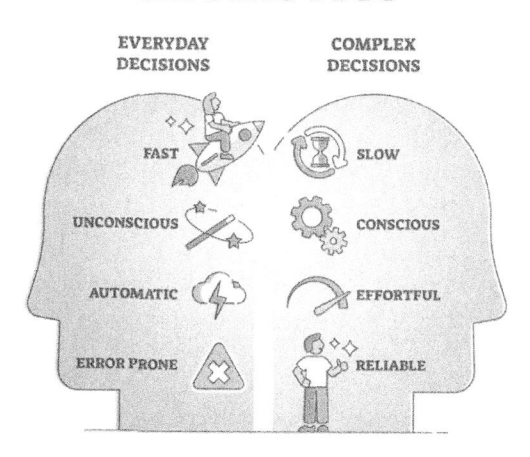

Heuristics

So why do we make these judgements? The answer lies with heuristics. We cannot keep all of the details of the world in our brains, so we use our beliefs and our mental models to simplify the complex into understandable and organisable chunks. Heuristics are a problem-solving method that uses shortcuts to produce satisfactory solutions given a limited time frame or deadline. Heuristics are used by the slower System 1 parts of our thinking. When we use these available shortcuts, we pay attention to how easy it is to think of examples. In other words, we pay attention to how available the examples are. Let's consider the shark attack/aeroplane part falling problem. When we are asked to ponder that question, chances are we try to think of recent examples of falling aeroplane part deaths as well as deaths from shark attacks. Most of us would find it hard to think of any examples at all of aeroplane part deaths. The easier one of the two to gravitate to is shark attacks. Examples of shark attack deaths are more available to us in our memories than are aeroplane part deaths. Therefore, more often than not, we decide that death by shark is far more likely. This combines with the fact that TV channels air shows such as *Shark Week* and films like *Jaws* are etched into our consciousness. They don't tend to televise *Parts Falling from Aeroplanes Week*!

Finally, which British animal is more dangerous? Dogs or cows? Sleep on it and I'll put you out of your misery later in the book.

LOST FOR WORDS

Consider for a moment the letter 'R' in the English language. If I asked you to pick up an average book, would you guess that the letter 'R' appears more often at the start of the words in this book, or would you estimate that it appears more often as the third letter of the words in this book? Or would you guess that they occur equally as often. Here are the choices again:

- The first letter
- The third letter
- Equally as often

If you guessed 'a', that the first letter is the most common, then you are not alone. In fact, the answer is (drumroll please) 'b' – 'R' occurs as the third letter more often. So why then do most of us guess the answer to be 'a'? The answer is simple. It is relatively stress-free to think of lots of words that begin with the letter 'R', but frustratingly, it is not as easy to think of as many words where R is the third letter of the word. So, it appears that 'b' is a less common answer, and therefore it's not considered a good option to choose. Once again, because of the cognitive strain thinking of words with 'R' as the third letter causes, our System 1 tends to solve the problem rather than handing it to the slower System 2 part of our thinking.

The above examples are all examples of the *availability heuristic*. This bias explains the tendency we have to use information that comes to mind quickly and easily when making decisions about our future plans. It is essentially a mental shortcut designed to save us time when we are trying to determine a risk. Smokers who have never known somebody die of smoking or a smoking-related illness, for example, tend to underestimate the health risks associated with smoking. In contrast, if you have a close relative and a handful of friends who have had various forms of cancer, then you might believe it is even more common than statistics tell us. This can either influence your decision to quit smoking or can cause the smoker to adopt the 'Well, I could get run over by a bus tomorrow!' approach and dissociate themselves from the obvious harmful effects of continuing to smoke. Essentially, the availability heuristic is a mental shortcut designed to save us time when we are trying to determine risk. The problem with relying on this way of thinking, as in the smoking example above, is that it can often lead to poor estimates and bad decisions.

MONEY FOR NOTHING

Could serious investors be influenced by availability heuristics? Perhaps the weirdest and funniest example of this is what has come to be known as the Anne Hathaway effect. Dan Mirvish of the Huffington Post observed a correlation between an increase in the share price of Berkshire Hathaway stock (BRK.A) and the release dates for movies starring the popular Hollywood A-lister, Anne Hathaway. Obviously these two entities have nothing in common other than the name. But why does this happen?

It seems that any news related to the actress influences people to think about investing in Berkshire Hathaway, driving up demand for Berkshire Hathaway stock. On the Friday before the 2011 Oscars, Berkshire shares rose a healthy 2.02%, and on the Monday just after the Academy Awards, they rose again, this time by an impressive 2.94%. Remarkably, it's not just an Oscar buzz, or something Warren Buffett may have said in the media, or even something the company itself has done. Just look back at some other milestone dates in Anne Hathaway's career and how they impacted the Berkshire Hathaway stock:

> 26 September 2008 – *Passengers* opens: BRK up 1.43%
> 3 October 2008 – *Rachel Getting Married* opens: BRK up 0.44%
> 6 January 2009 – *Bride Wars* opens: BRK up 2.61%
> 8 February 2010 – *Valentine's Day* opens: BRK up 1.01%
> 5 March 2010 – *Alice in Wonderland* opens: BRK up 0.74%
> 24 November 2010 – *Love and Other Drugs* opens: BRK up 1.62%
> 29 November 2010 – Hathaway announced as co-host of the 83rd Academy Awards: BRK up 0.25%
> 28 February 2011 – Hathaway co-hosts the 83rd Academy Awards: BRK up 2.94%

Maybe it's time to start looking at the IMDB website for better stocks and shares insight! Of course, today many investment companies use machine learning to study the news for the process of analysing the current stock market. The software then applies sentiment analysis to the news to determine whether a news story is positive or negative and accordingly estimates the future of the share prices of the subject company. But clearly machine learning is only part of the whole picture.

In a similar vein, one study has discovered that people are more likely to purchase newly offered initial public offering (IPO) stocks that have easily pronounced names than those that don't. According to Princeton psychologists Adam Alter and Daniel Oppenheimer, it's all about fluency. When people try to understand complex information, they tend to focus on the simplest aspects of the information. In simple terms, as individuals we naturally favour things that are more fluent, and easier to think about. 'We looked at intervals of a day, a week, six months and a year after IPO,' Alter said. 'The effect was strongest shortly after IPO. For example, if you started with $1,000 and invested it in companies with the 10 most fluent names, you would earn $333 more than you would have had you invested in the 10 with the least fluent.'

Similarly, the effect extended to the ease with which the stock's ticker code could be pronounced, indicating that a stock with the symbol BAL should outperform one with the symbol BDL in the first few days of trading. Oppenheimer states that, 'This research shows that people take mental shortcuts, even when it comes to their investments, when it would seem that they would want to be most rational'.

MYSTERY LADY

When we are faced with several choices, we tend to lean more to the one that makes the most sense for us, which of course outwardly seems to make perfect sense. But what if I asked you to picture a lady? This lady is middle aged, she has glasses, she loves reading, is quite introverted and enjoys her own company. If then if I asked you to very quickly make a guess at her profession, would you guess that she is more likely to be a librarian or a nurse? If you instinctively chose librarian, then you are not alone – that is virtually always the option the majority of us opt for. Why though? With some 24,000 librarians and almost 700,000 nurses in employment in the UK, the statistical likelihood of this lady being a librarian is pretty small. But the way heuristics influence us to stereotype makes the likelihood of us choosing the nurse much smaller in likelihood. This is an example of a *representativeness heuristic*. This mental shortcut helps us make a decision by comparing information to our mental stereotypes.

Finally, a base rate heuristic allows us to make decisions based on probability. It refers to how we have a tendency to rely more on specific information than we do statistics when making probability judgements. For example, if you were to be asked to evaluate whether smoking is good for you or not, you would most likely make an estimate on the average of 1000 smokers and compare that with 1000 non-smokers. Chances are you would estimate that the health of non-smokers would be more favourable compared with that of the smokers. However, if you happened to be a smoker yourself, then you may be influenced by individual anecdotes, such as a 40-a-smoker who lived until she was 102. Such a story may possibly influence someone to ignore base rates, and to focus on the long-living smoker and her story. In doing so, they would fool themselves into believing that smoking can't be all that bad for them. Therefore, base rate heuristics are very much about weighing up what we believe and what we want to believe, as well as what we have personally seen and experienced, rather than using statistical data to evaluate our judgements. One of my favourite stories around formulating a decision based on what we believe rather than looking at the problem from a different perspective involves pilots returning from combat in the Second World War.

SOLE SURVIVOR

Often with our belief systems we can hold a belief about something so readily because we trust that the evidence presented to us is unquestionable. So, therefore, why would we consider an alternative viewpoint on that belief? A fantastic example of believing something to be plainly obvious when in actual fact the complete inverse is true, is the story of Abraham Wald and his team of mathematicians and statisticians.

Born in 1902, Wald had graduated in mathematics and eventually came to lecture in economics in Vienna. As a Jewish family, Wald and his family faced persecution from the Nazis and so they immigrated to the USA when he was offered a university position at Yale. During the Second World War, Wald was a member of the Statistical Research Group (SRG) – a team of some 18 of the world's leading mathematicians and statisticians. Based at New York's Columbia University, the SRG focused on trying to solve complex military problems using research methodology.

References

One problem the US military faced was how to reduce the number of downed aircraft and subsequent casualties that would cause. They researched the damage received to the planes returning from conflict, asking the returning pilots to mark on a card the places on their planes where they had received damage from enemy bullets. By mapping out damage they found their planes were receiving most bullet holes to the wings and tail; it was looking like the cockpits and engines were spared.

To the US military's high command, the deduction drawn from these data was simple: the wings and tail are obviously vulnerable to receiving bullets, and they need to increase armour to these areas. Knowing that you could not armour the whole plane due to the weight that would add to a plane, it became glaringly obvious that they must recommend reinforcing just the vulnerable areas on a plane.

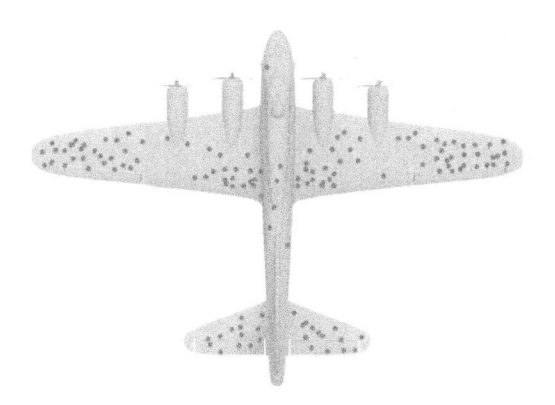

Damage to a World War II bomber

It was at that point that Wald stepped in. His conclusion was surprising: don't armour the wings and tail, armour the engine. Wald's incredible insight and reasoning had been based on understanding what we now term *survivorship bias*. In the case of the US military, they were only examining the planes that had returned to base following a conflict or, in other words, the planes that were not shot down by the enemy. What the drawings of bullet holes actually showed was the areas their planes could sustain damage and still be able to fly home.

So why did Wald see what the officers, who had vastly more knowledge and understanding of aerial combat, could not? It comes back to his maths-trained habits of thought. A mathematician is always asking, 'What assumptions are you making? And are they justified?' In the case of the returning planes, the officers were unwittingly making an assumption: that the planes that came back were a random sample of all the planes.

Abraham Wald eventually emigrated to the United States, where he met and married Lucille Lang. In 1950 as a result of his work, Wald received an invitation from the Indian government to visit and lecture on statistics. Tragically, in a rather cruel twist of fate, whilst on this trip, Wald and wife both died in a plane crash.

How often do we focus on individuals' successes rather than their failings? Lots of books focus on certain celebrities and personalities and how they have risen to fame and stardom. Rarely are we interested in the journeys of people who have made mistakes though we could learn a lot from the mistakes others have made. It's as if, if we avoid associating ourselves with those unlucky individuals who make mistakes, then somehow their errors and failures will not rub off onto us. As Henry Ford once famously said, 'Those who never make mistakes work for those of us who do'.

If you have ever visited a great restaurant and thought to yourself that you would quite like to open a restaurant yourself, and of course make the sort of money that restaurants of this calibre can make, then you may have fallen foul of a cognitive bias. After all, how hard can it be? Lots of restaurants do well. The facts, however, speak for themselves and the statistics on this are pretty unpleasant. A frightening 60% of restaurants don't make it past their first year, and a whopping 80% go out of business within 5 years! It is almost as if we are hardwired to look at the successes without considering the journey they have been on and the sacrifices they have perhaps made to get to where they are.

Similarly, ask anyone who has ever had an idea for a product or business that has failed, and ask them in the early weeks and months how many people told them what a great product or what a great idea they had. In other words, we tend to associate with people who reinforce our beliefs and who tell us what we want to hear. Perhaps only when we associate with others whose beliefs are not aligned with our beliefs and how we see the world can we truly grow and develop.

At their core, heuristics are essentially examples of what psychologists refer to as cognitive biases. We will be digging deeper into more of these biases, and how they impact our beliefs and our lives later in this book.

ANOTHER DAY IN PARADISE

It may seem at this stage that it is obvious that if we begin to observe our thoughts, we can potentially begin to change them. But, sadly, common sense is often not common practice, and that is why we more often than not need some help in beginning to be the active observer of our beliefs.

When we visit a therapist, often we already believe that we know the origins of our particular problem or problems. We have perhaps spent many hours thinking about them and ruminating over their possible origins. Frustratingly, however, rumination over one's particular symptoms and their origin has been implicated in the development, maintenance and aggravation of both anxiety symptoms and episodes of major depression. In other words, giving substantial time over to thinking about our problems can often have a huge detrimental effect on our mental health and our general wellness.

It is often the hidden, almost overlooked, beliefs that we hold about ourselves that can frequently create for us the most anxieties and feelings of low mood and depression. Dispute and disrupt these beliefs and you can potentially change how you think and feel day by day. Use this book to start to uncover those potentially 'hidden from plain sight' beliefs that underpin so much of our thinking and emotions. Together, let's begin to take out those bottom-level bricks, and in doing so watch the wall start to tumble. Importantly, we will only be removing the limiting belief bricks, the harmful ones, the unwanted ones, the ones that have limited your life in some form.

Think of this book as if you initiating an update of the software of your subconscious mind. You wouldn't want your computer to run on Windows 95; why then would you not desire to upgrade your own cognitive software? In doing so, allow yourself to perceive your world and the world around you differently.

SUMMARY

In this chapter, we look into how our different systems of thinking and mental shortcuts affect us daily. An experiment looking into activations in different parts of the brain found that there was stronger and longer brain activity when an individual was doubting a statement than if they were agreeing with it. In essence, we work harder to disbelieve. When we hold two opposing beliefs, it is known as *cognitive dissonance*. It is natural for us to wish we were in cognitive ease, otherwise known as System 1 thinking. System 1 thinking is unconscious, automatic and has the purpose of quickly assessing situations. This makes up 98% of our daily thoughts. The other 2% is made up by System 2 thinking – slower and more deliberate and allocates attention to mental processes. This puts us under cognitive strain. System 1 thinking, and the decisions it makes, takes this strain off our System 2. Heuristics – mental shortcuts – break down the detail we receive every day into more organisable and understandable chunks. There are different types of heuristics, or cognitive biases: availability, representativeness and base rate. An availability heuristic is the mental shortcut of using information that comes to our mind quickly, and a base rate heuristic uses information to make decisions based on probability. A representativeness heuristic helps us quickly make decisions by comparing the information presented to us with our pre-existing stereotypes.

CHAPTER FOUR

WHAT YOU SEE IS ALL WE BELIEVE THERE IS

Changing your mind is probably one of the most beautiful things people can do. And I've changed my mind about a lot of things over the years.
– PAUL AUSTER

IMAGINE

Imagine for a brief moment that you are visited one day by your future self. In that meeting the future 'you' articulates to you that all of your hopes and wishes, all of the dreams and desires for your life have actually materialised. Your future self speaks of all the amazing and monumental events that have actually happened, and how incredible they have been.

Now ask yourself this: would you in fact believe them? If the answer is no, then consider for a moment how likely it is for those things that you have planned to happen if you don't actually believe that they could happen. Or if there is any doubt in your mind. Perhaps also you haven't given yourself any time to imagine and dream about the things that you would like to happen in your life – the things you would like to accomplish, the events and places you would like to experience. Perhaps in fact you haven't given over any time to think about the things you would like for your future life. Let's imagine then for a moment that you have imagined some future successes, and that you have achieved some of the goals you have set for yourself.

Now ask yourself this: if indeed you don't or in fact can't believe for a moment that some amazing future event, experience or success could happen, what is the likelihood of those incredible things actually manifesting in your life? I would hazard a guess that it would be quite unlikely.

In reality, how often do we take time every night before we go to sleep to actually imagine what we want for our lives? Also, how often do we wake up thinking about what could go wrong in the day ahead rather than all of the positive experiences that may occur? Similarly, do we ever take a moment to think about what we will learn from an event or experience, regardless of how it will turn out for us?

Often, we are distracted in the day from our worries and anxieties, only to face them in full as we attempt to go to sleep at night. Psychologists believe that the cognitive function is hardwired within us as a way to protect ourselves from harm. In hunter-gatherer times if we didn't pay enough attention to any potential danger, we could potentially be killed. Focusing on a lovely sunset is far more dangerous than focusing on a potential tiger attack or the possibility of falling off a nearby cliff.

Part of this anxiety is about being ostracised by our own tribe, which would mean almost certain death for us. Perhaps then that is why we spend more time analysing other people's responses to events than the events themselves.

But what if you could change how you think when your head touches your pillow? What if you could indeed focus on what you want turning up in your life, rather than the things you don't want to happen? What if you did meet your future self and you were thrilled rather than disappointed about the future events that had happened in your life? If right now part of you can't actually believe good things can show up in your life, then why would you be surprised when indeed the things you don't want in your life are consistently presenting themselves?

In fact, do you find that your incredible, virtually limitless mind is more like Velcro for bad experiences and like Teflon for the more positive experiences in your day – dismissing the positive experiences promptly in favour of the events of the day that didn't have the outcome you desired?

If the answer is yes, then this book is for you. Reading this book regularly will, I promise you, transform your life beyond your wildest imaginings. Dare to dream and dare to imagine what your future self would say to you. Believe it and it will indeed happen for you. As the author Robert Brault states: 'We are kept from our goal not by obstacles but by a clear path to a lesser goal'.

Once again, by beliefs we do not mean religious or political beliefs, but the limiting beliefs imposed on us, often as children. At their heart the systems that define who we are, and how we fit into the world around us.

LIFE'S A HAPPY SONG

When it comes to happiness, we all have a tendency to return to our own personal 'set point' no matter what ups and downs we experience in our lives. For example, those lucky individuals who have a lottery win tend to return to roughly their original levels of happiness after the novelty of the win has worn off. There is naturally an initial splurge of ecstasy, but after about a year winners tend to experience the same general sense of happiness as non-winners.

Inversely the same is true for those unlucky enough to find themselves in a major accident and perhaps lose mobility or lose a limb. The change in ability can be devastating at first, but people generally tend to return to their pre-accident levels of happiness after the adaptation period.

This happiness treadmill, if you will, is referred to by psychologists as our hedonic adaptation – our general tendency to return to a set level of happiness despite what happens to us in our life, whether good or bad. We can quickly become accustomed to the pleasure of something, so that the same mood-lifting little treat doesn't bring the same flood of joy as it once did. For example, the first bite of something delicious is experienced as more pleasurable than the third or the tenth mouthful. How often have you tried someone else's food, such as a few chips, and found that the pleasure you obtained from the few shared chips far outweighed any enjoyment you would have obtained if you were to be tucking into your own full bag?

Similarly, when say you purchase a new car or move into a new house, there are usually lots of positive events happening as a result. You enjoy making additional purchases for your new car or home, you feel proud to display your new acquisitions off to others, and you enjoy a long, hot soak in the bath in your new house or the relaxing drive to work in your shiny, new car. But over time there are fewer positive events to experience. You rapidly become accustomed to your home's new features and the smell of your new car perhaps begins to be replaced with the smell of your child's backseat food preferences. With fewer positive events, and thus fewer positive emotions (excitement, pride, happiness), your newfound sense of contentment can't be sustained. In the same vein, have you ever achieved a major goal, only to find yourself feeling empty once you have reached it? Or have you ever gone on a shopping spree and felt happy for the rest of the day, but not the next day? If so you have experienced this 'hedonistic treadmill' phenomenon.

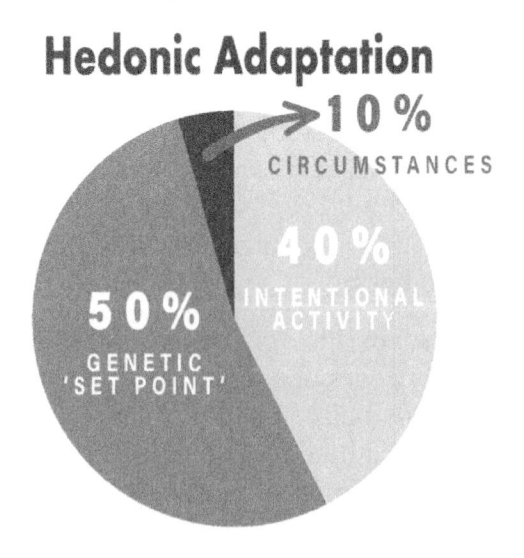

Hedonic Adaptation

10% CIRCUMSTANCES

40% INTENTIONAL ACTIVITY

50% GENETIC 'SET POINT'

Numerous researchers have examined hedonic adaptation and have attempted to determine how much of our happiness is really under our control. Researcher Sonja Lyubomirsky examined this set point and came up with a specific percentage for the control we have in our happiness, and that figure is 40%.

Lyubomirsky determined that a full 50% of our happiness set point is due to our genetics, while 10% is affected primarily by circumstances such as where we were born and to whom. The final 40% is what is very much under our control. This has come to be known as the 50-10-40% formula.

So why pursue happiness when we all go back to neutral anyway? Research carried out by psychologist Ed Diener into what he called subjective well-being (SWB) states that 'believed happiness' is a process and not a destination point. He believes that the key to experiencing happiness is to enjoy the moment that you are in, rather than constantly looking towards the future. This causes your happiness set point not to be neutral, but instead to change positively over time. Even if you return to a previous point, it's positive instead of neutral.

Diener believes we all have individualised happiness set points that are dependent on our personality traits and our heredity. He believes it is better to achieve happiness earlier in life if you are able to as this can generate a life of more positivity. He also believes that everyone is born with a predisposition to a certain set point of happiness, which may work in your favour or against you.

Later in this book we will look at how we can get more out of life by creating the illusion of slowing down time, something I refer to as 'Time Distortion Moments'. But with regard to happiness the paragraph that follows describes some ways in which you can move away from the effects of hedonic adaptation and engage in activities that can actually create a greater sense of happiness and contentment in your life.

As a rule, we tend to be happier if we spend money on experiences rather than just on 'stuff', and we seem to be happier if we spend money on others rather than on ourselves. Similarly, if we feel in control of our lives and are doing something that we feel we are good at, we tend to feel much happier. If we try and savour our positive experiences, this is a great way to enjoy life more without needing anything else to change. The approach we take in this book is very much about living more in the moment and processing the positive events that happen in our lives each day. So, you begin to notice and enjoy that special cup of coffee more, whether it's alone or shared with friends. You enjoy the experience of fresh new bedding more than you did before. You find pleasure in a phone call with a friend where you share a laugh. In essence you find pleasure in the things you may not have noticed previously. You begin to see how much joy and pleasure there are to be experienced in the world.

In 2002, Diener conducted a study at the University of Illinois with fellow psychologist Martin Seligman (more about Seligman and his work on learned helplessness later in this book). What the two uncovered was that the students in their study with the highest levels of happiness, and lowest levels of depression, were the ones who had the strongest ties to friends and family and committed to spending time with them. Diener went on to state, 'It is important to work on social skills, close interpersonal ties and social support in order to be happy'.

SOMETHING TO BELIEVE IN

Next, we need to examine our strongly held core beliefs. Core beliefs are deeply entrenched assumptions that guide our behaviours. They can affect how we perceive ourselves and how we interpret situations and experiences in our day-to-day lives. These beliefs can impact on how we feel, our relationships with others, and they can determine our levels of happiness and perceived success in our lives. Core beliefs are the belief system that we really want to and, in many cases, very much need to hold on to.

Picture a core belief as being like a strong, standing oak tree: the leaves on the tree are like the other secondary beliefs we hold, just like the 'brick beliefs' we examined earlier. Unlike the tree itself this network of leaves (secondary beliefs) is much weaker than the tree (core beliefs) and, like a belief that is not strongly held, it can be knocked off and left to float away quite easily if necessary.

Similar to core beliefs the tree is unwavering and it would take a lot of time, effort and energy to weaken and to ultimately knock it down. Some of these limiting core beliefs can be akin to the infamous black walnut tree – a tree that despite being beautiful and valuable will use its roots to infect and harm those trees around it. Using a natural herbicide known as juglone the black walnut tree inhibits the many plants that grow under and around it, thereby limiting the tree's competition, the result of which will be more water and nutrients for itself. Our beliefs can be the same – they can become all-consuming and take the energy and power away from other, more positively impacting beliefs. For example, if your core belief is that you are helpless, losing weight could seem like a massive hurdle to overcome. Similarly, you may feel out of control around food, allowing you to make bad eating decisions. Interestingly, according to a 2012 survey conducted by the International Food Information Council (IFIC), some 52% of Americans believe it is easier to figure out their taxes than to figure out what they should and shouldn't eat to be healthier. Is this shockingly high statistic down to poor information around food perhaps, or possibly a sense of powerlessness around food?

Think of a core limiting belief such as 'I am unlovable'. That belief is akin to the black walnut tree, in so much as it will infect other less rigidly held beliefs that surround it. For example, if you believe the above statement, it would be almost impossible to accept that anything positive could happen in your life, such as being with someone who shows you love and affection. Similarly, it has an effect on other beliefs, shifting them to new, more damaging beliefs such as 'I am better off alone', or 'I don't matter', or the highly damaging 'If I love someone, they will leave me' belief. When something good does happen to an individual with this belief, because the experience of love doesn't match their internal belief, self-sabotage can occur. They may reject the relationship or even subconsciously manufacture ways in which it can come to an end. Slightly less weighty beliefs such as 'I have no willpower' and 'There aren't enough hours in the day', whilst potentially harmful, can be more like the leaves on the oak tree we discussed above. In other words, with a relatively small amount of effort, they can be challenged and changed. The flip side of this is that it is our nature only to invest energy into that which we believe will produce the outcome we seek. Therefore, if we don't believe we can overcome a challenge or belief, chances are we won't invest any time or energy into trying to change it.

The majority of trees communicate and share resources with each other (using a fungal network brilliantly nicknamed the Wood Wide Web), as do our beliefs. They support each other, and many of these are not harmful, but like the black walnut, a negative or limiting belief can impact other closely associated beliefs.

RIDING ALONG IN MY AUTOMOBILE

Take a few moments to imagine that you need to drive your car to the shops as usual, but this time unlike the thousands of other times you have been behind the wheel before you are no longer allowed to wear a seatbelt. I don't just mean you are no longer required to – you are banned from wearing a seatbelt completely. You can do everything else in the same way as usual, and drive in exactly the same way, the only difference is that there is no seatbelt for you and your children in the car. You child can just sit in the back seat without any restraining device.

Would you feel the same? Would you drive differently? I would wager a bet you would drive with a lot more caution than you have ever done before, like you drive when you have your mum in the car. But go back to a time before 31 January 1983 in the UK and the wearing of seatbelts was not compulsory. Nowadays that notion seems almost outrageous. In fact, it wasn't until 1989 that the seatbelt law was extended, and it became a legal requirement for children travelling in the back of a car to wear a seatbelt. Finally, in 1991 the law was changed to included adults travelling in the back of the car as well.

Anyone alive at this point in history (anyone who had not been killed in a car crash!) may remember that once we were encouraged to 'Clunk Click Every Trip', just in case it hadn't become a habit yet! Not surprisingly, not everyone took to the new technology with ease. According to car historians by 1947 some drivers in America were so displeased with the restrictiveness of the domineering seatbelt that they cut them out with razor blades! Unbelievably, successive governments prior to the law change had failed to deliver seatbelt-wearing legislation through the 1970s, and it wasn't until 1983 that it became mandatory. A delayed decision that seems somewhat unimaginable not to have taken today.

This seatbelt scenario is a brilliant example of how we can adopt a new belief, to the extent that when we attempt to go back to our old way of thinking it can seem preposterous to even contemplate it. Like getting in your car and immediately putting on your seatbelt, not to do it would feel alien to us.

As a young boy growing up in the 1970s I can remember the journey from our home in the south of England to the north to take the ferry across to Northern Ireland with me sitting on my mum's incredibly uncomfortable lap in the front of the car for a journey that seemed similar in length to the 30,000-mile Pan-American Highway (goodness knows how uncomfortable it must have been for my mum also!). Neither of us wore a seatbelt. Fortunately, my dad drove in a way that would make *Driving Miss Daisy* look like one of the *Fast and Furious* franchise movies, so I felt relatively safe. At no time did any child of the 1970s think any other way, this way of travelling was normalised by us.

SMOKE GETS IN YOUR EYES

Similarly, in the 1950s cigarettes were once advertised as being good for the 'temporary relief of paroxysms of asthma'. Yes, really! According to the not so appropriately named brand 'Lucky Strike' some 27,679 unnamed physicians recommended this brand of cigarettes for this condition! Unbelievably in today's world, one eminent scientist proclaimed that smoking a brand of cigarettes called 'Chesterfield' was as good for you as drinking 'pure' water from your tap. To be fair I suppose it depends on where you get your water from, if you were living in Chernobyl in April 1986, then he may have been making an honest argument!

So, what have the wearing of seatbelts and smoking cigarettes got to do with changing the way you think? What do they have to do with challenging and changing your belief systems? Well, as I mention above, any person who smoked or drove without a seatbelt prior to the introduction of the compulsory seatbelt law or the rise in information regarding the harmful effects of smoking would have considered it just a 'normal' thing to do. It wasn't questioned. Today, though, it would feel dangerous, anti-social and perhaps even irresponsible.

I wonder then, how many of the belief systems and patterns of thinking that we have about ourselves and the world around us are like my seatbelts comparison above. Without question we have normalised them. It's not until the status quo is questioned and we are thrown into a place where our belief systems are challenged that we can begin to examine them. Only then can we perhaps see how they have been limiting us for so long.

We regulate things in our life. We don't question their substantiveness, and so we don't move away from them or realise how potentially harmful they may be for us. They can limit us and put boundaries around what we are ultimately capable of. My hope for you is that after using the Alfred Technique we will discuss shortly, one day you will look back at the limiting beliefs you have held and think of them as if you were looking at photos of yourself from many years ago, where the fashionable clothes you were wearing don't seem quite as 'on trend' anymore, and you cringe a little remembering how 'hip' and 'cool' you once felt wearing them.

CAN'T GET YOU OUT OF MY HEAD

Let's take a moment or two to look deeper at the functions of our incredible subconscious minds. In essence the job of the subconscious is to keep us safe, and to that end it's never switched off. It never stops functioning, not even when we are asleep. Housed within it are all of our memories, good and bad.

Sometimes it may take hypnosis to retrieve them but believe me they are all there somewhere. Its capacity is virtually unlimited. No man or woman since the dawn of time has ever filled up their brain like my computer hard drive does frequently. Our subconscious minds hold our thoughts and beliefs, our emotions, memories, skills, instincts and our behaviours. Thank goodness they do otherwise you wouldn't be able to sip that cup of tea whilst you read a book or concentrate on listening to the news whilst you are driving your car (with your seatbelt on hopefully!). Our subconscious mind is our habit mind, and that is why we can drive a car, ride a bike, type on a computer keyboard, tie our shoelaces and breathe without thinking about it. They are subconscious programmes that are running in our habit mind – until the moment we think about them and bring them to our conscious, 'creative' minds.

By the time you are 21 you have already permanently stored more than 100 times the contents of the entire *Encyclopaedia Britannica*. The subconscious mind is subjective, it does not think or reason independently. It merely obeys the commands it receives from the conscious mind.

Your conscious mind can be thought of as a gardener planting seeds, and your subconscious can be viewed as the garden in which these seeds can germinate and grow. In this imaginary garden, as in real life, the weeds, like our beliefs, can often grow the fastest, and are often the hardest to remove! If you remove them, they will grow again unless they are replaced with something else that's perhaps stronger and more effective.

The majority of beliefs we have are deeply embedded in our subconscious, non-analytical minds. These beliefs were formed from birth to age 6 or 7 when we looked to our parents for love and approval. Our parents, caregivers and teachers teach us how to be a good person, not to steal, where to look when we cross the road, to be kind to others and to share. We are taught how to make sense of the world, whether we have control or whether we are powerless within it. We are taught about love, we are taught curiosity, sociability, resilience, self-awareness, integrity, resourcefulness, creativity and, importantly, empathy for others.

When it comes to these early-formed beliefs, motivational author Louise Hay describes them perfectly when she says: 'We learn our belief systems as very little children, and then we move through life creating experiences to match our beliefs. Look back in your own life and notice how often you have gone through the same experience.'

Our beliefs affect what we think about ourselves, others and the world at large. They underpin everything that influences our emotions and our actions. Consequently, they are of primary importance when it comes to how successful and happy we are.

A belief is something we consider to be a statement of fact. It is anything that we assume to be true. We use our beliefs to understand and navigate our world. We use our beliefs to keep us safe and to keep us happy. That is why we commonly try to preserve our beliefs after they are formed and safeguard them cautiously.

Our beliefs serve to function as our subconscious autopilot – once formed we tend not to think about them again, we take them as fact. Beliefs once formed become integral in how we make sense of the world. Our beliefs determine if we consider something or someone to be good or bad, right or wrong, beautiful or unpleasant, desirable or undesirable, safe or dangerous, worthy or unworthy, acceptable or unacceptable. Our beliefs also dictate what we consider to be imaginable or attainable.

Few if any beliefs are based on absolute truths. For example, if you dropped the book, kindle or iPad you are reading this on now, it would without a shadow of a doubt either fall on your lap or, worse, hit the ground (please don't try it, you know what happens!). None of us would argue that gravity is anything other than a truth – there is no grey area, it's not something that's open to debate. I doubt if any of your friends or family have ever proclaimed that they don't believe in gravity – that they think it is one big conspiracy to sell shedloads more protective iPhone cases. No, gravity is an absolute truth. How many of our beliefs can we say that about though? How many are subject to grey areas? Incidentally, if you do have friends who believe gravity is a conspiracy theory, then you may wish to start getting new friends, and if it's your family, well, sorry, you're stuck with them, perhaps have a DNA test!

Our beliefs are commonly formed in two ways: by our experiences, interpretations and judgements, or by accepting what others tell us to be true. It is a strongly held opinion that the majority of our core beliefs are formed when we are children.

When we are born, we enter this world with a clean slate and without any fixed beliefs. Our brain is neutral, we don't hold any biases or judgements. From that moment onwards the programming begins. Like lines of code in a computer programme, as the days, months and years go by more lines of code are added as well as viruses that often run in the background without us being aware of them. These viruses are the self-limiting beliefs, and like a computer virus, we are often not aware of their presence until something bad materialises. You can think of the ideas we discuss in this book as a type of anti-virus, seeking out these little critters, and placing them gently into quarantine until we can examine them and probe deeper into exactly how harmful they may potentially be.

When we are young, we are impressionable and highly suggestible (more about this later!) and look for meaning in practically everything because we are naturally inquisitive. We are learning machines. Our parents, teachers and caregivers, the media in all its forms as well as our environment play an immeasurable part in shaping and forming our beliefs from a very young age. At school our friends can also play an important part. Who can't remember being told something by a friend as a child and believing it to be true without question? Talking of which, if I ever see snotty-nosed Clive Swatton again, I will inform him in no uncertain terms that he is wrong about something he once told me. Clive, if you are reading this, if you eat a watermelon seed then a watermelon does not grow inside you! It doesn't, Clive. I have eaten thousands of watermelons and to date I have never had one grow in me!

Similarly, what young kid did not believe that their teachers actually lived and slept at school, to the extent that if you ever saw them in town, it was as if they had just left their school to be there? We could not see or care for anything beyond our own little world. We believed implicitly what grown-ups told us. If they told us we could be anything we wanted when we grow up, we may quite have fancied being a cat. To a child there is nothing out of the ordinary in that. To a child, superhero films aren't fiction, they are like looking at careers options. Lastly, how many children have attempted to glance surreptitiously at the back of their teacher's head to see if they could actually observe the eyes they claimed were there?

Because we are unable to discern between truth and myth when we are young, we often accept what we are told as truth. After all, why would an adult lie to us? We are also greatly influenced by what we experience.

In this regard I am often reminded of one of the Facebook support groups for one of our weight loss apps. Some of the beliefs our app users have shared with us over the years have been staggering – particularly the beliefs around eating and losing weight. A whole generation of children grew up thinking that if they didn't eat everything on their plate, they would somehow be affecting the starving in another continent, mostly Africa.

Remember when your parents told you about Santa Claus or the Tooth Fairy? As children we take on without question the belief in the existence of these characters. At no point as a child do you look at a picture of the sack of toys in Santa's sleigh and think to yourself 'Hold on a second, there aren't enough toys there to give gifts to the 2.2 billion children on the planet! Never mind, I've got presents at Christmas for the past number of years so he must exist, after all Mum and Dad would never lie to me, they love me!'

When we get older and start to attend school and meet new friends, our beliefs start to be influenced by a whole new environment and set of people. Our teachers tell us things that we accept as fact. We begin to believe that we are either good or not so good at something – perhaps that we have a particular talent for something, or that we will never be any good at maths or languages. Beliefs that can last a lifetime.

We are also greatly influenced by our classmates in school. Let's assume you are bullied by another kid in your school. They may continually tell you that you are fat, weird-looking or that you talk funny – basically you are different from them. After a while, you might start believing this to be fact, and start perceiving yourself as the very person you wish not to be identified as. These labels can, even subconsciously, become part of your identity, regardless of whether you want them or not, and irrespective of whether they are true or not.

When we accept something to be fact and form a belief, it is stored in our subconscious, habitual mind. Our subconscious mind does not know or care if the belief is true or false. It simply stores it as fact for later use. Our subconscious mind acts as our autopilot to make our life easier and to keep us safe and free from harm in whatever form that takes, be it physically or emotionally. It serves to help automate our actions and reactions to certain situations.

One area of beliefs that is always fascinating to look at, as it is pretty much universal, is beliefs relating to money, particularly as money, or more often the lack of it, affects almost every single person in the world regardless of culture and religion.

FOR THE LOVE OF MONEY

Many of us at some time in our lives have heard someone say, 'Money is the root of all evil'. The first recorded instance of this damaging phrase is believed to originate from the King James version of the Bible, where in Timothy 6:10 it reads: 'For the love of money is the root of all evil: which while some coveted after, they have erred from the faith, and pierced themselves through with many sorrows'. At some stage in the early 20th century, some unknown, inflammatory individuals decided to omit the 'love of' part of the sentence and later the new, far more rousing phrase came into common usage. But I suppose 'the ends justify the means', which incidentally was also never actually said either. What Italian writer and philosopher Machiavelli actually reportedly said was, 'One must consider the final result' – which is nowhere near as catchy. It does make you begin to wonder about the veracity of other famous quotations from the past. Next they will be saying Forrest Gump never said 'Life is like a box of chocolates'.[1]

Often when taking my own son to the shops, particularly a toy shop, I listen to the things other parents say to their offspring and I find myself imagining how, unwittingly, that child may be taking on the beliefs of that well-meaning parent. On numerous occasions I have heard parents affirm to their offspring that 'Money doesn't grow on trees, you know', and the classic 'You must think I'm made of money'.

Recently, at our practice in Hampshire I worked with a young man, initially to help him stop smoking, but later to upgrade his thinking and challenge his self-limiting beliefs. During our sessions he would often speak of his beliefs around money. He had often spoken about how he would have compulsions to spend and waste money needlessly, often buying expensive items for the sake of buying them. His belief was that if he was to keep money it would be harmful. When we spoke about the beliefs he held around money, he mentioned some of the statements that had been voiced to him growing up. Beliefs such as 'More money, more problems' and 'You can always make more money, but you can't ever make more time'. Other belief statements included 'Anything good can always be taken' and the timeless standard 'You can't take it with you!' It perhaps will be of no surprise that after this charming client started to question his beliefs around money his financial circumstances improved rapidly.

Take a moment now to think about your own education and the well-intentioned teachers who taught you. For most children we were forced to dress in the same way from the moment we started school. We were taught to think like everyone else. Don't forget not to laugh too loud; always keep your creativity within the confines of other people's expectations; also, never forget that geniuses are cut from a different cloth to you, play small, don't think too big.

As a result, we can end up living in a box, both bodily and metaphorically. We live in a box, we drive in a box to work, where more often than not we work in a box, we eat our lunch from a box, we go home and watch a box, and finally we die in a box. We continue the cycle of beliefs that have been propagated within us, from one generation to the next – we haven't seen outside of the box and therefore we don't know what might be there. Considering this paradigm, I am reminded of the Chicago chef Charlie Trotter, who once owned the most respected and revered restaurant in America. Trotter would regularly invite groups of underprivileged children to eat at his restaurant for free, to give them aspirations and goals. Trotter received much criticism for this gesture. Some felt it was unfair on these children to introduce them to something they would never likely experience again. Trotter believed, however, that introducing this sort of experience to these young kids would inspire them, as indeed it did, with many of them going on to study culinary skills. As Robin Sharma once brilliantly stated, 'Stop being a prisoner of your past. Instead, become the architect of your future.'

ALWAYS ON MY MIND

As a parent I am extremely hypervigilant regarding what I say to my little boy, and the beliefs I impart to him about life and about money. I often find myself debating the best way to say something. Will what I say to him nurture a 'growth mindset' or a 'fixed mindset' in him? There will be more about mindset and beliefs and how they are formed and how they affect us later in this book.

Of course, the real magic of the subconscious mind is that is can process 40 million bits of data from the environment every single second. Compare that to the conscious mind, which can only process 40 bits of data per second. It is estimated that the subconscious is a million times more powerful than the conscious mind. The subconscious is like an emergency station that can kick in immediately when we encounter danger, as it can process a lot of data quickly.

The fact is that 95% of the life you are living right now comes from the subconscious programmes. So, by definition, your life is a reflection of those subconscious programmes running constantly in the background. Therefore, the things that you like and that come easily to you are there because you have a programme that allows them to be there. By contrast, with anything that you have to work hard at, put a good deal of effort into, or anything you have to struggle for to make happen, chances are it is because your subconscious programmes are not supporting those things right now.

Often as individuals we have a lot of difficulty trying to change the programmes of our subconscious mind. The fact is our two minds, conscious and subconscious, learn differently. The conscious mind is the creative mind and can learn by reading a self-help book for example, or going on a self-improvement course, or perhaps by watching a motivating video. It is creative, it goes, 'Aha! I have an idea, now I can change my mind.'

The subconscious mind, on the other hand, is the habit mind, and the thing of paramount importance with the habit mind is that ideally you don't want it to change too rapidly, because habit changes don't often endure as the subconscious can be somewhat resistant to change. Put simply, the subconscious mind is not as easy to change as the conscious creative mind. So how do I change my subconscious mind? As you read this book and take time each and every day to start to challenge your self-limiting beliefs, you will begin to notice some of the beliefs that you have held for so long have not served you well. You may not believe that right now, but I promise you if you follow the approach we take in this book and take time each day to challenge your thinking, you will indeed create the life that you have always dreamed of. You will achieve happiness, contentment and a passion for your life. As his holiness the Dalai Lama states in this brilliant book *The Art of Happiness*, 'I believe that the very purpose of our life is to seek happiness. That is clear. Whether one believes in religion or not, whether one believes in this religion or that religion, we are all seeking something better in life. So, I think the very motion of our life is towards happiness...'

References

The fantastic news is that when you have challenged a belief enough times, and you have seen enough contradictory evidence, then it's virtually impossible to return to your old, redundant way of thinking. For example, most adults in the Western world can remember their beliefs around the existence of Santa Claus. He just existed! you never questioned his existence, you wanted him to exist. That is, however, until perhaps you were older and someone made you question whether the jolly, rotund gift-giver did actually exist. He was kind and generous and cared for all of the children in the world – why would anyone lie about him not being real? When you eventually found out the truth, for a while you may have questioned it, wondering why you had been deceived. A large part of you still wanted to believe he was real. But eventually you accepted it and now you see Christmas and Santa differently. At no stage as an adult do you ever find yourself thinking, could he actually exist? You never have an urge to go and sit on his lap when you see him at a shopping mall or garden centre and communicate to him what you want for Christmas. In essence your beliefs around his existence have altered and will never revert back to your original beliefs. Chances are when you eventually came to the realisation of his non-existence, your only thoughts on the subject were around how your parents and caregivers managed to deceive you so convincingly for so long! So what else have they lied about?

[1] Forrest Gump never actually said 'Life is like a box of chocolates'. What he actually said was 'Life *was* like a box of chocolates'. Sometimes what we think is an absolute certainty isn't one, and perhaps those long-held beliefs you have are no different. Let's dig into them a little deeper... You'd better get your shovel; it's going to be quite an expedition!

CHAPTER FIVE

BEYOND BELIEF

The human understanding when it has once adopted an opinion draws all things else to support and agree with it. And though there be a greater number and weight of instances to be found on the other side, yet these it either neglects and despises, or else by some distinction sets aside and rejects.
– FRANCIS BACON (1620)

At around 11am on Wednesday, 19 April 1995, a 5 foot 6, 270-pound man walked audaciously into a Pittsburgh bank to rob it. It was one of the two banks that he robbed that day. Security cameras at the bank managed to capture a good image of the man's face. He wore no mask or facial disguise and could clearly be seen holding a gun to the teller, demanding money. Police broadcast the footage on the local 11 o'clock news and, within minutes, a positive identification of the robber came. Just after midnight on that day, the police were knocking on the suspect's door – 44-year-old McArthur Wheeler. When Wheeler was arrested and charged, he was incredulous, exclaiming 'But I wore the juice!'. When questioned, Wheeler explained to the police that he rubbed lemon juice on his face to make it invisible to the security cameras. Detectives concluded he was not delusional, not on drugs, just incredibly mistaken.

Wheeler's logic was that as lemon juice can be used to write invisible letters that become visible only when the letter is held close to a heat source, the same technique would also work on his face. By smearing lemon juice all over his face, he thought that his face would become invisible. He did not just think that it might work, he was certain it would. He even checked his 'lemon face' idea by taking a selfie with a polaroid camera. He confided to the police that he was not sure if the film was defective, or the camera wasn't operated properly, but the camera did give him a blank image. The blank image made him absolutely sure that this undetectable face strategy would work. The only downside to his masterplan was that the lemon juice had stung his eyes so badly that on occasions he could barely see what he was doing.

This 'lemon face' incident inspired psychologists Dunning and Kruger to dig more deeply into why we as humans might undertake such a deluded act. The two psychologists were interested in studying what gave Wheeler the confidence to do what he did. He had the confidence, but he clearly wasn't competent enough. They wanted to know why he was so positive he would succeed.

Their study finally demonstrated that the less competent an individual is at a specific task, the more likely they are to inflate their self-appraised competence in relationship to that task. This phenomenon is known today as the Dunning–Kruger effect. The Dunning–Kruger effect is a type of cognitive bias in which we believe that we are smarter and more capable than we really are. As a result of this bias, we tend to have a propensity to overestimate our knowledge or ability in a particular area – particularly if it is a subject or area in which we have little to no experience. Very much like a cognitive blind spot, we don't seem to be able to see what we don't know about something. In many ways, we are all fools who are blind to our own foolishness.

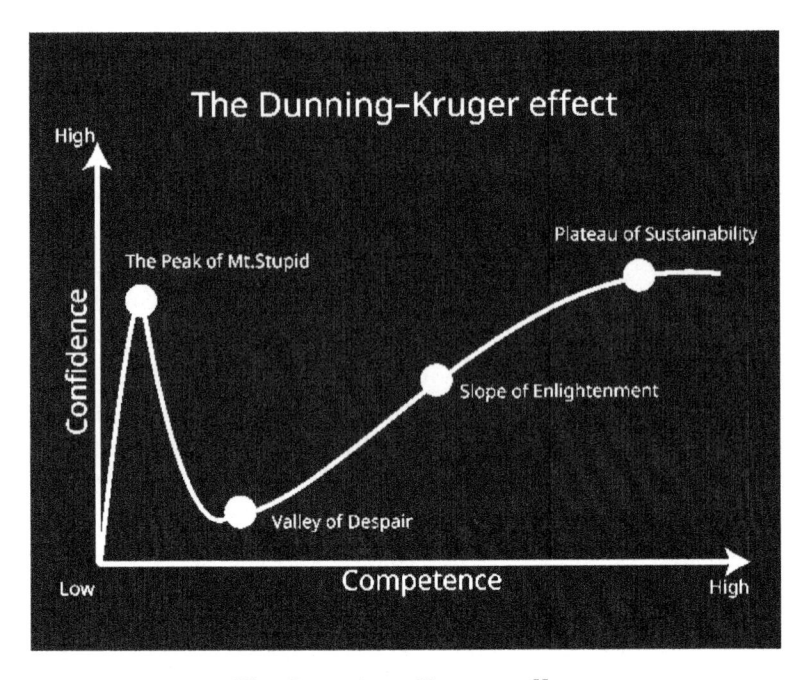

The Dunning–Kruger effect

How many of us have witnessed examples on TV shows such as *The X Factor* where the contestant's level of confidence and self-belief doesn't quite live up to their actual ability and talent. With this form of 'car-crash TV' we perhaps can find ourselves feeling uncomfortable for enjoying how the judges attempt to ground the contestant in some sort of reality. We may ponder as to the origin of this unusual, 'self-deluded' behaviour. Of course, when a contestant's beliefs have been propagated by a parent or carer, then the rejection by the judges and audience fails to shake their unwavering self-belief. As Charles Darwin poignantly writes in *The Descent of Man*, 'Ignorance more frequently begets confidence than does knowledge'.

The Dunning–Kruger phenomenon is not solely the domain of individuals we would perceive to be of lower intelligence or more deluded than the average person. On the contrary, politicians, actors and celebrities, CEOs, inventors and investors, astronauts, and teachers, in fact all of us without even realising it, can fall prey to the Dunning–Kruger effect. The dual irony is that at times we are all not only incompetent, but our incompetence robs us of the mental ability to realise just how incompetent we are, myself included.

Fooling others yields obvious benefits, but why do we so often fool ourselves? In his book *Deceit and Self-Deception*, author Robert Trivers provides us with possible answers. Put simply, the more we believe our own lies, the more sincerely, and hence effectively, we can lie to others. 'We hide reality from our conscious minds the better to hide it from onlookers', Trivers explains. But our illusions can have devastating consequences, from the ending of a marriage to a stock market collapse, and even the devastating commencement of a war.

DELUSIONS OF GRANDEUR

Our perceptions can have a massive impact on our beliefs and can trick us into thinking something that simply isn't true. Beliefs are powerful. They can influence us to think there are benefits to all kinds of products, therapies and services that may have no real value at all. For example, who among us has ever believed our car drives better and possibly even goes faster after we have had it cleaned? Similarly, as determined by a study published in the journal *Pain Medicine*, the 'consciousness areas' of the brain perceive less pain when taking a 'name-brand' placebo pain-relieving tablet as opposed to a 'generic' placebo. In other words, the perception of effectiveness of a placebo can have a huge impact on how efficient it is. Brain scans show that deep levels of awareness bias us towards familiar and popular items. Our belief that generic aspirin is inferior causes us to prefer another product based only on its familiar name. In the case of a placebo, these misconceptions can, in a sense, work for or against us.

Our belief systems are an invisible force underpinning all our behaviours. Along with our personality, genetic make-up and habits, our belief systems are one of the strongest forces affecting any decisions that we make in our lives. As we discussed earlier, we tend to call these types of beliefs 'core beliefs'. Core beliefs are just that – *core* to our identity. They can feel as deeply entwined with it as our gender or our name. If you had to think about choosing a different name for yourself for the rest of your life, it wouldn't feel right for a long time, until, by repetition, you finally got used to being called that new name. The same is true with our beliefs – we've worn them for so long that adopting new beliefs doesn't feel right, thus it can take time to change. That is why repetition is so vital in reprogramming the reptilian part of our brain.

Our core beliefs feel like absolute truths. They can be responsible for our feelings of insecurity and self-doubt. They can also be linked to feelings of depression as well as the constant desire for external validation and approval. They can lead to unproductive behavioural patterns such as perfectionism and the need to be a people-pleaser.

We go through our lives continually watching for events and situations that support and confirm our core beliefs, and ignoring and even challenging those that are contrary to our core beliefs. Our beliefs are like inner prison cells that have no doors and restrict us from experiencing new possibilities in life.

During our lifetime we accumulate thousands of beliefs about all aspects of our lives. Some good, some useful, some unhelpful, some destructive, our beliefs are the mental architecture that allows us to interpret our experiences.

When we enter this world, we are like a blank canvas. We have just two fears: falling and loud noises. Fear is adaptive because it protects us and, perhaps more importantly, it protected our ancestors. Because we had these innate fears, our distant ancestors who were afraid of heights didn't fall off cliffs, and those that feared wild animals didn't get eaten by a tiger.

Unlike these two fears, we are not born with a predetermined set of core beliefs. Belief systems are formed throughout our life, but especially during the time from birth through early childhood. Our core beliefs around *love* and *security* are usually formed by the time we are 4 years old because those two areas are essential for survival. If we aren't loved and cared for enough, or if we aren't safe, then we instinctively know we can potentially die.

The majority of our belief systems are naturally updated and changed as we go through life. We learn how to walk, ride a bicycle, tie our shoes, to read, to drive a car, get a job, and so on. Most of our belief systems work for us in a positive way and help us navigate through life.

However, when a belief is formed early and with strong emotions, it can remain unchanged in the subconscious until such time as it's consciously challenged and changed. It's these beliefs that are formed early in childhood and remain unchanged that can cause us difficulties as adults, and we will discuss those later this book.

Take a moment or two to cast a glance at the picture below and ask yourself what it is. You may recognise what it is immediately, but if not, you will certainly not be alone, as most people would not be able to recognise what it is. Now, what if I told you it was a creature – would this be any help? When you've given up, just go to the end of the chapter and you will be put out of your misery.

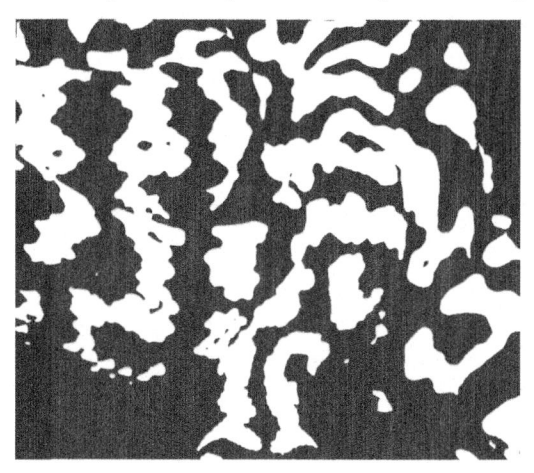

FIGURE B.

Now you know what it is, do you believe it is possible not to see the 'true' full image ever again when you look at this picture? Has your perception of it changed forever? No matter how many times you return to view this image you will always see the 'true' image, not the 'disguised' version. You may even wonder how you didn't see it in the first place (assuming you didn't). It can be the same with our beliefs. Once we have changed them and our perception has changed, it can sometimes be impossible, or indeed unnecessary to go back – to return to the original way we saw the world.

ROSE-COLOURED GLASSES

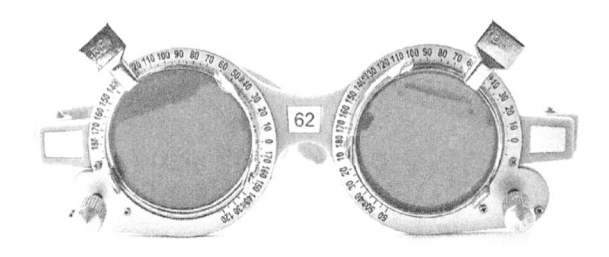

Optometrist glasses

Envisage, if you will, the following scenario: when we are born, we are given special glasses – the type that you get to wear briefly when you visit an optometrist. The heavy, metallic, round glasses that you can place other lenses into – in the case of an optometrist, the type used to assess the type of glasses you may potentially require. But, rather than being fitted with different glass lenses, imagine instead that different-coloured, transparent sheets are being placed in your glasses. Each one is so lightly coloured as to not be outwardly noticeable, unless pointed out to you by someone else.

Unlike the glasses, these coloured sheets remain permanently. Week after week, month after month and year after year, new coloured sheets are placed there on top of the other sheets, each with a slightly differing shade of colour. At the end of this time, what you see looks different, but you don't know or concern yourself with why it looks different. In fact, you can't even remember what it used to look like when you looked out through these, once unspoilt lenses. To you the world has always looked this way – the change has been so gradual.

Now, every other person you meet also has these glasses, but the colours and shades in their glasses are different to yours – to the extent that when you observe and experience the same situation as someone else, it is as if you are each witnessing something quite different. You only know and understand the manner in which you perceive it. To you it is an unarguable truth.

I am sure by now you have appreciated that what I am referring to here in this analogy is our belief systems and how they are formed. Without even realising it, we have been influenced by our parents, our caregivers, our teachers, friends and the media virtually since the day we were born. Each one placing a different tinted sheet in front of us and altering our perception of our world, potentially, if unchallenged, until the day we die.

By the time we are a young adult, we have a plethora of different colours that taint and blemish our world view. Some good, some bad, some empowering, some restrictive and limiting. One alters the other, like placing a blue on top of a yellow and getting green. No longer can we independently discern the colour blue or yellow; now all we can see is the green – almost to the point that it seems like the other colours never even existed. And all this has happened without us being aware that anything has even changed. Unsurprisingly, if we were to look through the lenses that our parents and caregivers possess then chances are we would be looking at the same-coloured view. Perhaps unsurprisingly, with a few exceptions, we enthusiastically take on the beliefs of those whom we know, like and trust.

If over time you are exposed to thoughts and beliefs that are in contradiction to your belief system, then there is a good chance that you will start to question some of your existing beliefs. In essence, that is at the centre of what this book are focusing on producing for you – providing you with enough insight and the tools to begin to challenge old paradigms, old models of thinking, and, in doing so, begin to peel off the coloured lenses that have limited your thoughts and beliefs. In many ways, to shift away from the cultural hypnosis that many of us have been exposed to all of our lives.

MAD WORLD

The economist and diplomat John Kenneth Galbraith once brilliantly stated that 'Faced with a choice between changing one's mind and proving there is no need to do so, almost everyone gets busy with the proof'. To that end, I am reminded of the Flat Earth Society. If you have not heard of them, just do a quick Google search to see the hundreds of sites dedicated to the idea. The most public group of writing is perhaps 'the Flat Earth Society'. The society boasts thousands of members worldwide and a Twitter following just shy of 94,000. In 2018, they held the first Flat Earth Convention in Birmingham, UK. The convention's organisers appeared on ITV's *This Morning* show, as well as being featured in the aptly titled 2018 Netflix documentary *Behind the Curve*. The number of 'Flat Earthers' is definitely on the rise around the globe, or rather across the flat plain as they see it.

Flat Earthers believe that the Earth is not round, but in essence flat, like a pancake. That it is surrounded on all sides by a huge impassable wall of ice and protected by a dome. Similar to a massive version of the Truman Show! Also, they believe that it is not hurtling through space at great speed but rooted still somehow – an immovable mass, the very epicentre of the universe.

Other Flat Earthers believe slightly different models of a flat earth. Some suggest the Earth is in fact diamond-shaped and supported by colossal columns. Seemingly, if you happen to walk off one edge, through a quirk of space and time, you'll appear on the other side, which, if you think about it, is really handy! Flat Earthers believe photos of the Earth are all photoshopped; GPS devices are rigged to make aeroplane pilots *think* they are flying in straight lines around a sphere when they are actually flying in circles above a disc. There is some contention as to the motive for why the world's governments would conceal the true shape of the Earth from us – the majority believing it is probably financial: in a nutshell, it would logically cost much less to fake a space programme than to actually have one, so those in on the conspiracy profit from the funding NASA and other space agencies receive from the government.

Remarkably, cricket star and TV personality Andrew 'Freddie' Flintoff believes that the world could be 'turnip shaped'. On his BBC Radio 5 show, which he co-hosts with Robbie Savage and Matthew Syed, Flintoff has previously said he thought the Moon landings could have been staged, once stating on the TV Show *Loose Women*, 'If I haven't seen it with my own eyes, I don't believe it.'

The Earth in Hindu mythology

Not believing the Earth is a globe isn't a new thing. In Hindu mythology, the Earth is supported by four elephants standing on the back of a turtle (which of course is a great idea for the main balancing animal as a monkey would have been a terrible choice). The Hindu deity Vishnu was reincarnated as the turtle Kachhapa, which carried the weight of the world on its back. Essentially, it consists of a large disc (complete with edge-of-the-world drop-off and consequent waterfall). Similar objects can be found in Chinese mythology and the mythologies of the Indigenous peoples of the Americas. So basically the Flat Earth Society is a little behind the curve (excuse the pun), as these ideas have been floating (or not floating depending on whom you believe) for thousands of years!

Intriguingly, interest in the Flat Earth theory spiked when NBA player Kyrie Irving said in a podcast that he believed the Earth to be flat. Also, when rapper Bobby Ray Simmons Jr, otherwise known as B.o.B, launched a crowd-funding campaign to send satellites into orbit to determine the Earth's shape, curiosity about the theory spiked again.

Perhaps unsurprisingly with all of the media attention given over to the subject, data from Google Trends show that since 2019, searches for 'flat earth' have more than tripled. While an overwhelming majority of Americans (84%) believe that the Earth is round, at least 5% of the public say they used to believe that, but now have their doubts. Flat Earthers have found traction in their beliefs among a younger generation of Americans. Young millennials, aged 18 to 24, are far likelier than any other age group to say that they believe the Earth to be flat (4%).

Perhaps not surprisingly, at this moment in time an astounding 65% of the population believe in conspiracy theories, and the vast majority of that 65% believe in more than one conspiracy theory.

EVERYBODY WANTS TO RULE THE WORLD

As we discussed previously, the Flat Earthers were not the first to suggest such a bold claim. In the 19th century, English inventor and writer Samuel Birley Rowbotham (1816–1884), penned a book called *Zetetic Astronomy: Earth Not a Globe.* Rowbotham's method, which he called zetetic astronomy, models the Earth as an enclosed plane centred at the North Pole and bounded along its perimeter by a wall of ice, with the Sun, Moon, planets and stars moving only several thousand miles above the surface of Earth. Sound familiar? The best part of the whole story is the fact that Rowbotham used a pseudonym, he called himself 'Parallax', and in doing so made himself sound like the coolest DJ of the 19th century.

Rowbotham ('Parallax') was convinced of the flatness of the Earth and began to lecture on the topic. He took a little time to learn his trade, running away from a lecture in Blackburn when he couldn't explain why the hulls of ships disappeared before their masts when sailing out to sea. However, he persisted and, charging sixpence a lecture, he began to fill halls where he asserted his bizarre theories.

In 1864 in Plymouth, England, Rowbotham was finally pinned down to a challenge by assertions that he wouldn't agree to a test. Undeterred, he appeared on Plymouth Hoe at the appointed time, witnessed by Richard A. Proctor, a writer in astronomy. He then proceeded to the beach where a telescope had been set up for him. His challengers had claimed that only the lantern of the Eddystone Lighthouse, some 14 miles out to sea, would be observable with a telescope. In fact, only half the lantern was visible, yet Rowbotham claimed his opponents were wrong and that it proved the Earth was indeed flat, leaving many of the onlookers to believe that some of the most important conclusions of modern astronomy had been seriously invalidated.

Proof then, perhaps, that no matter how much evidence an individual is presented with, if you ultimately want, and may even need to believe something you will see the world how you wish to see it. Be it flat, rounded or parsnip shaped! Never let the truth get in the way of your need to believe something.

It was Aristotle who first claimed that the world was a sphere sometime around 350 BCE. Plato agreed with him, as did Pythagoras and Archimedes. In 240 BCE, the astronomer Eratosthenes also concurred with them. He was also among the first to estimate the Earth's circumference. It was confirmed in the 1500s when a Spanish expedition, led by Magellan, circumnavigated the globe. Most of us have believed ever since that the world is indeed a globe – though not all apparently.

With regard to the Flat Earth movement, American astrophysicist Neil deGrasse Tyson stated, 'There are people who think that Earth is flat but recognize that the moon is round. Mercury, Venus, Mars, Jupiter, Saturn, Uranus, Neptune and the sun are all spheres. But Earth is flat ... something doesn't square here.'

Tyson explained that, because of the laws of physics and the way energy works, the universe 'favours the sphere' when forming planets and other bodies. Sometimes, a sphere might be distorted because it's rotating very fast, but almost everything in the universe is spherical, or almost spherical. The exception being asteroids, which are small bodies of ice and rock and are irregularly shaped, as they have a gravity too low to pull their mass into a sphere.

There's even more evidence that the Earth is round, Tyson said. During lunar eclipses, the Moon passes into the Earth's shadow and lies directly opposite the Sun. The shape of the Earth's shadow is always round in these eclipses. If Earth were a flat planet, at times, you would see a flat shadow on the Moon. But that's never happened, Tyson added. The Earth must be a sphere, because that's the only thing that casts a perfect circle every time.

Tyson went on to state that, 'If you think about a ship sailing toward the horizon, it gradually disappears, because the Earth is curved'. Tyson further described an experiment by the aforementioned Greek mathematician, geographer and astronomer Eratosthenes, who lived in Alexandria around 250 BCE. Eratosthenes noted that, in the Egyptian city of Syene (near modern-day Aswan), on 21 June that year, during the summer solstice, you could see right to the bottom of a well at noon. On the same day, you couldn't see to the bottom of a well in Alexandria, a city some 500 miles away. Tyson goes on to discuss that there are two possible explanations for that observation. The first is that the Earth is flat and has a small sun, close to the planet. The second is that the Earth is curved, with a sun further from the planet. He added that, if you were of course to extend the experiment to three wells, there's no way a flat Earth's geometry would fit the experiment's results.

So, why do people still believe the Earth is flat despite the overwhelming evidence to the contrary? Tyson believes that people believe in a flat Earth for two reasons: first, that in the United States the right to free speech is protected; and, second, its educational system doesn't teach students to think critically about the evidence. Physician and writer Atul Gawande summed it up perfectly when he stated, 'it's not so much about mistrust of science, as it is about mistrusting scientists'.

To understand Flat Earthers, and other individuals who hold unconventional beliefs, we need to first consider what it means to 'believe'. A belief, as we have discussed previously, is a cognitive representation of the nature of reality, encompassing our inner experiences, the world around us and the world beyond.

The reason I have examined the Flat Earth Society in this book, and that I have dedicated so much of this chapter to it, is not to denigrate the believers, but to highlight why perhaps sometimes we 'need' to believe something, to the extent that we believe it is part of our identity. It is 'who we are'. To no longer hold the belief would seem almost as if we were losing part of ourselves –it would shake up our perceptions of our world so much, the world would no longer make sense to us.

To this end, it is sometimes necessary to fight tooth and nail to hold onto and maintain those beliefs. Questioning the status quo is fine, in fact it's good, but when you are presented with solid scientific evidence then, conceivably, you have to consider why the need for a particular belief is there in the first place. Is it perhaps to fulfil the need to be part of a break-off group, almost as if you are liberating yourself from 'the matrix'? Perhaps unsurprisingly, as we discussed above, rarely, if ever, do individuals who have a fascination with conspiracy theories believe in just one. Often there are multiple conspiracy theories being examined and considered.

Imagine for a moment that we have offered to fund a manned rocket launch to go up into the Earth's atmosphere to witness first-hand the curvature of the Earth. On this expedition, we invite as many Flat Earthers as we can possibly accommodate. After the journey has taken place and the spaceship, its passengers and crew have returned to terra firma, how many of the Flat Earthers have changed their belief about the shape of our home planet? Many of these people are highly educated, and they have their own maths and logic to prove their belief. I would hazard a guess that the substantial majority would still maintain their original belief. Maintaining that perhaps the trip itself had been somehow faked, and that what they viewed through the window of the spaceship was indeed a spectacular special effect.

Of course, this speaks greatly of the need to believe. We may mock them for their belief, but you and I also have our own beliefs we 'need to maintain' and nobody can change those except ourselves. Our minds are like crazy machines that only show us what we want to see. Leo Tolstoy sums it up perfectly when he writes, 'The most difficult subjects can be explained to the most slow-witted man if he has not formed any idea of them already; but the simplest thing cannot be made clear to the most intelligent man if he is firmly persuaded that he knows already, without a shadow of doubt, what is laid before him'.

FIGURE B.

SUMMARY

Cognitive biases alter our perception of things daily without us realising. One common such phenomenon is the Dunning–Kruger bias: the belief that we are smarter or more capable of something than we perhaps actually are. In other words, the overestimation of our own abilities. We can often easily notice this altered perception in the shortcomings of others around us, but it is much harder to notice in our own behaviours, purely because our minds are brilliant at tricking us. When we truly believe something, when it is deeply engrained in our belief systems, it is near impossible to challenge it, despite any evidence that contradicts it. The example examined in this chapter is those who believe that the Earth is flat. Despite hundreds, if not thousands, of physicians and astronomers providing evidence for the spherical shape of the Earth, Flat Earthers still believe that it is flat. Is this because they need to believe it? Is it because of what that have been led to believe their whole lives? After all, we all have different belief systems, and they all alter the way we individually look at the world.

CHAPTER SIX

CLOSE ENCOUNTERS OF THE HERD KIND

You know, it's funny; when you look at someone through rose-coloured glasses, all the red flags just look like flags.
– WANDA FROM THE TV SHOW BOJACK HORSEMAN

At 6 o'clock on Christmas Eve, 1954, a small group gathered on the street outside the home of 54-year-old housewife and spiritual medium Dorothy Martin in Illinois. The group sang Christmas carols. But this was no customary Christmas gathering. The group were not celebrating the birth of Jesus but waiting to depart the Earth in a spaceship that Martin had predicted would come for them. Members of the press and some 200 spectators had gathered to watch the event unfold.

The day before, Martin had received a message informing her that her group was to wait at that place, at that time, for a flying saucer to land. The group waited eagerly for the aliens to collect and save them. They had packed their bags following the strict packing instructions. These included making sure all tinfoil was removed, even from the gum wrappers they may have with them. They waited and waited and when no spaceship arrived, they went back inside.

Martin had informed her followers, a group known as 'the Seekers' or the 'Brotherhood of the Seven Rays', that a catastrophic flood was imminent, but that the true believers would be extracted from the Earth by spacemen, much like the Noah story in the book of Genesis. Dorothy Martin had begun to receive what she believed were messages from the spacemen through a form of automatic writing. A form of writing believed to be formed by a spirit, the occult or the subconscious, rather than by the conscious intention of the writer (see Chapter 15 on the Law of Reversed Effort). Quintessentially, Martin believed the words she was being inspired to write were being channelled directly from the alien supreme beings on the planet Clarion. These alien beings predicted an impending apocalypse, and that the human race would be annihilated on 21 December 1954. Every member of the Seekers, being true believers, had to get themselves ready for this impending cataclysmic event. Members had left their jobs and their families in preparation. They had given away their money and parted with their worldly belongings – those things would not be needed on Clarion.

Strangely, this was the fourth time the group had been commanded to stand outside and wait for their interstellar taxi to arrive. Each time they waited with bated breath, but their spaceship never materialised.

Each time the extra-terrestrials didn't show up, Martin informed her followers of a message that had been relayed from the aliens as a reason for their lateness. Martin always seemed to manage to muster up a plausible reason for the absence. Similarly, the waiting group convinced themselves each time there was a 'no show' that it must have been a practice session.

By midnight of 21 December, unsurprisingly the world still had not ended. As the deadline for the rescue had passed, the gathered group became increasingly anxious, sitting motionless in Martin's living room, waiting for further instructions on what to do next. It was not until 4.45am that Martin, at last, received another communication. This time it was from the God of the Earth. This new message claimed that the faith demonstrated by this group of true believers had shed so much light onto the Earth that the coming disaster had been fortunately averted. By the afternoon of 22 December, the group's mission had changed. The new objective was to spread their message of hope to the world.

The events that unfolded in December 1954 fascinated social psychologist Leon Festinger. Festinger had managed to infiltrate the Seekers. He was intrigued as to what would happen if you believed in something so much, you were willing to reject reality to the extent you would reject your friends, sell your house and car, and give up everything to do so. Working with a team of two other psychologists, Festinger wanted to study the individual members of the cult over time to see how they would cope once they realised their prophecy was not going to materialise.

One main area Festinger and his colleagues wanted to examine was the so-called 'foot in the door' paradigm. This is a compliance tactic which assumes that when an individual agrees to a small request, they are then far more likely to agree to a second, much larger, request.

When cult members essentially crossed the threshold by sacrificing their family, jobs, money and belongings, the idea that their commitment to their beliefs might be false if the prophecy were not genuine led to potential extreme anxiety. The only way to overcome the obvious anxiety was to modify the belief and justify the sacrifices that had been made. Festinger's work was the first to shine a spotlight on the mechanisms at work behind members of cults and extreme belief systems – in particular, how members can continue to maintain a belief despite great personal loss.

The term cognitive dissonance is now used to describe the mental discomfort that we experience when, as individuals, we try to maintain two conflicting beliefs, values or attitudes. As humans we tend to seek consistency in our attitudes and perceptions, so this conflict can cause feelings of unease or discomfort. This inconsistency between what people believe and how they behave motivates people to engage in actions that will help minimise feelings of discomfort. People attempt to relieve this tension in different ways, such as by rejecting, explaining away or avoiding new information that contradicts those beliefs.

Smoking, for instance, is a good example of cognitive dissonance. Without any doubt, smoking has been shown to cause numerous health complications. However, individuals who smoke will rationalise to themselves, and often others, why they still have the compulsion to smoke despite the obvious consequences. At a subconscious level, individuals will often struggle with the clash between reason and the beliefs surrounding maintaining the unhealthy habit.

In 1959, Festinger followed up with another ground-breaking experiment, where he asked 71 male students to carry out a particularly monotonous task: turning pegs on a board for an hour. Participants were then given a choice: repeat the task again and earn another $1, or go into the waiting room and tell the next waiting participant that the task was 'lots of fun'. For doing this they would be paid a healthy $20!

You will not be surprised to learn that most participants took the $20. They perhaps justified it to themselves by reasoning that getting more money was worth lying. Fascinatingly, the few participants who stayed and earned the $1 also maintained to themselves that the task was more interesting than it actually was. In both cases, the experiment further demonstrated that we all have natural mechanisms for coping with cognitive dissonance. We tend to do this by modifying our beliefs to reduce the anxiety that arises from holding two contradictory beliefs.

Although the Seekers was a relatively small group – it had some 30 members – it was made up of individuals whom you would not normally associate with such magical, mystical beliefs. Amongst them was a former staff physician at Michigan State, the aptly named Dr Charles Laughead. After the alien visitation had failed to transpire, Dr Laughead went on to state, 'I've had to go a long way. I've given up just about everything. I've cut every tie. I've burned every bridge. I've turned my back on the world. I can't afford to doubt. I have to believe. And there isn't any other truth.'

When faced with the prospect of admitting you're wrong, or looking for a better explanation, most people get busy looking for an explanation. In fact, everyone experiences cognitive dissonance to some degree, but that doesn't mean that it is always that easy to recognise in ourselves. We are far more likely to witness examples of cognitive dissonance in the actions of our family and friends.

Incidentally, Dorothy Martin faced several police charges after the incident in December 1954. She went on to change her name to Sister Thedra and continued to practise as a channeller of extra-terrestrial entities until her death in 1992.

Psychologist and author Steven Pinker sums up perfectly why as individuals we feel the strong need to belong to a group of fellow believers in his book *How The Mind Works* when he writes, 'People are embraced or condemned according to their beliefs, so one function of the mind may be to hold beliefs that bring the belief-holder the greatest number of allies, protectors, or disciples, rather than beliefs that are most likely to be true'.

SUMMARY

Chapter 6 looked in detail at spiritual medium Dorothy Martin and her group of followers, the Seekers. When Martin was contacted by otherworldly beings and told that the world was going to end for everyone except those who had devoted themselves to the cause, she set about gathering a group of individuals – the Seekers. They were told that those who truly believed would be saved by a spaceship from the impending floods. This raises the question of how far would you go and what would you be willing to sacrifice for your beliefs? And if these beliefs end up being false, would your objective or explanation change in order to save face? When we are in this state of cognitive dissonance, we are often faced with a choice – to change our explanation, or admit we are wrong – in order to avoid the anxiety that is brought about when our sacrifices are made in vain.

CHAPTER SEVEN

JUST AN ILLUSION

*Reality is merely an illusion,
albeit a very persistent one.*
– ALBERT EINSTEIN

Take a moment to picture your mobile phone. Now, imagine opening your phone so the apps on your home screen are clearly visible. Can you picture which app is in the bottom left? How about the top right? Now can you picture how many apps there are horizontally across the screen? How about vertically? Out of interest how many of the apps on your home screen can you actually recall? Can you remember what your wallpaper is at present on your phone?

Now pick up your mobile (unless you have been frustrated enough to do so already!) and have a look.

So, how did you do?

Now you've had a moment to look at your device, obviously checking your emails, texts and social media feed as well. 'I might as well,' you say to yourself, after all you picked it up anyway! Now can you remember what time was shown on your screen?

I would imagine, unless you are fortunate enough to have a photographic memory or an eidetic memory and had glanced at your phone quite recently, then you were surprised at how vague your recall of your home screen is.

The average person picks up their phones 58 times a day, spending an average of 3 hours and 15 minutes each day on their device, with the top 20% of smartphone users spending upwards of 4 hours and 30 minutes on their devices. Assuming you don't change your home screen daily, that's a whopping 1740 times, at least, a month we gaze at our home screens. Yet, the majority of us (myself included) only have a vague semblance in our heads of how the screen we see so often is laid out. The question therefore is this: do we look at the things we see consciously, or does familiarity lead us to not actually process what we are seeing? In other words, do we disregard the things that are common to us, that we know are there, without actually observing them? If someone hacked into your device today and changed one app, would you notice? How about three of your apps? In fact, while you have been reading this my team has remotely logged into your phone and done just that! Go on, take a look!

Okay, you know that's not true. But if you did look, then please send £100 now to the address at the end of this chapter. Oh, and your car keys.

So, do we see things as they actually are, or do we see things as we believe they are? Do we miss things that are in plain sight?

The work of Harvard professors Christopher Chabris and Daniel Simons proves brilliantly that we don't always see things the way we believe we see them. Particularly if the stakes are high. Take a moment now to go online and search for the 'The Hidden Gorilla' on YouTube.

Chances are, as you now know the title of this famous psychology experiment, there is a pretty good chance that you spotted the gorilla as soon as it appeared. Now show the video to a partner or friend but offer an exciting prize if they spot how many times the people wearing white pass the ball. The likelihood is (unless they are familiar with the video) they missed the unfamiliar thing that was in plain sight, namely the 6-foot gorilla. If you did see the gorilla, did you notice in one version of the experiment the background changes colour as well? Or Donald Trump in a tutu on the top right-hand corner of the screen?

I'm kidding about Mr Trump, of course, but did you watch it again just to make sure, not believing what you had previously watched?

References

So why is offering such a significant prize so important? Simply because it has the effect of focusing our attention. We don't want to lose out. Our brains are hardwired to fear potential loss. Think about a time when you've had the good fortune to discover money in your pocket. Remember how you were momentarily filled with bliss. Now recall a time when you accidentally lost some money, perhaps the same amount as you found. You were probably angry and annoyed for hours, if not the whole day – maybe even regaling others with the tale of your misfortune for weeks! This fascinating cognitive bias, known as loss aversion, was first identified and studied by cognitive mathematical psychologist Amos Tversky. Specifically, his research demonstrated that losses are twice as powerful compared to their equivalent gains.

For a fascinating example of the power of loss aversion, we can look to the drivers in Italy. Like other European countries, Italy has a penalty point system for driving licences. However, unlike other countries, since 2003, drivers in Italy don't just lose points for poor driving. Italian drivers start with 20 points and receive a bonus of 2 points for every 2 years of driving well – up to a maximum of 30 points. Each traffic violation, however, incurs a specific point penalty and, should the driver lose all points, the driving licence is revoked. This powerful use of loss aversion in this example, along with other factors, has greatly reduced the number of road traffic accidents in Italy.

So, regarding counting the folks in white t-shirts, the greater the potential prize, the greater the likelihood your friend or spouse will not have spotted the gorilla in the ball-passing frenzy. I just hope they don't get too angry when they realise there is in fact no actual prize.

BICYCLE RACE

Again, do we see what we actually see, or do we see what we expect to see? It is believed that the disproportionately high number of motorcycle-related traffic accidents may be linked to the way the human brain processes, or rather fails to process, information. The term inattentional blindness was first coined by psychologists Arien Mack and Irvin Rock, who observed the phenomenon during their ground-breaking perception and attention experiments.

The perfectly named inattentional blindness is the surprising phenomenon whereby a person fails to notice an unexpected object located in plain sight. This strange occurrence is believed to explain the prevalence of looked-but-failed-to-see (LBFTS) crashes, the most common type of collision involving motorcycles.

According to researchers, LBFTS crashes are particularly worrying because, despite clear conditions and the lack of other hazards or distractions, drivers will look in the direction of the oncoming motorcycle, and in some cases appear to look directly at the motorcycle, but still pull out into its path.

So why does this happen? It is believed that when we are driving, there is such a huge amount of sensory information that our brain must deal with we simply can't attend to everything because this would consume enormous cognitive resources and take too much time. So our brain must decide what information is most relevant to the task at hand. The frequency of LBFTS crashes suggests perhaps that there is a strong connection with how the brain filters out information.

Of course, the irony of the situation about driving is that, even though more than 90% of crashes involve human error, we all believe we are much better drivers than we actually are. In fact, a recent survey found that over 70% of Americans drivers claimed that they were better-than-average drivers. Men in particular fall foul of this driving skill bias, with a perhaps unsurprising 8 in 10 considering their driving skills better than average.

A similar study was carried out in 1980 by Swedish psychologist Ola Svenson. He asked American and Swedish college students to rank their driving ability among their peers. The results were striking: 88% of the Americans and 77% of the Swedes ranked themselves in the top half when it came to driving safely. When they were asked to rank their driving skill, 93% of the Americans said they were better than average, compared to 69% of the Swedish students.

This and numerous other studies demonstrate the same human fallacy – namely that as people we all have a tendency to overestimate our own abilities. Similarly, in another study, 90% of college professors thought they were above average teachers, while another established that, out of a whopping 800,000 high school students, only 1% thought their social skills were below average.

This illusory superiority is a cognitive bias whereby we overestimate our own qualities and abilities relative to others – something that has come to be known as the Lake Wobegon effect, named after a fictional town in Minnesota, where 'all the women are strong, all the men are good looking, and all the children are above average'. This cognitive trap prevents us from seriously examining our own skills and thus overlooking opportunities for growth. From a personal development standpoint, the illusory superiority fallacy can be a barrier to self-improvement on many fronts. Its origin is of no surprise though.

Remember in school when just about everything you did was in relation to others? Competitions had first, second and third place. You were constantly compared to others in terms of ability and talent. No surprise then that we all grow up still comparing ourselves to others, often with our self-esteem being solely reliant on our perceived position in society. Clearly, we cannot all be number one, so to reduce the anxiety related to the feelings of disappointment this can evoke, we perhaps delude ourselves as to our abilities – be it our intelligence, sense of humour, driving ability or desirableness as a partner. Outwardly this may seem to be a good thing, a positive self-delusion, but what potential negative effects may lay beneath its shiny veneer? As author Robert Trivers says in *Deceit and Self-Deception*, 'even before we can speak, we learn to cry insincerely to manipulate our caregivers'. As adults, we continually employ 'confirmation bias', looking for and seizing on facts that bolster our preconceptions and overlook contradictory information. Often, we can become a master dissembler,[1] hiding not only from others, but from ourselves and our true thoughts and feelings. Think of the individual who defends an alcoholic and abusive parent or partner. Or the parent who defends the poor behaviour of their offspring. Again, we can often aim to deceive ourselves, in order to deceive others.

All of us can have a tendency to overestimate our skills, believing that we miss very little from the observable world. But what if I told you that you were blind for around 40 minutes each day? Would you believe me? Probably not.

Let's try this little experiment...

ONE MOMENT IN TIME

Find an analogue clock in your home, then try to observe what happens when you glance at it for the first time after, say, you have been reading a book or watching television. Did the second hand seem to linger for just a moment longer than it should, as though it had been frozen right before you looked up at the clock? This is known as the stopped-clock illusion, and it's an example of chronostasis. The reason behind this common illusion is actually an unbelievable act of coordination between your eyes and your brain. This illusion is a perfect demonstration of the fact that our brain is as much a part of how we perceive time as the reality of time itself. Similarly, have you ever wondered why, as your eyes dart from one place to another, your eyes don't blur like a movie being filmed from a moving car or train?

As our eyes move, there is a blurring of the image on the retina. To counteract this so that the image stays clear and sharp, a part of the brain, believed to be the cortex, cuts off the processing of images. What happens is that we go momentarily blind as the visual information is no longer going to the brain, therefore stopping the blur. We can't see this happening as it is done automatically and quickly thousands of times a day.

Now try this if you can. Take a moment to look in a mirror, ideally with your nose about 6 inches away from its surface. Now pass your gaze from one eye to the other. Observe that as you do this you are unable to see or feel your eyes moving. Now have a friend watch your eyes as you do this test again. They will see your eyes moving back and forth. The truth is that we cannot see our eyes in motion. We can see other people's eyes in motion, and other people can see ours, but we cannot see our own eyes move – a phenomenon known as saccadic masking.

Researchers believe that we don't notice these skips because the brain lets us experience vision as one continuous movement. Essentially, it fills in these gaps in vision the way it fills in a blind spot. Sometimes it does this by making us believe that certain moments last longer than they actually do in reality. This stopped-clock illusion for example, occurs following a rapid eye movement (REM) where the brain produces a still image rather than a blurred one.

The incredible thing is that, in the case of the stopped-clock illusion, it might only seem like a second before the hand starts ticking again; however, these lost fractions of a second can add up to an incredible 40 minutes a day! In reality, whilst this illusion does technically happen every time we move our eyes rapidly, a lot of the time it is undetectable.

CAN'T TAKE MY EYES OFF YOU

Of course, we often assume that if our eyes are open, we are seeing absolutely everything. But that's not the case. If you've ever experienced someone getting annoyed with you because they saw something and they think you should have too, then you know exactly how that is. The fact is even large objects in our visual field can pass our attention and go unnoticed. Think of the number of TV shows dedicated to mistakes in movies. When we watch these 'bloopers', how often do we question how we could have missed something so obvious?

Seeing is very much about attention, perception and focus. Two people in the same room may take in completely different features, based on what they are expecting or what they are focusing on. Our perceptions can very much depend not only on our vantage point, but the expectations we have about what we are seeing. Of course, it's not about doubting everything that comes through our senses, but perhaps more about looking for our blind spots, with the goal of becoming better thinkers.

In conclusion, our inattentional blindness perhaps causes us to see far less of our world than we think we do, and it's empowering to be aware of that fact. As Daniel Kahneman describes brilliantly in his book *Thinking, Fast and Slow*, 'What you see is all there is', evidencing how irrational we are in making decisions based on what we believe we are seeing, when, in fact, what we are seeing has an inherent cognitive bias to it. Indeed, if we base our decisions on what we believe we are seeing, then it is like breaking up a fight between siblings and only listening to one side of the argument to ascertain what has occurred.

It perhaps goes without saying that we can often base our beliefs on what we see. But can we believe what we have come to believe based on what we have seen?

[1] Dissembler – a person who professes beliefs and opinions that he or she does not hold to conceal his or her real feelings or motives.

SUMMARY

Do we see everything we look at? Do you consciously process everything you look at, or do you fill the gaps based on what you expect to be there? A lot of the time, we disregard something, and assume it to be there because it always has been. This familiarity is comforting but can lead us to miss vital pieces of information in a day. This chapter looks into the thought biases that lead to this happening, loss aversion and inattentional, and raises the question: for how much of the day do you think you are blind?

References

CHAPTER EIGHT

WE BECOME WHAT WE THINK ABOUT MOST OF THE TIME

Some people grin and bear it.
Others smile and change it.
– ANON.

In 1952, in an interview in London, Nobel Prize winner and peace activist Dr Albert Schweitzer was posed a question by a journalist: 'What's wrong with men today?' Dr Schweitzer paused for a few moments, thinking carefully, and then replied, 'Men simply don't think'. Clearly women had not been invented in the 1950s so this was a problem just for men to overcome! Today, in the early part of the 21st century, the problems we all face are not so much linked to not thinking, but perhaps more to thinking too much, as we live in an age of information overload. In 1952, I'm sure Dr Schweitzer could never have conceived of an age where an individual could access all of the information they could ever want or need on a device not much larger than an average purse or wallet. In a world where we have the ability to be more connected than ever before, paradoxically, people are now feeling more insular and isolated than ever before.

Of course, what Dr Schweitzer asserted was not that the average person was not thinking at all, but that they paid little consideration to the path that their life took.

Perhaps it isn't so much that 'Men don't think', but that we don't think of the things that will lead us to a happy and fulfilled life – living more in the past, and looking more towards the uncertainty of the future than actively living in the moment. The moment you are now in. Not the past, not the future, but right now. Because really, that's all there is, the present moment. Not that we shouldn't think and plan ahead, but if you are permanently 'living' in a potential future, then you by definition are not being present in the moment now.

In Earl Nightingale's pioneering audio book *The Strangest Secret* he quotes Dr Schweitzer and goes on to discuss this condition further. I do recommend Googling the above, as there are lots of free versions of the classic 1956 audio book to listen to and digest. Almost 70 years on it is still relevant.

In 1947, W.H. Auden wrote the poem 'The Age of Anxiety', and it appears to be almost prophetic in its prediction of life in the modern world. Indeed, never before in the age of man (and now women fortunately!) have people experienced the unprecedented levels of anxiety and stress in their day-to-day lives as now in the 21st century. Here in the UK, a staggering one in four of us will experience a mental health problem of some kind each year – with one in six of us reporting experiencing a common mental health problem, such as anxiety and depression, in any given week.

In many ways, the problems we are facing nowadays are not so much down to the fact that men (and women) just don't think, but are more than likely down to what and how people think. Indeed, think about your own education and ask yourself, did you spend any time learning skills around how to manage your thinking, how to lower your stress and anxiety levels, and how to focus on gratitude and happiness in your life? Sadly, I doubt you will have, unless you were very lucky and had an extraordinary teacher.

In his seminal book *The Monk Who Sold His Ferrari*, author Robin Sharma writes of meeting a high-profile trial lawyer, Julian Mantle. In this fable, Julian's life is centred around power, prestige and the desire for money. Near the beginning of the book, while arguing a case in court, Julian collapses from a heart attack and nearly loses his life at just 53. He survives and is given a second chance at life. He knows his life needs to change and he abandons his lavish lifestyle in search of one with greater meaning and

References

significance. He journeys to India for spiritual answers. In the Himalayan mountains he meets a Sage of Sivana named Yogi Raman. The wise Yogi then begins to teach Julian seven virtues.

After several years with the Sivana, Julian returns. Renewed and transformed, Julian begins to share everything he has learnt on his journey with his former co-worker and friend, who is still on the treadmill at the law firm – a friend who was potentially destined to end up the same way Julian did, fighting for his life on the courtroom floor.

One of the most poetic chapters in the book is when Julian speaks of what he learnt from the Sages of Sivana, and how we as people must learn to manage our thinking. He speaks of our minds being akin to gardens, gardens that we can nurture and cultivate, and will, given time, blossom far beyond our expectations. However, if we let the weeds take root, lasting peace of mind and deep inner harmony will always elude us. Sharma writes: 'To live life to the fullest, you must stand guard at the gate of your garden and let only the very best information enter. You truly cannot afford the luxury of a negative thought – not even one.'

When you are experiencing challenges in life, such as anxiety or depression, well-intentioned advice such as 'Why don't you try and pull yourself out of it?' or 'It can't be that bad' can have a detrimental effect on the individual sufferer, potentially causing even more feelings of helplessness, powerlessness and guilt. Similarly, when someone is experiencing the symptoms of the above, trying to meditate or attempting to use popular techniques such as positive affirmations can actually have a detrimental effect. So why is that the case? After all, everyone raves about how great meditating is for you – just about everyone is doing it nowadays it seems. After all, research has shown that practising meditation for a period of 6–9 months is believed to reduce anxiety by up to 60%!

So, here's the rub. If you are experiencing anxiety or depression, then, almost by default, you are very much 'living in your head'. The likelihood is that you are not living in the present moment, but either living in fear of the future, or trying to come to terms with possible traumas of the past. In essence, you are living in an almost constant state of 'fight or flight'. Of course, mindfulness is fantastic for helping you to live in the moment more; to be, as the name suggests, more 'mindful'. However, regardless of whether those traumas are conscious or subconscious, attempting to meditate or even be mindful during these periods can have the effect of creating even more anxiety. At those times perhaps it's not the panacea for anxiety and depression it is often thought to be.

The individual can then often feel even more of a failure, as they feel that they are unable to meditate effectively. Of course, meditation is often very much misunderstood in our Western world – its Indian and Chinese origins often being muddied by Western understandings of its powerful therapeutic processes.

Indeed, a study carried out at University College London discovered that there could be a dark side to meditating. In an international online survey of more than 1200 regular meditators, the researchers found that more than a quarter have had a 'particularly unpleasant' psychological experience related to the practice, including feelings of fear and distorted emotions. However, the study did not assess possible pre-existing mental health problems, which could have a huge bearing on the research. Again, if one in four of us experiences mental health problems in any given year, then this figure fits perfectly with this research.

In their ground-breaking book *The Buddha Pill*, Dr Miguel Farias and Dr Catherine Wikholm discuss in detail the pros and cons of meditation and mindfulness, putting their effects under the microscope and challenging the mainstream perception of what they are for, in addition to who should be practising them. According to Dr Miguel, it is believed that around 1 in 12 people who try meditation will experience some unwanted negative effect – usually a worsening in depression or anxiety, or even the onset of these conditions for the first time. Dr Miguel goes on to say, 'For most people it works fine, but it has undoubtedly been overhyped and it's not universally benevolent'. Perhaps Guru Swami Venkatesananda states it best when he says, 'Meditation is

References

like cooking — and, you know, in cooking scum comes up to the surface'.

For my clients in our practice, whilst I don't actually suggest *not* meditating, I do recommend that if they are experiencing the symptoms of depression or anxiety, if they are willing, they should endeavour to undertake what is known as the Wim Hof breathing technique. In addition to this technique, I also suggest that some clients start having some cold exposure, such as a cold shower or, if possible, an ice bath.

Better known as 'the Iceman', Dutch extreme athlete Wim Hof has not only helped advance scientific understanding, but also accomplished extraordinary feats of human endurance, including some 21 Guinness World Records. Wim's unbelievable achievements include climbing Mount Kilimanjaro in shorts, running a half-marathon above the Arctic Circle barefoot and standing in a container while covered with ice cubes for more than 112 minutes. The Wim Hof method is a combination of breathing, cold therapy and commitment to change, and can improve your health and happiness levels. It has been shown to have a profound effect on the symptoms of depression and anxiety in individuals who undertake its protocols.

At present, at least two of my clients sit in a cold river regularly, and others have purchased their own ice baths, as well as several who enjoy cold-water swimming regularly. When I say enjoy, I do mean enjoy – the process of cold exposure can become addictive due to the post-cold endorphin release. The cold-water exposure has the effect of sending many electrical impulses to your brain, which increases alertness, clarity and energy levels. Endorphins, more commonly known as the happiness hormone, are then released into your system. This effect can lead to feelings of well-being and optimism, which is incredible for anyone experiencing depression or anxiety.

I view using the Wim Hof method as one of the possible 'Circuit Breakers' we will discuss later in this book as part of the § Method.

A CHANGE IS GONNA COME

At this stage in your life, are you feeling that you have not achieved the levels of success and happiness that you hoped for? Have you read every new self-help book that hits the mainstream, attended life transformation courses, visited a range of therapists and done 'lots of work on yourself' for it all to be in vain? It could be that something needs to be challenged in your thinking and belief systems.

What if I were to tell you that it is estimated that an impressive 90–95% of change comes from real insight into the workings of our psyche – your conscious and unconscious minds working in harmony for your benefit, free from self-sabotaging behaviour? Indeed, I sincerely believe you can change your personality – you can literally reprogramme your mind for happiness and success. My heartfelt hope for you is that by the time you finish reading this book, every night your brain, due to neuroplasticity, will be vastly different from when you started.

In 1949, in his ground-breaking book *The Organization of Behaviour*, neuropsychologist Donald Hebb first used the phrase 'Neurons that fire together, wire together'. The intriguing phrase was used to describe how pathways in the brain are formed and reinforced through repetition. Hebb famously said that 'any two cells, or systems of cells, that are repeatedly active at the same time will tend to become "associated," so that activity in one facilitates activity in the other'. Otherwise known as Hebb's law, it describes how the more the brain does a certain task, the stronger that neural network becomes, making the process more efficient each successive time. The more we do and think something, the more that process creates and strengthens pathways in the brain for it to occur again. Likewise, the more we do it, the more ingrained the practice becomes and the easier it is for our brain to process it, be it a positive or negative thought, or activity. Sometimes it's good to be reminded why we need to manage our thinking daily.

TOYS IN THE ATTIC

I call difficulties in making lasting transformation the 'Stretch Armstrong effect'. One of the 'must-have' toys of the 1970s was a character called 'Stretch Armstrong'. No matter what you did to muscle-bound Stretch in his tiny blue trunks, he would return to his original shape. For some, transformation can be just like Stretch – no matter what you do, or learn, nothing seems to change. I often think this about the lovely clients I have met over the years in our practice here in Hampshire, particularly the clients who I have helped to quit smoking. On average, I will see a client to help them stop smoking for just 2 hours. What I have noticed is in the 2-hour session we have together, most clients have an 'aha moment'. What I mean is they just suddenly 'get it', and from that moment onwards they are essentially a non-smoker. In essence, their belief system around smoking has changed. Sometimes, however, the client's fear of becoming a non-smoker and what changes and challenges that may bring can be enough to hold onto the habit of smoking. This, of course, is much rarer. Sometimes, there are clients who are in the middle, and those clients need just a little more help to help shift their beliefs. So why is it so easy for some, but for others more of a challenge?

Of course, all smokers believe they want to quit smoking when they book their session, but the anxiety around quitting can, for some, be too much. Just like Stretch Armstrong they return to their original, and perhaps safe, belief systems. Essentially, if we fight for our limitations, we get to keep them.

The majority of the stop-smoking clients I have the pleasure of working with leave the session and never think about, or have the desire to, smoke ever again. Occasionally, a client who has stopped smoking can sometimes find that after a few weeks or so they can begin to feel uncomfortable, as if something is dreadfully wrong. When this happens, it can be the success itself that can be their downfall. Guided unconsciously by the uncomfortable feelings their success brings, they can experience the compulsion to return to smoking. So why would someone carry out such a self-defeating behaviour? This is the complex act of self-sabotage.[1] If an individual's self-image doesn't match up to the success they are experiencing, then they can be unconsciously driven to destroy any success they may have had. Think about the celebrities and public figures you have seen or read about that have sabotaged themselves, often at the height of their success.

On occasion, the powerful thoughts related to these episodes where clients sabotage themselves are related to what is known as 'imposter syndrome'.[2] Again, their success does not match with their self-image and their self-identity; therefore, they feel it is undeserved. This can happen with smoking, it can happen with weight loss, in business and just about any other area where we can be flung beyond what we believe we deserve for ourselves.

I often think of the concept of self-sabotage when I see the beautiful cruise liners moored here in Southampton. These immense ships, beautiful in their structure and design, are often moved into position by rusty, worn-out old tugs. In many ways, that is how some people view themselves, not as the majestic liner, but as the tarnished old tug. This book is a way to create a level playing field, to remove the blocks that can hold people back, and a way to transform lives in ways I never believed possible – becoming that luxury liner and not the rust-ridden tug.

We can only bring about a change in our lives when we start to view what we see in our day-to-day lives differently, understanding the effect that our perception and interpretation of the world can have on how we feel. For example, here in the UK, today it is cold and wet with a good deal of rain, as it has been all week. We can now view this from various perspectives. If we were in a drought, rather than feeling despondent about the poor weather, we would be longing for it. If our garden had dried up as a result of a long, hot summer, then we would be delighted to see the garden coming back to life and looking lush and green once again. Nothing has altered other than our perception of the event.

Everyone will experience negative events at some point in their lives, be it an illness or disease, the breakup of a relationship or loss of a loved one. Most of us will experience hurtful words from others, trauma of some sort, and many of us will experience lack of love and affection from a supposed caregiver. Many of us will experience the effects of depression and anxiety in our lives also.

It seems almost human nature to reflect on the past, wishing the past could have been different. Often, we can think of the person, or persons, who have harmed us, wishing to exact revenge on them as retribution for what has been done to us. However, such experiences lead to feelings of anger, bitterness, resentment and aggression. Whilst we often look for ways to distract us from our feelings, the effect of these sublimations can often be short lived – with the anger and resentment coming back with vengeance. Of course, these emotions exist for a reason. Carrying a grudge and wanting to seek revenge show we're not a pushover.

A much better, and much more effective solution to this dilemma is what is called 'benefit finding'. This was first discussed by Michael McCullough and his colleagues at the University of Miami, who asked some 300 undergraduates to think about an incident in their lives where someone had caused them great upset or distress in some form – from infidelity to insults, rejection to abandonment.

The participants were then divided into three groups. One group was asked to take time to describe the event in detail, focusing on how the incident had affected their lives and how angry it had made them. The second group were asked to do the same thing, but this time focus on the benefits that had resulted from the experience, including, for example, how the experience had helped them become more resilient or wise. The third and final group was simply asked to describe what plans they had for the following day. Finally, at the end of the study, all the participants were asked to complete a questionnaire that measured their thoughts and feelings towards the individual who had upset and wounded them in some form.

The surprising results of this study revealed that just a few minutes of focusing on the positive benefits that had arisen from the ostensibly hurtful experience helped participants deal with the anger and upset that the situation had caused them. The victims felt significantly more forgiving towards those who had hurt them and were less likely to have a desire for retribution or to avoid the offenders.

'Humans,' said McCullough, 'have a propensity for anger, grudges, and revenge when they're harmed. The capacity for revenge is a built-in feature of human nature – expressions that sometimes serve to solve problems, particularly the problems that arise from living around other people.' He goes on to say, 'One of the more fascinating aspects of feuds and the desire for revenge, is its universality across human culture. Concepts of resentment, feuds, and revenge appear in approximately 95 percent of all ethnographic material on all the societies studied by anthropologists, psychologists, and behavioural scientists.'

This approach is a powerful technique I use with my own clients in our practice. Recently, I had a young client who had the misfortune of being raised in an unloving, and sadly, abusive home. I asked this client to take a few moments to reflect on the benefits that had arisen from growing up in such an environment – a task that outwardly you may think would bring no positives to reflect on. Quite quickly he was able to share how living in a home where fear was ever present had inadvertently forced him to spend a good deal of time in his bedroom where he would direct his attentions to writing, no doubt as a way of blocking off what was happening within the four walls of the turbulent family home. The positive side of him applying such concentrated effort to his craft has meant that he is now an extremely talented writer. He also was able to consider how those traumatic experiences had helped him have great empathy for others and would lead him to one day be a great parent himself. Out of this tragic and destructive commencement to his life, he was able to create something incredibly positive. I often think of and refer to a quote by the late Napoleon Hill. Hill writes, 'Every adversity, every failure, every heartache carries with it the seed on an equal or greater benefit'.

ANOTHER ONE BITES THE DUST

Imagine for a moment that you are walking down a path and suddenly you happen upon a rhumba of rattlesnakes (yes it really is called a rhumba!). Most of us would like to believe that we would momentarily freeze on the spot before calculating the best, most effective way to escape without harm. However, most of us would bolt out of there as fast as our legs would take us, knocking everything and everyone out of the way in the process. If you were, however, a herpetologist, then you might freeze on the spot for a completely different purpose. The evident reason being that if you study and love snakes, in all their wondrous varieties and species, you would not be able to believe your luck that you have come across such a miracle of nature. Your heart rate may increase, not through fear of being bitten, but through sheer adrenaline-filled excitement. In essence, the same experience viewed from a completely different standpoint. Nothing has changed about the experience other than the way we view it through the lens of our beliefs about these magnificent creatures.

I like to think that we all see things either from a '*but*' or from a '*wow*' perspective. When we look an experience or a situation, we can reframe it to either see what is missing or what there is to gain and perhaps take from it. For example, if you know someone who has just bought a possession, such as a house, car or mobile phone, and all that individual focuses on is what is lacking, rather than how incredible it is that we live in an age where such things are possible, then chances are they are living in the 'but' zone, not the 'wow' zone. How often have you asked someone how their new possession, holiday or experience is, only to hear 'it was good, but ...'? Or if you ask someone something like, 'How was your meal last night?', they may reply, 'Yeah, it was good, but ...'.

When you focus on what is missing rather than what is present, you are living in the 'but' zone. (For hopefully obvious reasons I think the word 'zone' is probably better than 'hole' when referring to a 'but'!)

When we see what is wrong rather than what is right, we are focused on this rather than the possible 'wow' of any experience.

Even with a challenging experience we could say something like, 'Boy that was tough, but, wow, I certainly learnt something valuable from it'. If you measure where you formerly were compared with where you are now and don't see any change then potentially you are living in the 'but' zone. For example, someone might say, 'Yes I have improved my fitness since last month, but ...', or, 'Yes, I enjoyed that seminar, but...'.

Try and live in the 'wow' and avoid focusing on the 'but'. Never forget that happiness is a journey and not a destination. Author and motivational speaker Wayne Dyer stated it perfectly when he said, 'If you change the way you look at things, the things you look at change'.

THE HEAT IS ON

We can think of our belief systems as being similar to a thermostat. If we deviate too far from the midpoint, we can perhaps feel uncomfortable as if something is not quite right, and we pull ourselves back to the set point quite quickly, even if the feelings are generated from our unconscious, rather than our conscious, intellectual minds. For example, if we suddenly achieve some success, expected or unexpected, win an award or prize, or perhaps we meet the person of our dreams, if these experiences don't match up to what we envisage for ourselves, what we in fact believe we deserve, then directed unconsciously by our belief system, we can begin to sabotage our successes, much like the experience of the smokers we discussed earlier in this chapter.

Like a thermostat set at 50 degrees, if it rises to 60 or 70, it can fall back to the midpoint of 50 quite quickly as it can almost feel uncomfortable to be up at such a high setting. Likewise, when life throws us a challenge, then more often than not, for some mysterious reason, we begin to find the resources within ourselves to overcome the adversity. Again, akin to the thermostat dropping down to a 30 or 40, we are pulled back up to the midpoint of 50, often without knowing how or why. As humans we love being in a place of homeostasis and being flung too far out of what we know can make us feel uncertain, and indeed uncomfortable – similar to the idea of hedonic adaptation and how it affects our levels of happiness. We all have a set point for the success we believe we deserve in our lives, and sometimes it can take determined effort to move away from its unconscious influence.

To begin to challenge our belief systems, we need to push ourselves to these higher thermostat temperatures and remain there for more extended periods, making the uncertain and uncomfortable feel more comfortable and pushing ourselves beyond what we believe we are worth and what we deserve. This concept is perhaps best explained by author Shannon L. Alder when she writes, 'It is not until you change your identity to match your life blueprint that you will understand why everything in the past never worked'.

I HAVE CONFIDENCE

A question I have often been asked over the years by clients who have challenged their belief systems and have discovered a new sense of self and a new self-image is this: 'if I am more confident will I become more arrogant, almost to the point of being a narcissist?' Often, it can be beliefs such as these that can prevent us attempting to transition into a more self-assured self with a 'higher thermostatic temperature'. My reply is always the same. I state that if you have come from a belief system of feeling 'less than good enough', or 'lacking in confidence', then it is impossible to become a self-centred and self-satisfying narcissist, simply because you will have too much empathy and self-insight. In other words, you are far too grounded to do so. As Harper Lee writes in *To Kill a Mockingbird*, 'You never really know a man until you understand things from his point of view, until you climb into his skin and walk around it'. If you have compassion for others, when you shift and alter your belief system around who you are and what you deserve in your life it will come from a place of deep understanding. It will not be underpinned by neurosis. Therefore, your new sense of self will be free from the neurosis and neurotic behaviour that can drive much of human action.

When we confront our beliefs and our belief systems it's as if we set a new 'waterline' for our life, making it impossible to return to whom we previously were, and developing a new capacity for higher expectations of ourselves and our lives. Repetition is the key: only when we confront our beliefs repeatedly can we free ourselves from the negative and limiting beliefs.

I do believe that our personalities can change, and that we can become the best versions of ourselves. Indeed, research by neuroscientist over the past 15 or so years has shown this, and that the way we see ourselves now is not set in stone. It is not who we ultimately can become. One of the ways to do this is to, whenever possible, try to associate with people who will stretch you and help you to grow. Then, almost by osmosis, we will begin to challenge each other's beliefs, moving us to a greater place of thinking and questioning.

On that note, be aware that the people we are most likely to associate with will agree with us on about 98% of topics. If someone you know, like and trust has more fixed beliefs than you do about a particular idea that you broadly agree with, then you are far more likely to give those beliefs some serious consideration. But if someone you know has wildly different beliefs to your own, then it's much easier to dismiss them as a bit half-baked. It goes without saying that the further away a belief or idea is from your current standpoint, the more likely you are to reject it outright, without really giving it a chance.

One way to imagine these distinctions in our belief systems is by picturing beliefs on a spectrum. If you divide this spectrum into 10 distinct units and you imagine yourself at say, Position 7, then there is little point in trying to persuade someone at Position 1 to change, or indeed even challenge, their beliefs on a particular topic. The space between the two is far too wide. Likewise, the more time you spend with people who hold similar belief systems to you, the more your beliefs are likely to become cemented and inflexible. Those very beliefs may possibly hold you back from growing into the person you can potentially become.

If, however, you are at, say, Position 7 on the spectrum, your time is better spent connecting with people who are at Positions 6 and 8, as together you will allow each other to challenge those beliefs that you once saw as fixed. The most heated arguments often occur between people on opposite ends of the spectrum. However, the most frequent learning occurs from people who are close, in terms of the spectrum, to the beliefs you hold at this moment in time.

The closer you are to someone, the more likely it is that the one or two beliefs you don't share will, almost by association, bleed over into your own thinking and shape your own belief systems, allowing your own thinking to develop and mature.

As motivational speaker Zig Ziglar once famously stated, 'You can't scratch with the turkeys if you want to fly with the eagles'.

[1] *Self-sabotage* refers to behaviours or thought patterns that hold you back and prevent you from doing what you want to do.
[2] *Imposter syndrome* can be defined as a collection of feelings of inadequacy that persist despite evident success. 'Imposters' suffer from chronic self-doubt and a sense of intellectual fraudulence that override any feelings of success or external proof of their competence.

SUMMARY

In Chapter 8, we looked at how we can live more in the moment, in the present day, rather than dwelling on your past, or your potential future. This is encouraged frequently with mindfulness and meditation, but is this the one-size-fits-all approach it has been advertised as? Some may find it useful, however it is reported that 1 in 12 people who try meditation do not find it helpful and in fact some find it to be detrimental. With one in four of us experiencing a mental health problem at some point in our lives, and one in six experiencing this weekly, it is more important than ever to find effective methods of reducing the impact of these. The chapter also explored the Wim Hof approach – a combination of breathing techniques and cold exposure therapy. Although we all have a perceived ideal of where we want to get to when we change something about ourselves, it happens far too often that we will self-sabotage once we see some success. This can be due to imposter syndrome – when we feel we don't deserve this success, or when our self-image doesn't line up with it. In the final part of this chapter, we explored if you are in a 'but' or 'wow' mentality, and how you can begin to draw positives from negative life experiences.

CHAPTER NINE

QUIT THE 'BS-BS'

A bird sitting on a tree is never afraid of the branch breaking, because her trust is not in the branch but in her own wings. Always believe in yourself.
– UNKNOWN

In this chapter we are going to zone in on self-limiting beliefs. In simple terms, the BS-BS – the bullshit belief systems. Of course, when I use the term 'bullshit' or 'bull' for short, I am referring to the fact that when something is described with this slang term, it implies that the thing that is being described is in some form deceptive. It is misleading, disingenuous, unfair or false. Basically, it describes something that is nonsense or untrue, much like many of the beliefs we all hold.

I believe we all have virtually limitless potential, but often the results we are achieving in our lives don't reflect this potential. Why is this the case? As we have discussed before in this book, more often than not it is because our unconscious beliefs profoundly limit or sabotage our efforts to achieve. Beliefs have the power to create and the power to destroy. But what is a belief, really? It's a feeling of certainty about what something means. As we have examined in the previous chapters, most of our beliefs were unconsciously created based on our interpretations of painful and pleasurable experiences in our past. But our past does not have to dictate the present or indeed our future selves, unless we make the conscious decision to continue to live there. It seems then that if we fight for our limitations, invariably we get to keep them.

We can find experiences to back up almost any belief, but the key is to make sure that we are consciously aware of the beliefs we are creating. If your beliefs don't empower you, change them. Likewise, if they don't move you forward in your life, let them go – replace them with new more empowering beliefs. Will your beliefs be the reason you stop taking action towards the results you want in your life? Or will putting time, effort and energy into changing them create for you the ultimate opportunity to do something extraordinary for yourself and those around you?

Think for a moment of the poor African or Indian elephant back in the days when a circus would get a new, wild, baby elephant to train. They would train this magnificent animal by bringing the baby into an empty tent and driving an enormous iron stake into the ground. The elephant would then be tethered to the stake with a heavy metal chain where it would battle continually to get free, but to no avail. The chain was too heavy, and the stake driven too deep into the ground. As much as he tried, the little elephant could not break free and eventually he would surrender to his shackles.

Move forward 10 years or so. The same elephant, now colossal, and strong, is tied by thin rope, and a small piece of wood shoved in the ground. The elephant that could knock over a large tree if he so desired is now held in by only the smallest of means.

The rope is only tied tightly enough for the elephant to feel it and know it's there. In reality, this beautiful giant could easily walk away. He could break free in an instant. So why doesn't he attempt to escape? Simply because, for so long, he knew he couldn't. In an almost cruel form of learned helplessness, this most imposing of beasts still believes in the limitations imposed upon him when he was just a baby.

How many of us are just like the magnificent elephant? Despite phenomenal strength, we are limited by just a tiny rope and a stick in the ground. How many of us have learnt something in our childhood that we still hold to be true today? How many of us are capable of so much more than we allow ourselves to be? What are your sticks in the ground? Do you choose to maintain the belief

References

that you are perhaps not good enough or not intelligent enough? Perhaps you believe that you are not handsome or beautiful enough to ever be fully happy in your life?

On the subject of not feeling attractive enough, I am reminded of a particularly brilliant study carried out by Dr Robert Cleck, a psychologist at Dartmouth College. Cleck and his team devised an ingenious experiment that illustrates just how body image affects the way people feel about themselves – focusing in particular on the impact it can have on social interactions.

Using theatrical make-up, researchers fashioned a scar on the faces of a group of volunteer female subjects. The subjects then interacted with a confederate who was blind to the experimental conditions. Just as the women were going into the meeting, a researcher would ask if she could make a slight adjustment to the scar. Unbeknown to these women, the scar was then actually removed by the researcher. After the two interactants had a conversation, the study subject filled out various dependent measures that dealt with her feelings and perceptions of the interaction that had just occurred.

What was incredible about this experiment was that that the women commented that the stranger had stared repeatedly at the, now non-existent, scar. This imagined visual examination had made the participants feel extremely uncomfortable.

These studies are considered ground-breaking due to the fact that they visibly demonstrate that the simple belief of having a negative physical appearance leads to perception bias. In simple terms, it showed that individuals who believe they have a disability, or some perceived deficiencies, are far more likely to perceive other people's behaviour as related to their own negative characteristics – similar to the belief glasses analogy we examined earlier in this book. When you take on the tinted glass lens of a particular belief, you will see the world according to that particular belief. If you believe you are not worth of love, or lacking in some way perhaps, you will see the world reacting to you in the way you expect it to react.

121

Using the analogy of the elephant above, perhaps it's time to shake off the rope – to change directions. It's time to stop believing the lie.

DO YOU BELIEVE IN MAGIC?

So, what exactly are self-limiting beliefs? In their simplest form, they are the thought processes that constrain us in some way.

Many of our self-limiting beliefs and thoughts build up over time. In all cases, there will be an originating experience or thought. The belief can then be compounded over the years. Each time the limiting belief goes unnoticed and unchecked, it can be added to, like pushing more and more rubbish into a waste bin, rather than simply emptying it.

Let's consider for a moment now how a belief might have been formed. Let's say you come home from school, excited to see your mum and tell her about your day. You begin to talk excitedly about something that's happened to you during the day. Within a few moments, you notice your mum isn't listening and is not giving you the attention that you have demanded of her. She says to you that she is sorry, but she can't listen to you right now because she has a friend coming round and she needs to prepare. She asks if you would go to your room to play on your own. You comply with her request somewhat begrudgingly. At that moment in time, you're probably not thinking, 'I hope Mum has a nice time with her friend when she comes over'; all you are thinking is that you don't feel loved or valued. Perhaps you feel that your opinion doesn't matter and that the demands of a visitor supersede your own. You sit and play in your room, ruminating on the experience. You may then develop a belief that what you say isn't important. You may believe that you are somehow a nuisance to your parents, or perhaps even that you are not lovable as a human being.

Of course, what you're not considering from this perception of the event is the fact that the lady coming round to visit your mum could be an important work colleague; she could be somebody who is having difficulties within her marriage and is needing your mum's help; or the visit could be related to some health concern that either of them has. Naturally, as children, we are the centre of our world, and we see things from our perspective. That's not self-centred or narcissistic, that is just to be human. As children, we demand love, nourishment and security to feel whole as a human being.

If similar experiences and, perhaps more importantly, similar thought patterns occur, the chances are you have formed the foundations of a limiting belief. Namely that you are not important and that you are not enough. You may then go through your life attracting similar experiences, perhaps attracting a partner who views you in the same way you view yourself. Similarly, you may even unconsciously sabotage positive experiences to reinforce that underlying limiting belief that you are not worthy. As Oprah Winfrey powerfully states, 'You don't become what you want, you become what you believe'.

THE LITTLE DRUMMER BOY

I can vividly recall that once a year, when I was a teacher of music, I would unenthusiastically transport the department drum kit into my classroom – its tired, cream-coloured walls adorned with frayed-edged pictures of long departed composers, as well as the obligatory scatterings of musical terms and notes. Once the drum kit was in position, I would use it for the week's lessons. With each fresh, enthusiastic class, I would invite every pupil to have a go on the drums, just to 'get a feel for it'. This throbbing headache that I would have to endure for a whole week was temporarily relieved by the pure joy on the faces of the 400 or so children I taught, and by a dose of Advil.

The lesson involved demonstrating to my pupils a very simple 'bass, snare, bass, bass, snare' rhythm. Basically, the foundations of Queen's hit 'We Will Rock You' without Freddie doing the vocals! Each pupil then had a bash at playing the pattern (in some cases quite literally a bash!). Day after day and lesson after lesson this would go on.

I remember one of my year 8 pupils, a small, dark-haired, shy boy, who did not want to have his turn. I did not force the issue and allowed him to watch as the other pupils eagerly had their opportunity, many asking for a second crack at it, clearly enjoying the lesson enormously.

Like the majority of the kids that week, this young lad had never tried the drums, but clearly did not want to take his turn, fearing perhaps potential ridicule from his classmates. Eventually, bowing to peer pressure, brought about by a combination of excited egging on and 'That's not fair, Sir, I had to do it!' types of pleadings, he took his place at on the black plastic-covered drum stool. Before he lifted the drumsticks, he announced to me and the whole class, 'I'll be rubbish at this. I won't be able to do it, Sir.' He then paused, building up the confidence to start, dreading the inevitable mockery that would soon be flying in his direction. With little effort, he beat the snare drum once, and with the drum sound still vibrating in the air, he once again declared, 'I told you I couldn't do it, Sir. I'm rubbish at music!'

I once again reassured him and offered him the opportunity to try again. Something magical then happened; something that stunned me and indeed the whole gathering. This little morsel of a lad began to play – not just to beat the drum but to perform. His timing was faultless, as was his technique. It's as if his latent natural talent could breathe a sigh of relief that it had suddenly chanced upon its opportunity to finally be revealed to the world.

The whole class was astonished. No one, including myself if I am honest, expected to witness what we all observed that morning.

Not long after the lesson, I arranged drum lessons for this boy, and he went on to play the drums for years in many of the school performances. When his time in education ended, he went on to play in several bands, enjoying playing immensely. For him, it was as if nothing else mattered when he was playing the drums. No one could be mean to him; no one could belittle him; no teacher could yell at him. He was in his element when he performed, and the world could go to hell!

I often think about that day. Had I not encouraged him, had he flatly refused to attempt the drums, then he would never have discovered the talent that was unexpressed within him. How many of us maintain beliefs about the things we 'just know' we can't do, even if we have never even tried them?

SUMMARY

How many of us feel we have the potential inside of us to achieve something but, somehow, we don't quite get there. Unconsciously, our beliefs will hold us back from reaching this potential or, if we start to make progress towards it, will sabotage our efforts. This book will help you to identify these self-limiting beliefs and change them. If they are not moving us forward in the direction we want to go, they are useless and need altering. These beliefs, if unnoticed and unchallenged, can go on to be added to and compounded. How often do we maintain a belief about something we cannot do, or something we would be no good at, without actually trying it?

CHAPTER TEN

IT'S THE THOUGHT THAT COUNTS

You don't know who you are; you just know what they've told you about who you are!
– MADDY MALHOTRA

Imagine for a few moments that you are going to a party with friends, but you have simply forgotten to brush your teeth for the past 3 days or so. All of our senses are designed to face outwards on the world – your nose, being directly above your mouth, should, in theory, be the first to know of the unpleasant aroma. Chances are, however, everyone else in the room with us will know before we do. Of course, their social anxiety will prevent them from letting you know how unpleasant your malodorous breath is, so you remain utterly oblivious. In many ways this is how it can be with our self-insight: even though our senses should tell us something to our advantage, they tend to miss the most obvious, the things right in front of our very noses, in this case both physically and metaphorically. In other words, others see the blind spots in our personality before we ever become aware of them.

In this chapter, we are going to dive deeper into our self-limiting beliefs. Personally, I prefer the term auto-limiting thoughts as it hints at how little control we have over the thoughts that surround our beliefs. Self-limiting to some extent implies that we are forcing these beliefs upon ourselves, almost on purpose, whereas auto-limiting thoughts implies that perhaps these are predominantly belief-based thoughts that we give little or no attention to – they are just part of our identity, they are who we are. If your auto-limiting thought is that you are not any good at, say, sports, even if you have never tried a particular sport, then that is your identity, that is who you are. Often there can be a trigger point for gaining and maintaining a belief; for example, a negative personal experience such as being told that you can or can't do something or 'be' someone. Why then would you try something you know you will never be any good at? Perhaps like the 'little drummer boy' in the previous chapter, we must all open ourselves up to the possibility that latent skills, passions and interests lie within us, waiting to be teased to the surface. The question is: do you have beliefs that allow you to move through obstacles, or do you use your beliefs to avoid those very obstacles?

I believe one of the primary ingredients for lasting change is true self-awareness. Of course, the dichotomy that surrounds this notion is the fact that the majority of us believe we are very self-aware. Indeed, according to one 2018 Harvard study of around 5000 participants carried out by organisational psychologist Tasha Eurich, though most people *believe* they are self-aware, self-awareness is a truly rare quality. The researchers estimated that only around 10–15% of the participants actually had true self-awareness.

Internal self-awareness is about learning to better understand why we feel the way we feel, and why we may behave in a particular way. It is about understanding how our values, passions and aspirations fit with our environment. It is about understanding how and why we react to things the way we do. It is about understanding our thoughts, feelings, behaviours, strengths and weaknesses, as well as having an understanding of how we impact others.

According to the Harvard study, the positive benefits of having some internal self-insight include higher work and relationship satisfaction, personal and social control, and higher levels of happiness. Internal self-awareness is also related to decreased levels of anxiety, stress and depression.

Once you begin to understand this concept, you have the opportunity and freedom to truly change things about yourself, enabling you to create the life that you want and deserve. Unless you fully understand who you are, and why you feel the way you feel, it's fundamentally impossible to change and become self-accepting. Having clarity about who you are and what you want can be empowering, giving you the motivation and insight to become who you wish to be. Think of it as undertaking a long journey without a map to guide you: you may get to where you are going, but wouldn't having a map make the journey easier?

As you might imagine, there are many benefits to working on improving our internal self-awareness. First, it can make us more proactive, boost our acceptance and encourage positive self-development. It can also allow us to see things from the perspective of others, to practise self-control, work creatively and productively, and experience pride in ourselves and our work. In addition, it can lead to better decision making.

FROM A WINDOW

One of the best ways to gain a better understating of who we are and how we are viewed by others is by using a technique known as the Johari window. The Johari window, or Johari model, is a practical tool to illustrate and improve self-awareness.

References

THE JOHARI WINDOW

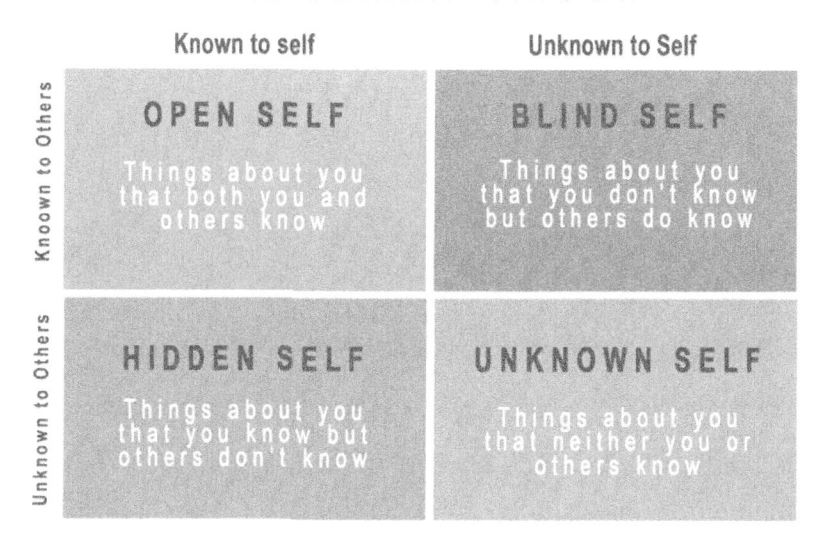

	Known to self	Unknown to Self
Knoown to Others	**OPEN SELF** Things about you that both you and others know	**BLIND SELF** Things about you that you don't know but others do know
Unknown to Others	**HIDDEN SELF** Things about you that you know but others don't know	**UNKNOWN SELF** Things about you that neither you or others know

The name derived from using the first names of the creators of this simple but effective technique: psychologists Joseph Luft and Harrington Ingham. The Johari window is a quick, insightful and useful technique often utilised by companies and coaches to help individuals gain insight about themselves.

Picture a house with four distinct rooms. Each room represents a different aspect of who we are as a person, in essence, our personality. Room one is the part of ourselves that we and others see, our 'open self'. Room two contains the aspect of ourselves that others see but we are unaware of, essentially our 'blind self'. Room three is the private space, where we hide things from others, our 'hidden self' or 'façade'. Finally, the fourth room is the unconscious part of us that neither ourselves nor others see, essentially our 'unknown self'. In summary two rooms represent your true self while the other two rooms represent the part that is known to others but unknown to yourself.

Now, take a look at this list of adjectives and choose 10 of them you feel best represent who you feel you are. Not who you would like to be, but your authentic self, if you will. Now write them down on a piece of paper.

Able	Accepting	Adaptable	Bold
Brave	Calm	Caring	Cheerful
Clever	Complex	Confident	Dependable
Dignified	Empathetic	Energetic	Extroverted
Friendly	Giving	Happy	Helpful
Idealistic	Independent	Ingenious	Intelligent
Introverted	Kind	Knowledgeable	Logical
Loving	Mature	Modest	Nervous
Observant	Organised	Patient	Powerful
Proud	Quiet	Reflective	Relaxed
Religious	Responsive	Searching	Self-assertive
Self-conscious	Sensible	Sentimental	Shy

All done? Great! Now ask a friend or partner to do the same for themselves and for you. Also, write down the 10 adjectives that you feel best describe your friend or partner's personality (If you are doing this with your partner it may be a good idea to have a good divorce lawyer on speed dial, things could suddenly get ugly!).

When you have completed the above task, take a few moments to discuss with each other the words you had on your lists. How many of the words that you used to describe yourself did they have on their list? Now, how many words that you pencilled down to describe yourself did they have written down? Assuming that you have not fallen out with each other, begin to think about how this newfound insight can relate to the Johari window pictured above.

You can now do the following:

Using the four-window model as your base, draw four squares on a piece of paper, and label them in the same way as the illustration above: Open, Blind, Hidden and Unknown:

References

The Open Self: Write the adjectives selected by both yourself and your friend/partner here, representing personality traits that are known to both groups. The Known Self is what you and others see in you. This is the part that you are able to discuss freely with others. Most of the time you agree with this view you and others have of you.

The Hidden Self: Adjectives selected only by yourself go here, representing aspects of your personality that others may not be aware of. The Hidden Self is what you see in yourself, but others don't. This is the side of your personality where you can hide things that are very private about yourself. This is the part of you that you keep hidden possibly for reasons of self-protection. It could also be that you may feel vulnerable and are anxious about having a perceived fault or weaknesses exposed. This area equally applies to those good qualities and talents that you are modest about and don't want advertised to others.

The Blind Self: Adjectives chosen by your friend/partner that you did not select go here. This box represents personality traits that are outside of your awareness. The Blind Self is what you don't see in yourself, but others see in you. You might see yourself as an open-minded person when, in reality, people around you don't agree. Or you might see yourself as a 'shy and reserved' person while others might consider you incredibly outgoing and extroverted. Sometimes those around you might not tell you what they see because they fear offending you. It is in this area that people sometimes detect that what you say and what you do aren't congruent. On occasions our body language can express this mismatch.

The Unknown Self: This is where the adjectives that were selected by neither party go, either representing personality traits that don't apply to you, or hidden traits of which neither party is aware. This box is particularly useful if you do the Johari window with more than one friend/partner, and new areas unknown to you are brought up. The Unknown Self is the self that you cannot see, and others can't see it either. This might refer to untapped potential, as well as talents and skills that have yet to be explored by you.

CHANGES

Once we have achieved a good level of self-insight, we can effectively begin to change our auto-limiting thoughts. If we are able to push ourselves beyond what we believe is possible, we can then get to the place where things seem easily obtainable for us. For example, when working with clients and challenging them to undertake something that once they felt uncomfortable doing, such as flying or driving, I always get them to process how achieving this goal will make the next thing they undertake much easier.

For example, if you, as most people do, find it difficult standing up in front of a group of strangers and delivering a presentation, then practising conversing with others at a social or network event will make the group presentation potentially somewhat more manageable, as it will feel more familiar to us to converse in that relaxed manner.

Often, we can change through association. In other words, if we associate with individuals who have a good deal of self-insight, and who are positive and resilient, then almost by osmosis, change will occur through association. A phrase I often use with my clients is 'get comfortable getting uncomfortable'. This is often where the philosophy of 'Stoicism' can be useful: the idea that through developing self-control and fortitude we can overcome any destructive emotions. More about 'Stoicism' later in this book.

Just know that everything you need is within you right now, but if our thinking patterns and behaviours don't change, then we don't change. Similarly, we must consistently be mindful of what we share out loud. Some experts believe that when we verbalise out loud a negative or limiting thought, that shared belief can hold four times the destructive power of a thought simply held within our own minds. Albert Einstein is often wrongly attributed as having said that 'The definition of insanity is doing the same thing over and over again and expecting a different result'. Actually, the origin is believed to be an article written by a journalist from Tennessee describing the 12-step programme used by Alcoholics Anonymous. The message, regardless of its origin, is clear.

Attempt whenever you can not to continue the same thought patterns and behaviour expecting a new outcome.

If we challenge and reframe our old redundant thoughts and beliefs, then we can change our beliefs rapidly. Here, for example, are some auto-limiting thoughts and how they can be positively challenged:

EXISTING THOUGHT AND BELIEF	CHANGE TO
1. I just don't ever have enough time...	*Time is a universal. It is the one thing everyone on this beautiful planet experiences in the same way. How can I make the most of the time I have every single day?*
2. I just can't...	*What am I fearful of, is it fear of failure, or making myself look stupid? Will anyone remember my mistakes in a few days?*
3. I can't because I am not...	*Is that a BS-BS? What lies have I told myself about who I am and what I am capable of?*
4. I'm just not good enough...	*That is a belief system, it is not real. It is just my perception, perhaps a reflection of my self-esteem at this moment in time. It can change.*
5. If I do that then I'll...	*Will I feel embarrassed? Will I make myself look stupid or silly? Will I show myself up? Those are just the beliefs and excuses people use to carry on living a life that they don't want for themselves.*
6. I will never be as good as others...	*This is just social anxiety. Most people live in their head and don't actually notice or care about the mistakes of*

	others. They are more worried about their own errors.
7. I have failed at so many things before...	*The past doesn't have to dictate the future. We all learn from the past; we are all growing and evolving every day. Life is about falling and getting up again.*
8. I'm a real idiot sometimes...	*Everyone feels like that sometimes, it's what makes us human. Only a sociopath or narcissist doesn't feel those sorts of emotions.* *If as a child I never undertook a task that I had failed at then I would never have made any progress.*
9. Somebody like me could never do something like that...	*That belief is simply based on how I feel about myself and my self-identity. I will work on improving my self-worth and overcome any adversity that I am faced with. It is a belief it is not real.*
10. I've never done it before.	*Great, here is an opportunity to try something new and exciting. Every day in every way I am getting better and better.*
11. It's far too complicated.	*I'll try and tackle it from a different angle. Sometimes when we look at things differently, we see new opportunities.*
12. I'm too lazy to get this done.	*I am not lazy at things I enjoy doing. How can I make this enjoyable and find the joy in everything I do, no matter what it is?*
13. There's no way it will work.	*I can try to my best to make it work. If I fail, then I will have learnt a great*

	deal for the next thing I undertake. As inventor Thomas Edison once said, 'I have not failed. I've just found 10,000 ways that won't work.'
14. I'm just too old...	*Think of Harland David Sanders, who started the fast-food giant KFC when he was just 65 years of age! More about Harland Later in this book!*

Let's briefly look at some of the auto-limiting thoughts that many of us have. Take time to read through the examples below and see how many, if any, apply to you. This list is by no means exhaustive but should inspire you to begin to think about your own auto-limiting thoughts, so together we can change them. As architect R. Buckminster Fuller perceptively wrote, 'You never change things by fighting the existing reality. To change something, build a new model that makes the existing model obsolete.' Use this book to create your new reality. Remember to challenge who you can be by not letting let fate determine your future self.

Let's start off with some general auto-limiting thoughts...

LIMITING BELIEFS ABOUT OUR SELF-WORTH

I am not good enough • I don't deserve anything good in my life • Bad things always seem to happen to me • I'm just a failure • I'm really not that clever • People won't like me if they get to know the real me • I just don't deserve nice thing showing up in my life • I'm not that attractive • I'm far too overweight • I'm far too skinny • I'm too shy • I don't like my body • I feel powerless • I just can't seem to make any changes in my life • I'm not strong enough • I'm not important enough • What I wish for just doesn't matter • Other people's needs are more important than mine • I never have anything good happen to me • People like me don't ever succeed in life • There's no point to anything • I don't know what I want • I never have any willpower • I will always get hurt by others • I can't trust myself • I'm just not very techy • I'll look stupid if I do something I'm not good at • I'll never measure up to others • No one ever supports or encourages me • One day I'll change • I'll never be successful no matter what I do • Eating healthily is really hard for me • I just don't have a good brain!

And so on. I think you get the picture by now of the thoughts we can have daily. Now let's break them down into more specific areas of auto-limiting thoughts.

AUTO-LIMITING BELIEFS ABOUT SUCCESS

Life just isn't fair • Nobody is interested in my ideas • I'll never pay off all these student loans • If I succeed, I won't be able to sustain it • I just don't have the skills • They'll never take on someone like me • I'm not going to be successful so there's no point in trying • People won't take me seriously because I'm ... [female, young, old, fat, thin] • I don't feel like I could give enough value to an employer • I've tried it before and failed, so I'll probably fail if I try again • I don't have enough money to start my business idea • I don't have enough support • I don't have the right connections • I'll always be broke • I mustn't get my hopes up as it always leads to disappointment • There's too much competition these days • Money is the root of all evil • Rich people are just greedy • Money is not important • I'm no good at selling • I'm just not any good with money • I just don't have enough experience • No one is ever going to give me an opportunity with my experience • Life is hard, that's just how it is • I'm just not creative • I'm not original enough • I'm sure somebody thought of this before •

Every good idea has already been thought of and done • I'm a procrastinator • Making lots of money requires sacrificing who you are as a person • Other people don't like people who are successful • If I become too happy or successful, I'll jinx myself and it will all go wrong • There's an earnings ceiling that I'll never go above • My plate is too full already •I don't have the right education.

AUTO-LIMITING BELIEFS ABOUT HEALTH

I just can't lose weight • I seem to always get sick • Being overweight runs in my family • I'm just not built to be an athlete • I don't like to exercise • I simply don't like fruits and vegetables • I'm too busy, I don't have time to exercise • What's wrong with me, I just can't stop eating! • I've got to have my ... [chocolate, bread, cake, sweets, soft drink] • I'm too far gone to start taking care of my body now • My mum used to say there are starving children in Africa • I'm absolutely addicted to sweet things.

AUTO-LIMITING BELIEFS ABOUT RELATIONSHIPS

All the good ones are taken • I'm just not good at relationships • I don't feel like I could give enough • I'd better not express my feelings if I want to be loved and accepted • I need someone to complete me • My family just doesn't understand me • Something is wrong with me • I need someone to take care of me • I'll always be on my own • No one will ever love me • Letting others get close just leads to pain and upset • Being honest leads to rejection • If I drop my guard I'll just end up getting hurt again • I'm too old to meet anyone new • I'm a mess, it's hopeless • I expect others to hurt me • Nice men (or women) are impossible to find nowadays.

As we have discussed previously in this book, unless we make the auto-limiting thoughts conscious, they will continue to guide our behaviours on autopilot. The best option is to bring the thoughts to the surface where we can begin to accept them and exercise more control over them. As author Nathaniel Branden writes, 'The first step toward change is awareness. The second step is acceptance.'

SUMMARY

Have you ever been looking for something unsuccessfully, only for someone else to find it right where you were looking? The same thing can happen with ourselves: often we fail to see things about ourselves that are right in front of our noses, yet others can identify them almost instantly. This can be likened to our limiting beliefs – they are so engrained that we often fail to see them ourselves. Though we feel like we have self-awareness, it is a very hard thing to achieve fully. This chapter investigated how we can become more self-aware, using the tool of the Johari window. Once we have gained more self-awareness, we can start to change the beliefs that are holding us back. The chapter also looked into the power our thoughts can hold – thoughts verbalised hold four times more power than those that remain in our minds – and how we can challenge our thinking to change our beliefs for the better.

CHAPTER ELEVEN
THE ALFRED TECHNIQUE

You'll see it when you believe it.
– Wayne Dyer

This book is not only about about thinking differently and seeing your world through a new, clearer lens, but also about detecting many of those 60,000–80,000 thoughts you are having every day and starting to become the conscious observer of them in order to discern just how many of them are akin to a harmful computer virus – often created innocently, but going on to infect many areas of our own personal operating systems.

Alfred Pennyworth

Just how many of these thoughts are auto-limiting? How many of them are redundant? Think of it as if you are disengaging the autopilot of your mind for perhaps the first time in your life.

There are several synergistic elements to changing your belief systems. The first part is what I call the the 'Alfred Technique'.

So, what is the Alfred Technique? If you have ever watched one of the Batman films, or seen the colourful 1960s TV show, then you will most likely be aware of Alfred, Bruce Wayne's ever-present, long-suffering butler. Full name Alfred Pennyworth, he is constantly deliberating over what is in Mr Wayne's best interests. He is very much a cross between a Zen master, a parent, a psychiatrist and a doctor.

According to Batman legend, Alfred is versed in martial arts, swordsmanship, archery and computer programming, as well as electrical, chemical and mechanical engineering, nanotechnology, biotechnology, rose breeding, first aid and many medical procedures. He is an ex-medic in the Royal Air Force and former member of the Royal Marines, British Secret Service and the British Army's Special Air Service, as well as an intelligence agent posted to occupied France in the Second World War. Not a bad résumé for any butler!

Alfred is exactly the person to look out for your best interests relentlessly. From today onwards I want you to imagine that Alfred is sitting on your shoulder requesting that you challenge every thought you have, his soft English accent asking you to question whether the belief you are having, that inner chatter, is a truth or is at some level an auto-limiting thought. In other words, is it a 'truth' or is it a belief that is holding you back? He's never brash, but he is persistent, and he always knows what is best for you, even if you don't. Like a child who wants sweets, but needs fruits and vegetables, Alfred will always give you what you need, which isn't always what you want.

In essence, he has your best interests at heart 24/7, 365. Deep down, he loves you implicitly, and most likely would die for you if push came to shove. Like one of the president's secret service men, if it were demanded of him, he would take a bullet for you.

References

Who would not like to have their very own Alfred to look after them and their best interests? Even if you don't always know what those best interests are! Often, we don't always get what we want, we get what, in the long term, is the best for us. We don't always know what is best for us until much later on. Alfred knows just what that is *all* of the time! Alfred, of course, is your powerful and virtually limitless subconscious mind.

So, the Alfred Technique is just that. He will insist you have your vegetables rather than the sweets, and one day you will thank him for it. When he is not monitoring your thoughts, he is repeating the following phrase to you: 'Sir, you are enough. You are enough.'

On the surface this may appear such a simple technique but, as with many simple things, its effect can be powerful. When we give over our thoughts to a 'third party', then, by default, our thoughts are being monitored by something outside of ourselves. Of course, if you would prefer another character rather than Alfred, that's fine, but do make sure that they would have your best interests at heart. If you would prefer more of a Downton Abbey-style butler then that is perfectly fine as well.

Here are the simple steps to the Alfred Technique:

THE ALFRED TECHNIQUE

Picture the benevolent butler on your shoulder or in attendance as you go through the day, assisting you in noticing your self-limiting thoughts. You can remember Alfred by using this acronym:

Always
Look
For
REDundant beliefs

Let's break it down a little further:

Awareness of Your Thoughts – Pause, Stop and Reflect – Take Back Your Power
Look for Evidence – Understand Your Thoughts Are Not the Truth Just Perceptions

141

Free Yourself from the Belief – Does This Belief Serve Me or Hinder Me?
Reframe your Belief and Build Your Resilience
Enlist the Help of Others to Support Your New Beliefs
Denounce the Old Belief – Publicly Declare It to Be unhelpful

– TALK TO YOURSELF!

Don't believe simple is more complex? Ask yourself what is the most 'complex' word in the English language? By 'complex' I don't mean the longest, I mean the word that has the most definitions. The more definitions a word has, the more situations it will inevitably be used in, hence the more 'complex' the word becomes.

On the surface, you may think that it is a long word such as 'supercalifragilisticexpialidocious', a nonsense word used by children to express approval. Or you may think it's the unpronounceable and ridiculously long 'pneumonoultramicroscopicsilicovolcanoconiosis', a lung disease caused by inhaling very fine ash and sand dust. However, it's neither of these words. There is one English word in particular that's deceptively simple – 'run'. As a verb, it boasts a record-setting 645 definitions. In fact, lexicographer and associate editor of the *Oxford English Dictionary* Peter Gilliver spent an eye-watering 9 months gathering its many shades of meaning.

Originally, when the first edition of the *Oxford English Dictionary* was published in 1928, the word with the most definitions was 'set'. Later, however, the word 'put' outpaced it, and 'run' eventually overtook them both as the English language's most complex word, thanks in part to phrases such as 'an iPhone runs apps'. Sometimes then, like the oft-cited 'duck on the water' analogy, just below the surface, simple things can be incredibly complex and powerful.

Part of the beauty of the Alfred Technique is that it utilises what is known as Solomon's Paradox. In simple terms, Solomon's Paradox explains how we are much better at giving sage advice to a third party than giving successful advice to ourselves, which is something we will look at in detail in Chapter 19.

TALKING TO MYSELF

Talking to ourselves may seem a little strange, mainly because we tend to see speaking out loud to nobody in particular as a sign of being a little unhinged. However, there's a growing body of research to suggest that self-talk can help with confidence, memory recall and focused attention. Often without even realising it we say a name out loud if we want to recall it, instinctively knowing that saying something out loud is an incredible retrieval cue.

People often talk to themselves – most of us do it at least every few days. Scientists have found many of us do it on an almost hourly basis. Self-directed speech can help guide children's behaviour and learning, with kids often taking themselves step-by-step through tasks such as tying their shoelaces, as if reminding themselves to focus on the job at hand.

To see if talking to oneself could also help adults, psychologists conducted experiments with volunteers who had to search for specific items. In one simple but brilliant experiment, volunteers were shown an image with 20 random objects pictured on it. They were then asked to look for a specific item. In this study participants were asked to look for a banana. In half the trials, participants were asked to repeatedly say what they were looking for out loud to themselves; in the others, they were asked to remain silent. Amazingly, the researchers found self-directed speech helped the subjects locate the object on the sheet objects much faster. In fact, faster by about 50–100 milliseconds. The average time for participants who did not state the name of the object they were searching for was 1.2–2 seconds.

CARELESS TALK

So, what should you say to yourself? Often when you want to bring about a change in your life, some books and motivation experts recommend using positive affirmations. The problem with this approach is that, with some exceptions, positive affirmations simply don't work – the foremost reason being that they focus on the conscious part of our minds, not the unconscious. If you are reciting a positive affirmation that is incongruent with a deeply held negative self-belief, all that will result in is an inner conflict and struggle – a form of cognitive dissonance if you will, the outcome of attempting to hold on to opposing beliefs simultaneously.

Let's say you hold the belief that you are 'unattractive and insignificant' – sadly a common belief held by individuals suffering from anxiety and depression. This belief may feel irrevocably true, despite what the reality may be.

For example, at the peak of her career, actress and fitness model Jane Fonda was held to be one of the most beautiful women in the world, yet, as her frank autobiography *My Life So Far* reveals, she judged her physical appearance as inadequate and struggled with bulimia for decades.

Fonda speaks of the day her mother, Frances Ford Seymour, showed her the terrible scars she had received from a kidney operation, as well as the results of a botched plastic surgery operation on her breasts. This life-altering, intimate moment came a few days after her mother informed Jane that she was getting divorced from her father, Henry Fonda. Believing that these physical impairments were the reason for the divorce, she vowed to do whatever it took to be perfect so that a man would love her forever.

In an interview with *People* magazine, Fonda said that she 'never felt pretty or confident' when she was growing up. She added, 'We develop addictions because we're missing something, and my addiction was food. I moved outside myself, left a big, empty space inside, and tried to fill it with food. I went through phases of bingeing and purging, and it was many years before I could sit at a table without feeling any anxiety. Bulimia is very easy to hide, but you can't be intimate with people if you're an addict.'

Imagine for a moment that Ms Fonda had been told by a self-improvement expert to stand in front of a mirror and recite affirmations related to loving herself and her body. Would that activity have made her feel better or worse? She reported that she would often cringe when she was being paid a compliment, believing that 'I know it isn't true'. Imagine how excruciating this exercise would feel: look at yourself in the mirror and say out loud: 'I am beautiful, inside and out. I love myself.'

If you believe deep down that you are ugly and worthless, it will set off an inner war. With each positive declaration, your unconscious will cry out, 'It's not true, it's not true!' Similar beliefs have afflicted supermodel Elle Macpherson. Macpherson would receive praise from millions of adoring fans, as well as the press and the modelling world, for the way she looked and yet she didn't feel that way about herself. In her own words she said, 'I have felt unhappy in my skin'. Actress Angelina Jolie once said, 'I know other women would kill for my lips, but I feel like they take over my face'. Similarly, Victoria Beckham once admitted, 'I've got so much saggy skin on my stomach and I've got no bum at all. I might fit into jeans, but I look really awful naked.'

BOB THE BUILDER – CAN WE FIX IT?

So, if affirmations don't work, what does? Well, a groundbreaking 2010 study published in the journal *Psychological Science* may hold the key. Researchers Senay, Albarracín and Noguchi have shed light on what has come to be known as 'declarative versus interrogative self-talk'. The good news is that this type of self-talk is something we can all adopt immediately for instant results. Think of the famous line from Watty Piper's children's classic *The Little Engine That Could*, in which the title character declares, 'I think I can. I think I can. I think I can.' Was the little engine using the best and most up-to-date psychological technique to motivate himself? Or does Bob the Builder have the right idea when he asks the central question, 'Can we fix it?'

Albarracín's team tested some 50 study participants, encouraging them to either spend a minute deliberating on whether they would complete a task or telling themselves they would. What they found was that the participants showed more success on a task when they *asked* themselves whether they would complete it than when they *told* themselves they would.

Further experimentation had students in a seemingly unrelated task write two sentences, either 'I will' or 'Will I?' and then work on the same task. What they found was that the participants did better when they wrote 'Will' followed by 'I' even though they had no idea that the word writing related to the task at hand.

So why does such a simple change of words bring about such an astonishing change in outcome? Professor Albarracín's team suspected that it was related to the unconscious formation of the question 'Will I?' and its effects on motivation. When participants asked themselves a question, they were more likely to build their own internal motivation.

In a follow-up experiment, participants were once again placed into either the 'I will' or 'Will I?' categories. This time however they were asked how much they intended to exercise in the following week. Participants were then asked to fill out a psychological scale measuring their motivation for exercising. The results of this experiment showed that participants not only did better as a result of the question, but that asking themselves a question did indeed increase their fundamental motivation for exercising. Amazingly, reversing two simple words can have a profound effect on our levels of motivation for a task.

'The popular idea is that self-affirmations enhance people's ability to meet their goals,' Professor Albarracín said. 'It seems, however, that when it comes to performing a specific behaviour, asking questions is a more promising way of achieving your objectives.'

So, let's put this idea into a real-life scenario. Let's say you are planning to join a gym to get fitter and perhaps lose some weight. You may say to yourself, 'I won't use the gym much because I haven't before and I always find it hard to lose weight, so why should this time be any different?' Alternatively, you may decide to motivate yourself by using a positive affirmation and say to yourself, 'I am good enough and I will get to the gym and lose the weight this time'. The problem with both statements is they are declarative statements that have a predetermined outcome, therefore creating an external pressure within us that can prevent us from accessing internal problem-solving resources. In addition, they can potentially limit us from creatively finding ways to achieve our goals.

Instead of using positive affirmations, try turning these statements into questions. For example, instead of saying, 'I won't get to the gym because I have joined in the past and I never used it, so this time won't be any different', try saying, 'I have joined the gym in the past and made a commitment to myself that I didn't follow through on, so what can I do differently to make it a success?'. Or, 'Am I good enough to lose the weight I no longer want or need? If I am not, then what can I do to make myself good enough to make a success of it this time?'

By using this method of interrogative self-talk, you are not only being inquisitive and seeking to solve problems, but you are also acknowledging your negative and auto-limiting thoughts, subsequently eliminating the potential need to challenge them. This in turn will then engage the unconscious mind, where the magic really happens. As we will discuss in detail in the next chapter, the unconscious mind is remarkable at coming up with solutions to our biggest and most difficult challenges. Adopting this method will stimulate our problem-solving creativity and hopefully put an end to that exhausting inner struggle, inspiring the thing that we all are in continual search of – more cognitive ease.

SUMMARY

This chapter encouraged you to disengage the autopilot that runs your mind and tune more into the little Alfred on your shoulder, who always knows exactly what is best for you. This is also known as your subconscious mind – a powerful force guiding you. The chapter also asked you to look deeper into how well the positive affirmations we are all encouraged to use in order to improve our well-being truly work. If they are incongruent with our self-limiting beliefs, they create cognitive dissonance. It may be better, in fact, to question ourselves rather than give ourselves imperative statements. The curiosity of our minds will help to seek solutions to the problems we're posing, whilst also acknowledging the limiting belief that is initially holding us back.

References

STAGE TWO

AWARENESS

CHAPTER TWELVE

IF YOU EAT ANY MORE, YOU'LL END UP LOOKING LIKE ONE!

My mom's favourite Stevie Wonder song is,
'I Just Called to Say Someone You Don't Know Has Cancer'.
– DAMIEN FAHEY

If you are anything like me, as you have become older you may have come to realise that much of the sage advice your parents and grandparents imparted to you when you were growing up was not always based on any scientific research, or even any objective reality. In other words, the pearls of wisdom were often based on superstitions, misplaced beliefs and, more often than not, old wives' tales. These well-meaning folklore-like gems were often invoked to discourage certain behaviours in us as children. Sometimes, they were there simply to pass on good advice, ease concerns or even reduce pain, such as the caring words shared after a tumble or minor accident – 'You'll live!'.

Let's be honest, though, some of the advice our parents gave us, particularly our mum's advice – and chances are she got that advice from her mum – was not the best. Peppered within the questionable old adages, however, were some genuinely good and useful concepts. From these nuggets of advice, many of us form beliefs – beliefs that many years later we still hold. Here are just a handful of them taken from the brilliant book *Mother Knows Best* by Michele Slung. Some of these may bring back some not so pleasant memories of your childhood, but just remember I am doing this for your own good! Oh, and remember to put on clean underwear, just in case you're in an accident! So, here we go:

'Don't go swimming for an hour after you have eaten, or you will drown!'
'Wash behind your ears or you'll have potatoes grow there!'
'Don't expect too much and you won't be disappointed.'
'Don't sit too close to the television or you'll get square eyes.'
'If you eat any more of that you'll end up looking like it.'
'Never drink out of a water fountain, you don't know who's drunk out of it before you.'
'Who got out of the wrong side of the bed this morning?'
'The bigger you are, the more stupid you are.'
'If only you were more like your brother.'
'You're too big for your boots, you are.'
'If you can't say anything nice, don't say anything at all.'
'Don't try and teach your grandmother to suck eggs.'
'If I had talked to my mother the way you're talking to me!'
'As long as you are under my roof...'
'If you're quiet, you must be up to no good.'
'Everyone else might be doing it, but you're not going to.'
'Put that down, you don't know where it's been.'

TOO MUCH TO THINK ABOUT

Some of the advice from our parents turns out to be great advice. For example, psychoanalyst Sigmund Freud advised: 'When making a decision of minor importance, I have always found it advantageous to consider all the pros and cons. In vital matters however ... the decision should come from the unconscious, from somewhere within ourselves.' Or, as our parents may have said, perhaps less eloquently, 'Sleep on it!'

The idea that unconscious processes may sometimes be more effective at decision making than conscious processes is not a new one. As we have observed in Chapter 2, a staggering one-fifth of the decisions we make, we end up regretting; that's 143,262 decisions in an average lifetime. It seems that often the more time we spend sitting and consciously thinking about a problem, the more we end up making a decision we are ultimately not happy with. It clearly helps to put a problem aside for some time in order to arrive at a better decision – to literally 'sleep on it'.

Creatively, this is often a good decision as well. As a composer, I will often work on a piece of music late into the evening but will somehow get 'stuck' as to where a melody or idea is going. I then go to bed, and when I return to the piece in the morning, it is as if my 'muse' has visited me in the night and imparted the complete piece of music to me. Of course, it is my subconscious mind that has continued the work while my conscious mind has got some shuteye.

Most of us have experienced decision fatigue at some stage of our lives, be it in a restaurant, when choosing a present for a loved one or buying clothes for ourselves. Also known as ego depletion, decision fatigue is the phenomenon surrounding our ability to make effective decisions. The theory surrounding decision fatigue is that our ability to make decisions can decline after making numerous decisions in succession as our brains can tire rapidly. Who among us has not spent a significant amount of time thinking about, and making, a decision about an important purchase only to regret it moments after we have made the purchase?

It was this concept of effective decision making that fascinated Dutch psychologist Ap Dijksterhuis and his team. In 2006, he conducted a series of experiments to examine how and why we make the decisions we do with the information we have before us. In one experiment, he had people choose between four hypothetical apartments. The information was assembled in such a way that one of the four apartments was somewhat more desirable than the other three, in that it possessed more positive and fewer negative qualities. These positive attributes, however, were not immediately evident as the apartments were described with a large amount of information. Participants were asked to read all the information about the apartments and then they were placed into one of two groups. One group was asked to choose their favoured apartment immediately, and the other group made their choice after a period of distraction during which they were asked to do something unrelated to the task.

The rationale behind the experiment was that the group who were doing the unrelated task would continue to 'unconsciously think' about the apartments while they were distracted. Indeed, the fascinating findings showed that 37% of the participants who decided immediately chose the apartment they believed to be most appropriate to them, whereas 60% of the unconscious thinkers chose the better one. Evidently, postponing a decision can help, even if one does not consciously think about it anymore. Similarly, by overthinking a decision we can we pay too much attention to the unimportant attributes of the choice we are making.

Traditionally, most academics studying decision making have assumed that thorough conscious thought is the best strategy to arrive at sound decisions. This is without doubt often true; however, conscious thought can sometimes lead to deterioration in the quality of the decisions we make. The idea that unconscious thinkers outperform conscious thinkers and immediate decision makers has been replicated many times in studies.

It appears, however, that when we have sufficient knowledge and experience in a particular field, we most certainly benefit from more conscious as opposed to unconscious thinking.

But why is unconscious thinking so useful in decision making? Ap Dijksterhuis believes this is down to two main reasons. First, it has to do with the different processing capacities of conscious and unconscious processes. Similar to the fast, System 1 thinking we examined in Chapter 3, our conscious mind has limited capacity for analysing concepts and problems in sufficient detail. That is, it can only do one thing at a time, and it can only work on a very limited amount of information. Our slower and more powerful System 2, unconscious mind, however, has the capacity to work on different things in tandem and can process a large amount of information.

Another fascinating study by Ap Dijksterhuis and his team involved interviewing individuals who had recently purchased a consumer product. They asked the purchasers if they had thought a lot about their purchase consciously, or whether they had followed the 'sleep on it' approach. Amazingly, they discovered that purchasers of products that only require limited information processing (books, CDs clothes, shampoo, etc.) experienced more post-purchase satisfaction after conscious rather than unconscious decision making. Conversely, purchasers of more involved products such as cars, cameras and furniture experienced more satisfaction after adopting the 'sleep on it' approach to their purchase.

The Bully In The Brain approach that we discuss in this book is very much about using the subconscious to make effective decisions and challenge our belief systems. Our beliefs lie within our powerful, habitual, subconscious minds. When we harness their limitless power and have clarity in our thinking, then we can truly gain internal self-insight and bring about powerful changes in our lives. So, when it comes to making that all-important decision, Mum was clearly right after all! Enjoy your nap!

SUMMARY

Our childhoods were filled with sage advice given to us by our mothers: 'If you can't say anything nice, don't say anything at all', 'Don't sit too close to that TV, you'll get square eyes' and, perhaps one of the most important ones, 'Sleep on it'. When we are faced with a difficult decision, it can often be hard to come to a conclusion we are happy with. If we take the example of a purchase – how many times have you bought something on an impulsive whim, and then come to regret it later on? Making a decision can be difficult, and the fatigue that comes with this, or ego depletion as it is otherwise known, makes it that bit harder. Therefore, taking a step back or some time away from a decision gives your brain that much-needed time to rest and, ultimately, come to a better decision in the end. So, maybe mother really does know best, and when it comes to making a difficult choice, sleeping on it is the best course of action.

CHAPTER THIRTEEN

THE BULLY IN THE BRAIN

The voices in my head, which I used to think were just passing through, seem to have taken up residence.
– ELIZABETH WURTZEL

As we have considered before in this book, our belief systems can be viewed as an invisible force behind our behaviours. Combined with other factors, such as our personality and our habits, our belief systems are perhaps the single most dominant driving force affecting the decisions that we make daily. They can impact how we communicate and how we react to things in our life, or indeed any aspect of our behaviour.

With regard to the idea of whether a behaviour is inborn (nature) or learnt through our experiences and our relationships with others (nurture), belief systems most certainly fall into the environmental (nurture) side of the argument. As we have discussed previously, as humans we accrue thousands of beliefs throughout our lifetime about all aspects of our life. We gain them through things that other people say to us, things we hear, things we read – usually from a trusted or authoritative figure. Many of these beliefs interact with one another, and in doing so, create layers of beliefs. This combination of beliefs can then be viewed as a belief system.

Beliefs can be 'held' at different levels of awareness. Some we can bring to mind easily whilst others are deeply ingrained. Those beliefs seldom, if ever, come into question, they are just accepted in the same way that a young child accepts the existence of Santa Claus and the Tooth Fairy. Sometimes, the need to maintain a belief can be so strong that when we think our beliefs are being challenged we can react with anger and even aggression.

Beliefs can be held with different levels of conviction or degrees of confidence. Beliefs vary in their degree of personal reference; for example, we may wish to maintain a belief as it suits the ego to do so. To challenge it may perhaps risk some damage to our self-identity or our self-esteem. Related to this, our conviction in some beliefs we hold may even fluctuate over time or across different contexts.

We also have internal pressures to keep our beliefs. No one wants to be wrong. Being wrong can make us feel silly or foolish. So, to protect our self-image, we ignore evidence contrary to our beliefs and look for evidence in support of them. In the realm of beliefs, there is comfort in company, so we seek out fellow believers to associate and align ourselves with.

Beliefs vary in the degree to which they are shared by other people. Some beliefs are very common, while others may be comparatively unusual (e.g. in the case of some delusions). In one famous study, social psychologist Milton Rokeach put three men in the same hospital ward who thought they were Jesus. Rokeach had previously heard word of a random grouping of two women who both believed themselves to be the Virgin Mary at a different psychiatric hospital. Eventually, one of the Marys realised that if another person was claiming to be the only Virgin Mary, then, logically, she must be mistaken about her own identity. She subsequently snapped out of her delusion. Rokeach held the conviction that the same shifting in beliefs might be possible for the three Jesuses. The study came to be known as The Three Christs of Ypsilanti – the name of the psychiatric hospital in Michigan where the study took place.

As time went on the men started to humour one another's delusions. The three Christs of Ypsilanti remained exactly that: three Christs. They argued every day and sometimes came to blows. When cornered, they accused the others of being crazy or being controlled by machines. With time, they became friends, defending each other against other patients. They stopped arguing and talked about more mundane things and avoided the subject of Jesus entirely.

After 2 years, Rokeach prepared to end the study. He had accomplished next to nothing. The only difference was that one of the Jesuses named Leon had changed his name to Dr Righteous Idealized Dung. Some progress perhaps?

Whilst Rokeach had failed to accomplish his mission of assisting his patients in overcoming their delusion, he began to see that delusion was indeed a condition he suffered from himself. He too had been under the false belief of omnipotence while at Ypsilanti. He explained that in the intervening years he had grown uncomfortable about the ethics of his experiment. Later, he admitted that he 'really had no right, even in the name of science, to play God and interfere around the clock with their daily lives'. Rokeach had come to the realisation that many of us fall prey to the belief that we can impose our beliefs on others. He saw first-hand how hazardous this can potentially be for others, even when that work is underpinned with good intentions.

In this chapter, we are going to look at how we can bring about changes in our own lives when a challenging experience can make us question how we may be viewed by others. We will look further into limiting beliefs (auto-limiting thoughts) and how sometimes the challenges we face in life can drive us to go beyond what others believe is possible for us.

CRAZY FROG

One day, Mr Frog was happily hopping along when he heard a voice come out of a hole a few feet away from where he had hopped. To find out who was calling to him, he hopped across the hole to peer over the side. In the hole, he spied his friend Mr Rabbit staring up at him. Mr Rabbit begged Mr Frog to help him get out of the hole he had unfortunately found himself stuck in. 'Mr Frog, please help me get out of the hole! I was hopping along and the next thing I knew, I'd fallen down this deep hole and I just can't get out. Will you help me?' said the rabbit to Mr Frog.

Mr Frog said to Mr Rabbit, 'Well, I can't get you out on my own, I'm just too small. I will need to get some help, Mr Rabbit. I will be back as soon as I can, I promise.'

With that, the frog hurriedly hopped off in search of assistance to help Mr Rabbit get out of his predicament. Some time passed and eventually Mr Frog was able to muster up enough help to get Mr Rabbit out of the hole. But when Mr Frog and his band of helpers returned to the hole, they were amazed to find that Mr Rabbit had somehow managed to get out and was nowhere to be seen. The frog was confused and apologised to his friends for wasting their time.

Suddenly, out of nowhere, Mr Rabbit hopped towards the group of friends as if nothing had happened. The frog quizzed the jolly rabbit, asking him how he had managed to get out of the hole that he had claimed to be stuck in. Mr Rabbit grinned and answered, 'Oh, I got out on my own. A snake fell in the hole and, without a second thought, I found I was able to jump out quite easily.'

Mr Frog looked at him and thought, 'What an absolute boondoggle you are, Mr Rabbit!'

Of course, this allegory is really about how sometimes we can bring about change easily when something is worth it for us or when there is a threat to us of some sort. Sometimes, we just need that push to get us going. Sometimes we don't need 'grit'; we just need to be gently pushed onto the right trajectory. In many ways, the simple tale of the frog and the rabbit reminds me of the origin of the world's most recognised prize for peace.

GIVE PEACE A CHANCE

On 12 April 1888, engineer and businessman Ludvig Nobel passed away in France from a heart attack. In the annals of history, his death would perhaps have been of little note other than for the series of extraordinary events shaped by his sad departing.

Alfred Nobel

Thanks to some poor reporting, at least one French newspaper believed that it was not Ludvig that had perished but his brother Alfred Nobel, the Swedish inventor and businessman. As a result, it printed a contemptuous obituary that branded Alfred a 'merchant of death'. It went on to assert that Nobel had grown rich by developing new ways to 'mutilate and kill', stating that he had become rich by finding ways to kill more people faster than ever before.

Unsurprisingly, the error was later redacted, but not before Nobel had the unpleasant experience of reading his own death notice. Historians have noted that it was this single, unfortunate occurrence that may have brought on a crisis of conscience, and steered Alfred to revaluate his business practices. Nobel, who was a self-proclaimed hermit, once wrote: 'I am a misanthrope and yet utterly benevolent, have more than one screw loose, yet am a super-idealist who digests philosophy more efficiently than food'. What Nobel read that day troubled him so profoundly that he then became obsessed with his posthumous reputation. In his last will and testament, he bequeathed the majority of his fortune to 'a cause upon which no future obituary writer would be able to cast aspersions'.

Nobel held an impressive 355 different patents, of which dynamite was his most famous invention. It was also the product he made the majority of his great wealth from. There is some evidence that Nobel believed that dynamite would be instrumental in bringing about world peace. He once wrote to Baroness Bertha von Suttner: 'Perhaps my factories will put an end to war sooner than your congresses: on the day that two army corps can mutually annihilate each other in a second, all civilized nations will surely recoil with horror and disband their troops'.

Known as the 'dynamite king', Nobel chose very a simple life and lived it isolated from society. He travelled constantly, which allowed him to remain distant from his relatives. He never married and had few female friendships. One day, he fell gravely ill and the only visit he received was from one of his employees. This solitary, compassionate experience, along with his potential obituary, drove Nobel to reflect profoundly on his life and on his legacy, and how he would be remembered.

The Nobel Foundation noted that he may have first got the idea for the science prizes in 1868, when he received an award from the Royal Swedish Academy of Sciences for 'important inventions for the practical use of mankind'. Nobel was also a voracious reader who spoke five languages and dabbled in writing plays and poems. It was this love of the written word that no doubt sparked his interest in offering a prize in literature.

Although Nobel may have provided the funds, it was chemical engineer Ragnar Sohlman who made the Nobel Prizes a reality. After Alfred Nobel's death on 10 December 1896, Sohlman was occupied for several years with the task of realising Nobel's intentions of establishing the Nobel Prize. He secured Nobel's assets and collaborated with the prize-awarding institutions. Between 1929 and 1946, he presided over the Nobel Foundation and helped make the awards a worldwide phenomenon, awarding prizes in physics, chemistry, physiology or medicine, literature and peace.

Just as Nobel's beliefs about how he was to be remembered drove him to take massive action, sometimes, our previously unshakeable beliefs in our own abilities can be challenged unexpectedly, forcing us to believe that perhaps we have been outsmarted, as in the following remarkable true story.

ONLY A PAWN IN THEIR GAME

It's New York in the May of 1997 and chess champion Garry Kasparov is sat challenging IBM's new supercomputer named 'Deep Blue'. Previously Kasparov had bragged that he would never lose against a machine. A year earlier, his certitude had been proved correct when had won against the supercomputer in a game in Philadelphia. This game was different though. At a certain point in the game Deep Blue made a sacrifice move that seemed to hint at a long-term strategy. Kasparov believed this move to be far too sophisticated a move for a mere computer, believing instead there had been some sort of human intervention in this cunning move. This unlikely move threw Kasparov into something of a tailspin, resulting in Kasparov being defeated in this milestone game.

Fifteen years after this legendary game, one of Deep Blue's designers revealed that in fact the move by the supercomputer was the result of a simple software bug. It transpired that when Deep Blue did not know what move to make, it was programmed to make a random move. It was undeniable that this random, out-of-context move shook Kasparov's beliefs about his skills as a chess player. Indeed, his belief system about what this artificial intelligence machine was in fact capable of had been shaken – the result of which was that he lost the game. He had formed a belief that the counterintuitive move by Deep Blue was in fact a sign of superior intelligence. He could, of course, never have conceived that the move was simply a result of a bug in the software. His previously unshakeable belief had been challenged. The bully in Kasparov's brain chiselled away at the belief he had so publicly asserted.

RUN LIKE HELL

Often when we overcome the bully in the brain, we can achieve something remarkable. In the following example, not only did an individual achieve something that had previously been viewed as impossible, but his achievement meant that limiting beliefs around such a feat had been destroyed, allowing others to achieve beyond what he had.

Often, when we think of belief systems in sports and other human achievements, we think of the incredible Roger Bannister – the first human being to run a 4-minute mile – and what he taught us about breaking new ground and achieving the impossible. Runners had been chasing the goal of the 4-minute mile since 1886, but it wasn't until 6 May 1954 on a cold, wet track in Oxford, England, that Bannister ran the incredible time of 3 minutes 59 and 4/10ths of a second. It was truly the pinnacle of athletic achievement. Bannister, a full-time student, was an outlier who had little use for coaches and who devised his own system for training and preparing for the race. What is most astonishing about the feat is that just 46 days later Australian runner John Landy beat the record with an incredible time of 3 minutes and 58 seconds. Just a year later, three runners broke the 4-minute barrier in a single race meeting. Over the past half-century, more than a thousand runners have conquered something that had previously been considered completely out of reach for a human being. This achievement speaks to us about human achievement and what we believe our abilities are – both in sports and in our lives. When a trailblazer like Bannister paves the way, the limiting beliefs surrounding what is possible are eroded away, leaving open the possibility of 'what if'. Indeed, our beliefs determine how high we set our sights. Often positive thinking alone isn't enough, but it creates a growth mindset and a belief system that allows the intersection of superior planning and execution.

OLD KENTUCKY HOME

Individuals can often hold limiting beliefs that they are too old to try something new or follow a dream they have had. The bully in

References

the brain is telling them that the opportunities of youth have passed them by.

To consider what is possible you need look no further than the sixth grade dropout, farmhand, locomotive fireman, railroad worker, insurance salesman, unsuccessful political candidate, aspiring lawyer, motel operator and finally restaurateur Harland David Sanders – better known to the world as Colonel Sanders.

What makes this story the more extraordinary is that at age 65, Harland David Sanders was reliant on a $105 a month social security check to live. He felt that the government was saying to him that he couldn't provide for himself. Deciding that his life wasn't worth living anymore and feeling like a failure, he decided to take his own life. Legend has it that, sitting under a tree to pen his last will and testament, he decided instead to write what he could have accomplished in his life, and what he could still do with his life. He thought he had tried everything at that stage, but there was one thing he hadn't learnt: how to cook.

He borrowed $87 against his social security cheque, and he bought some pans and utensils, and fried some chicken. The rest is finger lickin' history.

It was in his late 60s that the Colonel – an honorary title given to him, a Kentucky Colonel not a military rank – finalised his now legendary 'original recipe' for KFC, consisting of 11 different herbs and spices. At age 65, Sanders travelled door to door across the United States, visiting restaurateurs, and dealing with rejection after rejection, trying to convince them to franchise his distinctive chicken. His determination paid off, and by 1963 there were over 600 KFC restaurants open, making the company the largest fast-food operation in America. At age 74, Sanders sold his company to investors for a tidy $2 million (around $16 million in today's money).

Sanders was born in 1890 on a little farm in Henryville, Indiana. Sadly, when he was aged just 5 his father died, forcing his mother to take work at a local tomato canning factory and sewing for nearby families. She would frequently be away for days at a time. In the meantime, Sanders, who was the oldest of three siblings, took care of the home and his family. It was during this difficult time that he started to develop his cooking skills.

Sanders, who had been balancing his work as a farmhand with his full-time education, dropped out of school, having only completed the sixth grade. Later in life, Sanders would claim that 'algebra's what drove me off'.

Sanders' own family life was often tumultuous and peppered with tragedy. In 1908, he married Josephine King, with whom he had three children. His inability to hold down a job soon proved taxing at home, and Josephine would leave him for a short time, taking the children with her. The tragic loss of Harland Junior, Sanders' only son, greatly troubled Sanders and he was afflicted with depression for most of his adult life. Finally, in 1949, he married a woman named Claudia Leddington, whom he would remain with until his death in 1980.

By age 88, Harland David Sanders was a billionaire! Proving perhaps that regardless of your age and background, it's never too late to follow your dream and create a legacy.

I PUT A SPELL ON YOU

When we think of limiting beliefs, often we may think of the torture individuals can bestow on themselves, questioning their work and their achievements. Thinking their work is not good enough, or not worthy of public attention as in the case of the French composer Paul Abraham Dukas (1885–1935). You may not know his name, but you probably know his music. Picture if you will Mickey Mouse dressed in a blue hat with stars and moons adorning its sides, and a red cloak tied with a piece of rope. Now see his wand and the buckets of water being carried by broomsticks as they shuffle along, brought to life by his spells. Chances are you will hear in your mind a particular piece of music, one of the most well-loved and well-known 'classical orchestral' pieces of music of all time – the wonderfully descriptive 'Sorcerer's Apprentice' (L'apprenti Sorcier), made famous by Walt Disney's 1941 classic Fantasia.

Few will ever have given a thought to the origin of the piece, or indeed the torment and lack of self-belief that Dukas felt about his works. His absence of self-belief in his compositions was so strong that, as he neared his death in 1881, he set about burning all but a handful of his works. We can only wonder what works were destroyed – works that could have lived on and been adored by millions around the world for generations, as the 'Sorcerer's Apprentice' has been.

Dukas's pathological perfectionist tendencies have perhaps denied the world a wealth of classic works. Clearly the criticism and unrealistically high standard placed on his work only existed in his mind, in his belief system, not in the real world. It was his perception of the lack he saw in his work, not in fact the reality of the pleasure it would give others that prevented him from sharing more of his unique talent with the world.

Whilst a perfectionist thinking system is a powerful ally when it is managed well, its lack of flexibility and constant striving for unrealistic standards can be a destructive force that denies many a form of expression and creativity. Often rooted in a fear of disapproval from others, and massive feelings of insecurity and inadequacy, it can lead to procrastination and incomplete projects. In many ways, it can seem better not to try something at all rather than to try and fail. How many of us have not taken a risk in something for fear of what might happen if others don't approve of our work? The belief that it's too risky to try something is perhaps the most restrictive of all of the limiting beliefs we may have, as it stops us moving forward and expressing who we really are. As author and teacher Francis Chan explains, 'Our greatest fear should not be of failure … but of succeeding at things in life that don't really matter'.

EIGHT DAYS A WEEK

One of the areas we work with frequently at our practice here in Hampshire is to help our clients recognise and challenge their self-limiting beliefs. Of course, the very nature of a limiting belief dictates that you may not be aware that a belief is in fact a belief at all, let alone a limiting one. For example, if you hold the belief that you are not any good at say 'maths' or 'numbers' and live your life not questioning that assumption, then why would you need to challenge it? You assume it to be a statement of fact. After all, it hasn't impacted much on your life up to this point. For example, you may not make an effort to improve your maths skills, and you rely wholly on using a calculator – perhaps not even trying to do any maths in your head when needed. After all, with the invention of smartphones, you are never too far from a calculator anyway.

But think back to the formation of that limiting belief. Was it a belief that was formed for you by a teacher, a parent, a caregiver or even a friend? Was it a limiting belief you formed yourself because it was easier to hold onto? Does the anxiety of being asked to do maths in school still exist in your memory, unconsciously constraining you to distance yourself from the feelings such experiences generated in your formative years? Indeed, would taking time to improve your maths skills bring back some of those uncomfortable emotions? Or would avoiding improving a particular skill remove the responsibility attached to making a change in your skill level? Possibly even something that you may be quite good at as an adult?

I remember when I was at primary school I was placed on the 'special table' with other kids who often struggled with the work. Next to me was a boy called Lionel. Lionel also struggled with some of the learning required of us at that stage in our development, and I clearly remember the exasperated classroom assistant appointed to our non-high-flying table saying to my poor friend, 'Lionel, you will never be any good at maths!' At that point, two things could have happened: Lionel could have taken on that suggestion to his subconscious, and therefore his belief system, or he could have chosen not to. As we looked at previously in this book, children are highly suggestable until around age 7. For Lionel, he could have chosen to maintain the belief for the rest of his life that 'maths was not for him'. Alternatively, he could have thought, 'You'll see, lady. I am going to get really good at this maths thing!' In fact, Lionel did the latter:

he went on to get two degrees in maths and worked for a leading London financier. He also went on after this event to steal some of my Action Man's clothes, but I promised him on my life I would never mention that again. But if you do ever read this book, Lionel, can I have my silver Action Man's Apollo space suit back? I hear it's worth quite a lot now on the toy collectors' market!

Lionel's reasoning and beliefs in this situation are perhaps described by author Rachel D. Greenwell when she writes, 'If someone calls me stupid, I have to actually believe I'm stupid in order for it to affect me'.

On another occasion, a shy little boy sat a music test with the rest of his school designed to determine whether he could recognise if one note was higher or lower in pitch than another. The prize for the top achievers in this test was a beautiful, brand-new, free musical instrument and free tuition on that instrument. He had desperately wanted to learn any instrument, be it the flute, clarinet or trumpet, even worst case a not-so-cool violin! He didn't care; he just loved music and wanted to play an instrument. The day came when the teacher called out the scores for the test, the highest first, continuing all the way through the entire list of names right through to the lowest scorer in the test. Of course, she could have stopped at the first 20 as they were the delighted few who would be the recipients of the free instruments and lessons. But no, she continued right through to the bitter end, making the most of her ability to belittle children – a practice I'm sure she realised that would be frowned upon beyond the 1970s education system.

So, this little boy didn't get the instrument he so desperately wanted. At that stage, he could have thought to himself, 'I obviously don't have an ear for music'. Or he could have thought, 'I want to do this, and I can do it, what do I need to make it happen?' – like Lionel and his maths. The very thing that limited him became the driving force to push him beyond the limits of where his peers believed he could go.

This little boy went on to get a degree in music education, to write and have published several musicals, and to have several albums on Spotify. How do I know this? Well, because that little boy was me. Did the children who got those instruments that day ever go on to follow a career in music? Highly unlikely, perhaps because it had become all too easy for them. In many ways, Friedrich Nietzsche was absolutely on the money when he penned, 'Sometimes, struggles are exactly what we need in our life. If we were to go through our life without any obstacles, we would be crippled. We would not be as strong as what we could have been. Give every opportunity a chance, leave no room for regrets.'

I am sure there are lots of examples of this sort of happening in your own life, and in the lives of your friends and family. In fact, the challenges that outwardly seem to restrict us become the very thing that can drive us to achieve more in our lives, particularly if we have that all-important growth mindset.

As we will look at shortly, the Nova Effect highlights that every adversity we may experience in life can in fact turn out to be of benefit to us. It is impossible to establish if the outcome of any situation will be good or bad until the future has fully come to pass. The 'rear-view mirror' of life can often show us the benefits and advantages that have come from an adversity or challenge.

SUMMARY

This chapter looked at the title character of the book: The Bully in Our Brain.

The beliefs we hold at a much deeper level are rarely ever questioned, and if they are, it can be met with anger or aggression as we feel a strong need to maintain our beliefs. If there is something that challenges these strongly held beliefs, we can often ignore the contradictory information in order to save face.

When it comes to our self-limiting beliefs, we often don't realise they are holding us back. The majority of the time, it takes either an incentive or a threat to us for our beliefs to be challenged and our behaviours to be changed. This can also be made a lot easier if another individual paves the way first. The self-limiting beliefs we hold are more often than not imposed on us by someone external, whether this be a parent, friend or teacher. When faced with these beliefs, we can either let them define us and maintain them for the rest of our lives, or we can use this to spur us on and challenge them – proving the enforcing individual wrong.

CHAPTER FOURTEEN

ORIGINS OF CHANGE

*When solving problems, dig at the roots instead
of just hacking at the leaves.*
– ANTHONY J. D'ANGELO

The summer lockdown of 2020 gave many people many things. Lots to worry about, lots of time to think about their lives and also, for some, lots of opportunity to eat for comfort. Personally, it gave me a lot more time to spend with my 4-year-old, to meditate and to educate myself in my chosen line of work. It was whilst meditating one day that an idea came to me: to combine the benefits of meditation with the results that can be achieved in my day-to-day work as a hypnotherapist. As a practising hypnotherapist and hypno-analyst, I had seen incredible results with clients over the years – not just in our practice in Hampshire, but with people using our range of apps across the globe.

Something, however, had played on my mind for years with regard to one of our weight loss apps: why some users were experiencing extraordinary results, but others less so. Before I talk about that, I want to travel back in time to the first time Sue, my long-suffering business partner and friend, and I discussed creating a weight loss hypnosis app. Sue had already achieved great success with her weight loss clients in the practice. Indeed, the Virtual Gastric Band programme we had created together had become so popular that people from far and wide came to us to be hypnotised to lose weight, the vast majority doing so with breath-taking success. It was during a conversation one day that I mentioned creating an app that would allow users to follow the programme remotely, without our individual assistance and support, other than perhaps support on Facebook. We decided to

References

give it a go and, after several months of disagreements and arguments (we argue a lot!), the app was born! The 'EasyLoss Virtual Gastric Band – Lose Weight Fast!' app hit the iTunes store! (Many years later we changed the name of the app to '12 Weeks to Wow'.)

A few weeks passed, and we began to notice that strange things were happening – people were starting to report amazing results. So much so, that we launched a much improved and updated version less than a year later.

Years went by, app sales grew, Facebook support group membership flourished and the results that users were having left us speechless, and I mean literally speechless (not an easy feat for anyone who knows Sue!). Media interest in the programme grew and app users' success stories were regularly featured in media outlets such as the *Daily Mail*, *The Doctors* TV show (in the USA) and the popular *How to Lose Weight Well* on Channel 4 here in the UK.

Now, why am I writing about this, other than because it feels great? As I mentioned above, something played on my mind with regard to the app, and it was this: when we designed and built the app, we naively assumed app users would find 20 or so minutes in their busy days to sit down somewhere quiet and undisturbed to listen to the hypnosis sessions we had created for the app. Of course, the reality is that most people don't have 20 minutes in their day, particularly the busy mums who use our app. What mum has 20 minutes in her day?! So, what started to happen is app users would listen to the hypnosis session at night as they lay down to go to sleep. As a result, Sue and I were bombarded day after day with the question, 'Is it okay to listen at night and will it still work okay? Will I lose weight?' Understandably, we informed app users that, yes, it would work fine! But, to be honest, in the back of our minds we were thinking that perhaps it wouldn't work as well. However, we concluded that listening to it is still better than not listening to it! And also, to be totally upfront, we didn't want too many app users asking Apple for a refund!

In our extensive hypnosis training, going to sleep whilst in a hypnosis session was never fully discussed, other than to say that if it happens, try and make sure you raise your voice and wake the client up gently. There is a state called the 'somnambulistic state' where you could perform surgery on your client and they would feel little or no pain. In reality, these clients are few and far between, but when they are in this deep state of hypnosis, they're in such a comfortable relaxed state that they aren't keen on coming out of it to carry on living in the real, less comfortable world.

The questions about going to sleep whilst listening to the hypnosis played on my mind. Having composed the music for the apps, I congratulated myself, thinking that possibly it was my music which was so relaxing that no one could remain awake for more than a few minutes. Although, to be more accurate (and honest!), it was far more likely Sue's relaxing voice. Over the next few months and years, we were once again astounded by the results app users were having. In particular, the users who reported that they had lost a large amount of weight and had never actually managed to listen consciously to a whole session! Indeed, many app users still declare that they have never heard more than about 2 minutes of our 20-minute sessions. On a side note, when we rerecorded the audio in a professional studio as opposed to the front bedroom of my house, huge numbers of app users wrote angrily to us, claiming we had altered the hypnosis script and that the new version didn't work as well. Of course, in reality, the script was the same; the only thing to have changed was the metre of Sue's voice and the background music. Plus of course the audio quality (there is only so much you can do with an old microphone and a few pillows and cushions placed around the mic)!

So, the handful of app users who had experienced the 'nocebo' effect moved on, and a new wave of app users emerged, who were once again having incredible results. However, we were still intrigued by the app users who were having the results whilst asleep.

References

In 2010, a brilliant, one-off special by the incredible Derran Brown entitled *Hero at 30,000 Feet* revealed how Derran could take a young guy called Matt and turn him into a hero in just a few weeks. Matt, an unmotivated, uninspired, thirtysomething call-centre worker from Leeds, was unknowingly put through a series of smaller challenges to covertly inspire and uncover his 'hero' like qualities. The culmination of the show was when Matt, who previously had a fear of flying, volunteered to land the plane he was on after the captain was taken sick. Unbeknownst to Matt, the plane had not actually left the ground, and Matt was in a flight simulator. Obviously, the whole scenario was created when Matt was placed into a deep trance, the 'real, not in trouble at all' plane landed, and Matt was placed in the simulator safely on the ground, where he successfully landed the plane. Matt had no conscious awareness of any of this – he believed he was on a real flight and that he would be landing a real plane.

Part of the process for reprogramming Matt's mind was a series of early morning visits where Derran would speak slowly and positively to Matt's unconscious mind, suggesting he would be a good deal more confident and motivated. The results spoke for themselves as the protagonist of the show delivered, in bucket loads, true confidence and openness to opportunities. A remarkable TV show. It was apparent that Matt was one of those fortunate people who can achieve the powerful somnambulistic state (a state that, for the hypnotherapist, can be terrifying! Any hypnotherapist who has ever experienced it will tell you that, for a fleeting moment, you briefly fear that you may have inadvertently killed your client!).

This amazing Derran Brown show stayed with me, and I often thought about the concept of whether it is possible to reprogramme someone's mind while they are asleep – to the extent that they become a better, more confident, fearless and generally more 'go-getting' version of themselves. Can fears and anxieties, particularly social anxiety – the most everyday and life-damaging anxiety – really be reprogrammed that easily? Derran proved in this show without doubt that the mind can be reprogrammed for positive change, and that outstandingly positive results can be achieved by an individual willing to make those changes for themselves.

Of course, the deep state of hypnosis that Matt could achieve (with Derran's aid) undoubtedly helped, and it was made clear at the beginning of the show that the process to choose Matt for this episode had been quite extensive. But what about the average person? What could they achieve with the right amount of help using a perfectly crafted hypnosis session? After all, the astounding results we had seen with the Virtual Gastric Band app couldn't have happened by accident. Surely, this level of profound transformation had to be achievable in other areas of people's lives? We know weight loss cannot be achieved overnight – it takes time. But could achieving a greater level of confidence or a more relaxed, less anxious state be achieved after just a few days? I was intrigued to find out.

As I mentioned earlier, it was during one particular meditation session I undertook during lockdown that I had the idea of combining hypnosis and meditation to form a new transformative therapy: I call it the MediNosis Method. Meditation in its Westernisation has become more about being in the moment and focusing on the here and now rather than worries about the future (a very useful skill to acquire during a pandemic!). Some view it as clearing the mind but, of course, it's not that. After all, as humans we have spent millennia trying to think creatively – why we would want to switch that power off, even momentarily? Meditation is more about controlling your thoughts and letting them go when you need to. The human race has flourished and survived for thousands of years on the ability to think and to make decisions; trying to switch these though processes off would not be easily achieved for anyone, other than a master meditator.

Hypnosis, on the other hand, is more about bringing about a change in the individual's life by communicating directly with the subconscious mind – applying positive suggestion to bring about a change such as stopping smoking, overcoming addictions such as alcohol or gambling, overcoming fears and phobias or losing some excess weight! Different again is hypnoanalysis – a therapy more focused on resolving an unconscious conflict that is having an impact on a client's life. These repressed experiences, by their very nature, are more often than not outside of the client's conscious awareness. Indeed, the client will have little or no awareness of the 'thing' that is causing the issue, or issues, they are experiencing. By using hypnoanalysis, the client resolves the anxiety caused by the repressed emotion and goes on to live a more anxiety-free life. More about that particular therapy later in this book.

Hypnosis and meditation are already very close bedfellows. But what if you could combine the powerful elements of each of them in a way to bring about maximum change in a person's life? It was at this time that I discovered the work that had to be carried out on brain waves. Not the brain waves you think you are having when you have a good idea, but actual brain waves – the electrical activity of the brain.

During a typical day, an average person will move from the Alpha and Beta brain wave states of the waking day, to the Delta and Theta waves of sleep. With normal, waking activity, the brain moves through the relaxed Alpha brain wave state, shifting to the Beta wave state when we become involved in more thinking and problem-solving work. As we go to sleep at night, we move through the Theta wave state to the Delta wave, or deepest stage of sleep, state. In this state our brains and bodies can repair and process the activities of the day. It is in this Theta state that the real magic can and does happen, and the unconscious mind seems most open and receptive to positive suggestions, and therefore, positive changes. The Theta state is what is achieved in a good hypnosis session, and that is why visiting a good hypnotherapist can bring about such a positive life change for people. To help you bring about a massive change in your life, I have included several free MediNosis downloads on our website at www.bullyinyourbrain.co.uk/. I hope you enjoy them and get a lot from them.

IN MY LIFE

Children from the age of about 3–7 years old are in this Theta brainwave state for the majority of the time. Prior to this, from a baby to about the age of 3 years, the child is in the Delta brainwave state. This state is very much synonymous with the unconscious mind. In the Theta brain wave state, children are able to fluently mix regular play with imaginative play. Indeed, as any parent or carer who has ever spent time with a child of this age will attest to, when a child says 'You be Hulk and I'll be Spiderman', in their minds they don't see an adult before them; they picture a large, angry, green man with a ripped shirt! Naturally, in this Theta brain wave stage, kids are far more open to suggestion – either positive or negative in nature – shaping a child's beliefs about who they are in the world, what they deserve, how loved and cared for they are and what limiting self-beliefs they will hold for the entirety of their adult lives (unless as an adult they visit a good therapist!). As Aristotle once wrote, 'Give me a child until he is 7, and I will show you the man'. Again, women had not been invented in Aristotle's day; we had to wait till the 1960s for that to happen.

HUMAN BRAIN WAVES

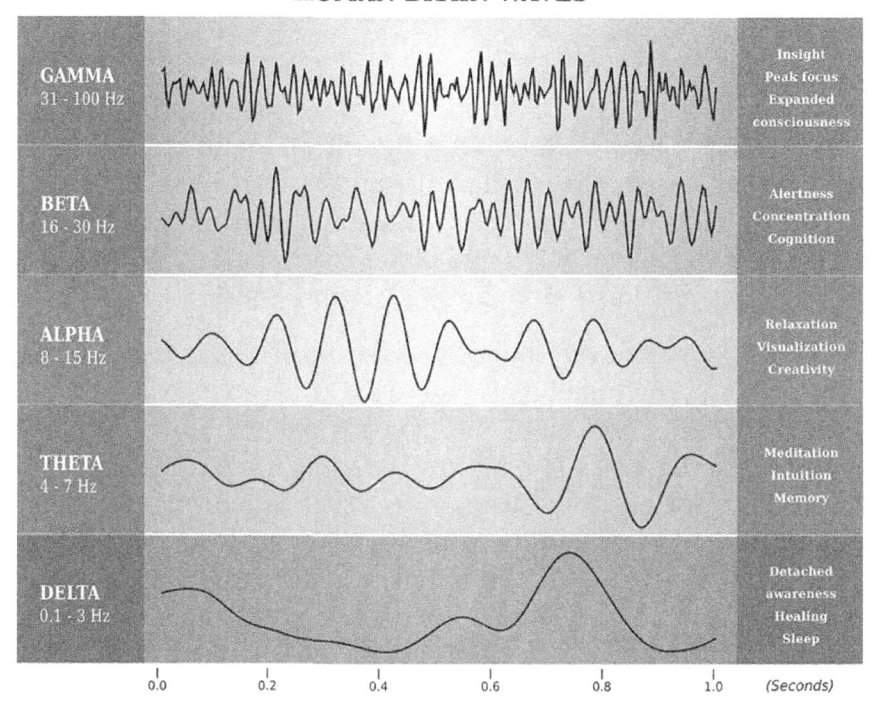

GAMMA 31 - 100 Hz		Insight, Peak focus, Expanded consciousness
BETA 16 - 30 Hz		Alertness, Concentration, Cognition
ALPHA 8 - 15 Hz		Relaxation, Visualization, Creativity
THETA 4 - 7 Hz		Meditation, Intuition, Memory
DELTA 0.1 - 3 Hz		Detached awareness, Healing, Sleep

0.0   0.2   0.4   0.6   0.8   1.0   (Seconds)

FIGURE C

So, given that children are highly suggestible in this Theta brain wave state, and our app users were having incredible results whilst going to sleep, then perhaps the brain wave state of Theta held the key to lasting transformation. But what about the folks who want to hold on to their beliefs or who are convinced that their distorted beliefs are serving them well? I often think of beliefs as being like a toy discussed earlier, 'Stretch Armstrong'. The premise of this toy was that no matter how hard you pulled his arms and legs, he would always go back to his original shape. No matter what you did, when you stopped stretching him for a few moments, his shape would revert back to how he looked when you first started playing with him. For many, this is a good analogy for an individual's beliefs: no matter how much work they do on themselves, their beliefs and self-identity will always return to their original form. Often, we seek out help and advice from lots of different channels, from friends, medical professionals and counsellors, but fail to act on their sage advice. Many of us hold onto old beliefs like a baby holds onto a comforter, perceiving that those beliefs are serving us well.

Frequently, clients would tell me how they would go to bed and brood and ruminate on the things that have gone wrong in their day. The arguments they've had, the injustices they have felt, the worries around work and money that may be happening in their lives. This destructive act would obviously impact on their sleep, further exacerbating their anxiety or depression.

I would always ask the obvious question of them: what if you were to spend the time before you went to sleep focusing on the things that had gone well in your day, no matter how small those experiences might be? In addition, what do you have in your life that you are grateful for? Alternatively, what about spending that time thinking about and focusing on your goals and what you would like to achieve in the following day, month or year? In simple terms, stop focusing on the negative experiences of your day and rather focus on the positive. The free MediNosis downloads at www.bullyinyourbrain.co.uk will help you make the changes you want in your life possible. They will assist you in channelling their thoughts in a relaxed and positive way, making full use of the suggestible Theta wave activity of our brains. Making that seemingly small adjustment to our thinking can have a profound effect on our mental health and our well-being. Think of the MediNosis downloads as making use of the royal road to the subconscious or imagination part of your mind, creating permanent and lasting change in the user.

In 1979, the Harvard MBA programme conducted a study in which graduate students were asked, 'Have you set clear, written goals for your future and made plans to accomplish them?' Amazingly, only 3% claimed to have written goals and plans. Some 13% claimed to have had goals but they weren't written down, with a substantial 84% stating that they had no goals at all. Ten years passed by, and the same group was interviewed again. The 13% of the class who had goals, but had not committed them to paper, were shown to be earning twice the amount of the 84% who had no goals at all. Incredibly, the 3% who had actually written goals were earning, on average, 10 times as much as the other 97% of the class combined!

I often say to my clients that if I were to wake them up at 3am and ask them what their goals are, they should be able to – allowing for understandable shock as to why their therapist is in their bedroom – state their clear and precise goals and aspirations for the future. But, to be able to put them down on paper, you need to have imagined them first. As Napoleon Hill famously penned, 'Whatever your mind can conceive and believe, it can achieve'. Use the MediNosis downloads at www.bullyinyourbrain.co.uk to do just that – to take time each night to imagine the possibilities that await you once you have freed yourself from your self-limiting beliefs.

SUMMARY

This chapter looked at the origins of the MediNosis Method. The method combines the benefits and results of both meditation – to control your thoughts and let go of anything you need to – and hypnosis – to communicate with the subconscious to bring about positive change. This chapter looked into the types of brain waves we have, and which are most conducive to positive suggestions, and answered the all-important question: can we really benefit from hypnosis while we're asleep?

CHAPTER FIFTEEN

I FOUGHT THE LAW, AND THE LAW WON

Nothing can harm you as much as your own thoughts unguarded.
– BUDDHA

Okay, let's have some fun. For the next 30 seconds, think about anything that you want to think about. You can think about the most recent TV show you've watched, a funny video you've seen recently, a chat with a work colleague or partner, or even what you're having to eat later. But, whatever you do, *don't* think about a pink zebra. Basically, you can think about anything you want other than a pink zebra. Remember, whatever you do, try to not to think of that pink zebra. Now try not to think of that very same pink zebra with a monkey on its back playing the banjo ... badly!

Okay, I'll wait. No cheating!

So how long did you last before you pictured the pink zebra? My guess is, only a few seconds. I bet you're wondering how that happened. I mean, when was the last time you thought about a pink zebra? In fact you're probably thinking that you have never even seen a pink zebra in your life! Particularly one with a monkey on its back playing the banjo! So why am I thinking about it?

In psychology, this phenomenon is known as the 'ironic process theory', which was first studied by social psychologist Daniel Wegner in 1987. Wegner states that the more you try to suppress certain thoughts, the more likely that they will resurface in your conscious.

Wegner found that the inability to inhibit certain thoughts could be worsened during times of stress and anxiety in individuals who were prone to anxiety or obsessive thoughts. For some, ironic mental processes can result in intrusive thoughts about doing something immoral or something very much out of character, such as stealing or harming one's own child – thoughts that understandably can be really distressing for the sufferer.

So, asking someone to just 'stop thinking about it', although well-meaning can often have the opposite effect. Particularly if that individual has a propensity for obsessive or ruminating thoughts. If only we could take Lao Tzu's sage advice and 'Stop thinking and end your problems'.

Likewise, have you ever gone to meet a friend of your partner/spouse having been told beforehand that your partner's friend has just broken up with their respective partner and that they are devastated? Whatever you do, you must not mention this ex-boyfriend/girlfriend. Of course, now the suggestion has been planted, you almost can't help yourself and end up mentioning the very person whose name you have been forbidden from speaking! Either that or you are completely silent for fear of doing just that and facing the wrath of an unhappy partner and partner's friend!

Similarly, if you are a parent, ask yourself if you have ever asked your child not to spill something they are holding. How often has that child gone on to do exactly what you have asked them not to do? And how often do we find ourselves saying the words, 'I just knew that would happen! I told you to be careful, didn't I?' Coincidence, or a psychological phenomenon? In fact, in order to mentally process your request, your offspring had to imagine the action of spilling the drink and in doing so created the very action you asked them not to do. Have your words just created the very outcome you wished to avoid?

In the same vein, have you ever played a sport such as golf, tennis or football, been playing well then missed a shot that should have been the perfect shot? Then each subsequent shot you take doesn't go anywhere near as well as it had been at the beginning of the match/game?

Have you ever experienced being tired, trying hard to go to sleep as perhaps you have an important meeting the following day, yet despite your strong will to go to sleep, the harder you try to sleep the more awake you are? Only to find the moment you are not 'willing' yourself to sleep, you drift off without any recollection of the actual process. Similarly, have you ever tried hard to remember someone's name, only to give up? Then suddenly moments later, as if by magic, when you are no longer trying to think of the name, the elusive name just pops straight into you head!

Although Daniel Wenger is credited with the first study of this occurrence, the 'ironic process theory' is at its heart undistinguishable from a phenomenon first written about over 100 years ago by Frenchman Émile Coué. It is more famously known as the 'Law of Reversed Effort', but is also referred to as 'Coué's law'.

Émile Coué (1857–1926) was a French pharmacist, psychologist, and all-round clever bod, who wrote several books on psychology and autosuggestion – *hypnotic or subconscious adoption of an idea that one has originated oneself.* The most famous of his books is *Self-Mastery Through Conscious Auto Suggestion*. Whilst working with his patients in France, Coué noticed a particular psychological phenomenon, which he very humbly gave his name to. Coué's law states the following:

1. When the will and the imagination are antagonistic, it is always the imagination which wins, without any exception.
2. In the conflict between the will and the imagination, the force of the imagination is in direct ratio to the square of the will.
3. When the will and the imagination are in agreement, one does not add to the other, but one is multiplied by the other.
4. The imagination can be directed.

References

In simple terms, when the imagination and the will are in conflict the imagination will always win the day!

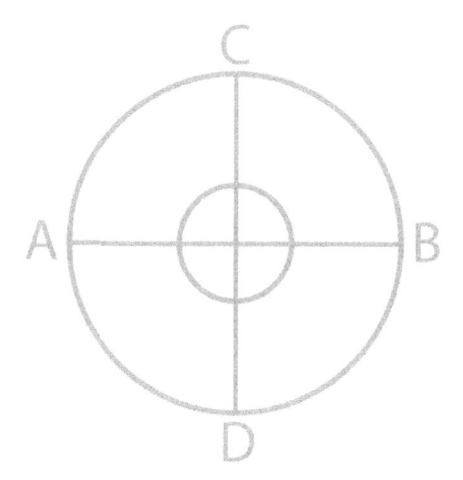

Try this little experiment. Take a piece of white, A4 paper and draw a large circle in the middle of it (as large as the space will permit). Draw another smaller circle in the middle of the larger circle, and then draw one vertical line and one horizontal line though the large circle, making a cross shape in the circle. Now mark each of the point that touch the circle A, B, C and D (see image).

Now take a weighted object such as a wedding ring or a fish weight and attach it to a string approximately 40 cm long, in essence making a makeshift pendulum.

Now take a seat and place your meticulously drawn piece of paper on the floor between your feet. Rest the elbow of your dominant arm on your leg towards your knee – right to right etc. Now hold the pendulum in your dominant hand between your thumb and first finger. As best you can suspend the weight over the centre of the circle, making sure it's nice and still.

Now do the following. Take a nice relaxing breath and start to imagine the pendulum moving gently from A to B, in a nice straight line. Without trying too hard just imagine it, just picture it in your mind. Just see it in your mind's eye, as If it is really happening.

183

Now, after a few moments, when you are ready, start to picture it moving across from C to D in a horizontal line. Again, don't try to overthink it too much, just picture it in your mind actually happening.

Now start to imagine the pendulum moving in either a clockwise circle or a counterclockwise circle – you can choose either.

Finally, just imagine it coming to a complete standstill, as if it's encased in ice, completely frozen, completely still.

What you should have found is that if you didn't overthink the activity or try and second-guess what you were trying to do, the pendulum would have started moving. For some it would move only a small amount; for others there will be quite significant movements. It can feel like it is something otherworldly, almost mystical. Fear not, it's all very explainable.

If it didn't move for you this time, then either try again later or check yourself into a hospital as you may be dead.

This little experiment is known as 'Chevreul's Pendulum', and it is a fantastic demonstration of Coué's law.

Now let's take it to the next level. Use your imagination once again, but this time imagine the pendulum being absolutely still at the centre of the piece of paper. Use all of your willpower to keep it absolutely motionless. Muster up all of the willpower you can and keep it completely still.

After a few moments have passed, at the back of your mind start to imagine once again the gentle swaying of the pendulum from A to B. Like the gentle rocking of a ship, swaying from one side to another, from A to B. Picture that thought coming from the back of your mind to the front, picturing the movement getting wide and wider with each passing moment.

Chances are, as much as you employed your willpower and resisted it, the pendulum started to move, even if it was only ever so slightly at first. Gradually the movements began to get larger and larger demonstrating beautifully that our imagination supersedes our willpower. Again, when our imaginations are in conflict with our willpower our imaginations will always win the day! Without fail!

Let's look at how Coué's law affects all of us, and how we can use it to change our lives for the better. Just for a moment imagine the following scene: picture a plank of wood about a foot and a half wide, and around 100 feet long. Imagine this sturdy plank of wood being supported about 2 feet off the ground. Now picture yourself walking the length of this plank. So far so good! Now picture the same plank of wood you have just walked along, but this time 100 feet in the air. Let's assume the weather conditions are the same at the elevated height as they are on the ground. Once again, imagine yourself walking its length.

Now, the likelihood is that one of two things happened. Either you pictured yourself walking its length with no problem at all, as you did when it was just a few feet off the ground, or alternatively you imagined the possibility of yourself losing your footing, tripping and falling, potentially falling into harm. So, what has changed? The conditions are the same; the plank was the same. You had no problem walking across it when there was little risk. Of course, what has changed is the level of risk, and, as we are hardwired to analysis the risk return ratio, understandably, we come to the conclusion that there is a higher level of risk associated with the task at hand. In essence we had imagined the potential negative outcomes of the walk. Think for a moment about how many times in your life you have imagined the negative and perhaps harmful outcome of something, giving little or no thought to any potential positive outcome of the experience. But here's the kicker: if you did imagine yourself tripping and falling, then there is a much greater chance that you would actually do just that – simply because you have imagined it first. You will certainly be significantly more likely to actually come to some harm if that is what you imagined happening. In essence you evoked Coué's law.

LADY WILLPOWER!

It is estimated that around 27% of the population believe they don't have enough willpower to make a lifestyle change. The good news is that willpower is a skill we can learn. Like a muscle we can exercise.

Believing you have no willpower can often be linked to what is known as a 'locus of control' (more about that later in this book). It is very much a limiting belief. Of course, as with any self-limiting belief you can challenge it and conquer it, allowing you to move towards the empowering belief of 'If I can't, I must; if I must, I can'. Coué's law is perhaps the best tool to utilise to begin to make these changes. In addition, you can make small changes to your life such keeping your trainers by your bed if you want to take up running, and not having sweet or junk food in your house if you are looking to lose weight (there are a plethora of books that cover simple hacks like these).

Coué's law states that when your imagination and your willpower come into conflict, your imagination will always win the day. Always; without question. So, the best way to utilise Coué's law is to begin to take time to imagine what you want, not what you don't want. I will say that again: IMAGINE WHAT YOU WANT, NOT WHAT YOU DON'T WANT. On the surface it seems so simple and so obvious, but as I have mentioned before in this book 'common sense is often not common practice'.

Take a moment now to think of times in your own life when something has happened, and you said to yourself, 'Damn it, I just knew that was going to happen!', implying that you had already spent some time picturing the potentially negative outcome to some event – perhaps a job interview, a date or giving a presentation at work.

Virtually every stop smoking client I have had the pleasure of meeting in the past 20 years has at some stage in the early stages of our sessions confessed to having no will power when it comes to stopping smoking. This proclamation is often followed by a list of areas where the client does have tremendous will power – just not quitting smoking, which is why they are there in the first place! After I reassure them that they don't need willpower to quit, there is often a visible sigh of relief. The soon to be non-smoker has virtually never taken the time to imagine themselves as a happy non-smoker. Often their thoughts are filled with the fear linked to giving up something that they once saw as a friend, a relaxant or even something rebellious. It seems almost too obvious, but isn't it much easier to achieve something if you have pictured it in your mind first?

In many ways Coué's law can also lead to creating for us our biggest fears. I had always realised the psychological power it can harness, but it wasn't until about 2010 that I experienced first-hand the real physiological impact it can have on our lives.

DOCTOR! DOCTOR!

In early 2009 I was diagnosed with a degenerative neurological condition. Life at that time was pretty rough. I woke up one morning and the whole left side of my body was completely numb, like I had 'slept' on it badly. After months of tests and a very painful lumbar puncture, I was diagnosed and informed that my condition would almost certainly get worse. To add to the misery, I was told that there was a strong possibility I would be in a wheelchair in a few years. I certainly wouldn't get any better, I was told. As you can imagine, particularly if you have experienced any serious medical condition yourself, I was swiftly thrown into a state of fear and anxiety. I suddenly felt despairingly uncertain about my future.

I would often feel like my head was 'cloudy'. I had weakness in my body and frequently felt dizzy and generally unwell. Life was not good. I made up my mind to get as well as I could, and I set out to 'cure' myself as best I could of this horrible 'incurable' disease. About a year or so after I was diagnosed, and I had made significant steps towards getting myself as well as I could at that time, I was invited to a 'club' for sufferers of this condition. The well-being nurse informed me that it would allow me to share my experiences and how I felt with others with this condition. Likewise, others with this disease could share with me how it has impacted their life. The meeting of this club was at a local hotel, so somewhat reluctantly I attended the event.

As I entered the room, I was met with an onslaught of wheelchairs and walking sticks. The room was full of individuals who had not only lost a significant amount of their physical capabilities but in some cases their eyesight as well. I was shocked and horrified at what I was witnessing.

'Oh f###!' I remember thinking to myself, picturing these physical limitations as being my future. I had always looked after my health, and now I was looking at what seemed to be a life sentence of disability and utter misery. I tried my best to keep positive and chatted cheerily with a girl in her twenties who had recently been diagnosed and had experienced episodes of blindness and paralysis. During the evening we were all asked to stand up (those who could!), introduce ourselves and talk about our experience of having this unkind disease. I stood up, said my name and stated that I planned to cure myself of this disease, no matter how long it took. To be honest the unspoken feedback I got felt like it was surprise. Like a parent telling a child that 'Well, it's okay to wish, but don't be too disappointed when it doesn't happen for you'. In my heart of hearts, I guess I didn't fully believe I could, but I felt like if I made this public declaration, then I would have to give it my best shot.

What happened next was extraordinary. I returned home and for the next 2 days the right side of my face was completely numb. Bearing in mind that prior to the 'club' meeting the only time I had experienced this sensation was when I was first got 'sick', a year or so before this event, I was puzzled. This was a real sensation, a real physical feeling; it wasn't just in my head or imagined.

Several days later when I was chatting with a colleague and I spoke of what had happened they said to me, 'It's Coué's law, mate!'

At that moment I realised that the anxiety I had felt attending this meeting had created in me my biggest fear. Namely, experiencing what had happened to me a year or so previously – the numbness and lack of feeling. Through my fear and anxiety, I had created these 'real' feelings. For me at that moment in time my biggest fear was to lose fully my mobility and eyesight.

Within the day the numbness had subsided, never to appear again in the 10 years or so since I was first diagnosed. I realised at that moment the almost unbelievable power of our imaginations. In particular, how we can either use Coué's law to our benefit or experience the potential havoc it can inflict on us. Once again, taking time each day to imagine what we want, rather than what we don't want.

Hopefully now you may have come to see how powerful our imaginations can be, both for positive and negative experiences. Finally, in the magnificent words of George Bernard Shaw, 'Imagination is the beginning of creation. You imagine what you desire, you will what you imagine, and at last, you create what you will.'

SUMMARY

Have you ever tried so hard not to think about something that it ends up being the only one thing you can think about? Perhaps you've met a friend after they've been through a break-up, and every ounce of your mind was trying to not say their ex's name, only to then go and blurt it out right in the middle of the conversation. Chapter 15 explained why this happens using the ironic process theory. Although in some situations it may just lead to some slight embarrassment or awkwardness, for someone with ruminating thoughts telling them simply to not think about something can end up being very detrimental. The chapter also looked into the Law of Reversed Effort, otherwise known as Coué's Law. Simply put, Coué's Law states that the more you imagine something happening, the more likely it is to actually happen – meaning we can put this to good use when it comes to bringing about positive changes in our lives.

CHAPTER SIXTEEN

PERCEPTIONS AND BELIEFS

The eye sees only what the mind is prepared to comprehend.
– ROBERTSON DAVIES

St. Charles Church, Vienna

Take a few moments to examine the beautiful painting above. The painting is of St. Charles Church in Vienna, and is a watercolour dating from 1912. It was painted by a young man who loved painting and was desperate to become a professional artist. Sadly, his dreams were ruined because he twice failed the entrance exam to study fine arts. Despite this failing, his desire to continue painting meant he often ended up sleeping in a homeless shelter or under a bridge just so he could remain in the same city as the Fine Art Academy. Eventually, with help from a friend, the budding artist started to earn a meagre living drawing postcards and selling them to tourists.

References

He was a thin, sallow youth, who wasn't cut out for physical labour. Nevertheless, despite this, he went to war for his country. He served in France and Belgium, and it was at the Battle of the Somme that he received a wound in his left thigh when a shell exploded in a dugout. He begged his superiors not to be evacuated. In October 1918, he and several comrades were temporarily blinded due to a mustard gas attack. The young artist went on to be decorated twice for his bravery.

Knowing some of the history of the artist, ask yourself how does the painting make you feel? Has learning about the artist changed how you feel about it? Indeed, does it make you feel anything at all? Perhaps it's not a work you would have hung in your own home, but can you appreciate the passion of the artist who painted it? Could you perhaps imagine seeing it hung in a nice hotel or restaurant? Now, just hold this image of the painting in your mind for a few moments.

GOODBYE YELLOW BRICK ROAD

More about the painting later in this chapter. But now, cast your mind back to the first time you saw the classic movie *The Wizard of Oz*. Most of us can remember the moment in the classic 1939 movie where Dorothy leaves her home in Kansas and steps through the door to the full-colour world of Oz. The stunning scene takes us from sepia tones to full wondrous technicolour. As CGI had not been thought of yet, and indeed neither had computers, you may not be aware that to achieve this remarkable scene the set was painted in sepia tones, and Bobbie Koshay, Judy Garland's double, was outfitted in a sepia dress and given a sepia make-up job. Then, when she steps back out of frame, Judy Garland walks through the door and replaces her. Put simply, other than the open door, we are witnessing a scene filmed entirely in technicolour but made to look sepia. That is until the door to Oz is opened and Dorothy steps through it. In other words, through clever trickery, we are momentarily brilliantly deceived. I think of this remarkable scene often and it makes me curious as to how often we are, in our day-to-day lives, living in vibrant technicolour yet our own perception has placed us in an almost sepia existence. Indeed, it's only when we open the door that we realise we were in fact living in technicolour already. It was our internal dialogue and our self-limiting beliefs that prevented us from experiencing what was already ours for the taking. As W.B. Yeats declared, 'The world is full of magic things, patiently waiting for our senses to grow sharper'.

In this chapter, we are going to discuss some of the perceptions we have and how, in fact, they may be limiting our lives. We are also going to examine the notion that often when we change our beliefs about something it can feel fundamentally impossible to return to our original belief. We are going to examine how the way we view something can profoundly change our beliefs about it. C.S. Lewis states it perfectly in his book *The Magician's Nephew*, when he writes, 'What you see and what you hear depends a great deal on where you are standing. It also depends on what sort of person you are.'

GONNA FLY NOW

As I write, approximately a third of Brits (some 21 million) have a fear of flying. Between 2.5 and 5% are unable to fly due to crippling fear about flying. Some 60% of sufferers experience generalised anxiety during the flight, which can be managed. Most notably, most people report their first fear of flying 'attack' on average at the age of 27. If you were to ask the average person whether air travel is safer or more dangerous than in previous decades, I would hazard a guess the majority would say that it's a lot riskier to travel now, with the fear of a terrorist attack being high on the list of reasons why. In reality, however, air travel has never been safer. According to research by the Massachusetts Institute of Technology (MIT), it has never been safer to travel on a commercial airliner. A study found that between 2008 and 2017, airline passenger fatalities fell significantly compared to the previous decade, as measured by individual passenger boardings. Globally, that rate is now one death per 7.9 million passenger boardings, compared to one death per 2.7 million boardings during the period 1998–2007, and one death per 1.3 million boardings during 1988–1997. So, we have to ask ourselves, why has the number of people with a fear of flying increased? Is it the prevalence of information from the media? Is it the general accumulation of the other threats in the world placed into one general fear, creating the misconception that the world in general is a much more dangerous place than in previous generations?

This is the concept discussed by Steven Pinker in his fascinating and insightful 2018 TED Talk entitled 'Is the World Getting Better or Worse? A Look at the Numbers.' In that talk he discusses that very question. Indeed, until the Covid-19 pandemic of 2019/2020 many people asserted that 2017 was the worst year ever, until 2018 happened, then that was the worst year ever. In his analysis of the data on murder, war, poverty, pollution and more, psychologist Steven Pinker finds that we're doing better now in every one of them when compared with 30 years ago. For many, though, the perception is that the world is far more dangerous than ever. But how does holding these beliefs affect us in the decisions we make day by day. In other words, is it good to be hypervigilant and on guard to potential threats? Or does taking aversive action prove to be even more harmful, as in the case of the next example I'd like to discuss.

COME FLY WITH ME

The official death toll for the September 11 attacks stands at a disturbing 2996 – including the 19 hijackers. However, research suggests that there is a further, indirect toll as a result of the fear-induced behavioural change brought about by the terrorist attack. Namely, that in the months after the 2001 terror attacks, passenger miles on the main US airlines fell by between 12 and 20% while road use jumped exponentially.

The dramatic change to the style of travel post 9/11 is widely believed to have been attributed to passengers opting to drive rather than fly – seemingly a good decision to make at that time in our history. However, travelling long distances by car is potentially far more hazardous than travelling the same distance by plane.

Of course, measuring the exact effect is complex because there is no way of knowing for sure what the trends in road travel would have been had 9/11 not tragically occurred. However, Professor Gerd Gigerenzer, a German academic specialising in risk, has estimated that 1595 more Americans died in car accidents in the year after the attacks, essentially becoming indirect victims of the tragedy. Gigerenzer ascribed the extra deaths to people's poor understanding of danger. Professor Gigerenzer stated that, 'We have an evolutionary tendency to fear situations in which many people die at one time. This is likely a hold-over from when we lived in small groups, where the death of a small part of the group could place the lives of everyone else in jeopardy.' Interestingly, is very difficult to elicit the same fear for the same number of deaths spaced over a year. For example, seldom do we give any thought to the number of smokers who die every year in the USA. Over 480,000 deaths per year in the USA are attributed to cigarette smoking, as well as more than 41,000 deaths resulting from second-hand smoke exposure.

Gigerenzer said governments shared the blame for excess deaths in the wake of terrorism or natural disasters due to efforts to reduce their culpability for any misfortune. Similarly, when British and French planes were grounded due to the Icelandic ash cloud in 2011, no threats to safety were discovered when planes did test flights through the ash. Politicians, however, would be held responsible if a plane had in fact crashed as a result of flying through the ash cloud. If people are killed on the roads because they are forced to take their car instead, no one would ever think to blame a politician.

Sometimes, how we perceive a potential threat can have a considerable bearing on how we make our decisions. Incredibly, those seemingly 'better' decisions can on occasions actually lead us into more harm.

EVERYBODY HURTS

Fascinatingly, when it comes to time, it seems the last part of an experience, particularly how pleasant or unpleasant it is, has a huge bearing on how we perceive the experience. This has come to be known as the peak–end rule. This rule is a cognitive bias that impacts how we think about and remember past events. Intense positive or negative moments (the 'peaks') and the final moments of an experience (the 'end') are heavily weighted in our mental calculus. According to the peak–end rule, our memory of past experience – pleasant or unpleasant – does not correspond to an average level of positive or negative feelings but to the most extreme point and the end of the episode. Basically, the better it is at the end, the more favourably we perceive the experience.

Imagine the following. You are asked to place your hand in freezing, ice-cold water for around 1 minute. After a short break, you are then asked to place your hand once again into freezing, ice-cold water but this time for a minute and a half. On this occasion, for the last 30 seconds the water is warmed up to a slightly less freezing, but nevertheless painfully cold temperature.

Finally, you are asked to choose between doing the first or second task again. Obviously, the most logical choice would be to repeat the first 1-minute round of the experiment, particularly as the water for the final 30 seconds of the second round is still somewhat unpleasant. As it turns out, the slightly less uncomfortable final 30 seconds of the experiment seems to change how people perceive the entirety of the second round. Indeed, in a study of this phenomenon, in the region of 80% of the study participants preferred the second round and chose to repeat that condition in the final trial, clearly demonstrating that how we perceive the end of something has a massive bearing on how we perceive the whole task.

This peak–end rule research conducted by Daniel Kahneman and Barbara Frederickson perfectly highlighted the fact that human memory is rarely a perfectly accurate record of events. It would seem that the evolutionary purpose of the peak–end rule is to helps us avoid devoting more brain capacity to memories than we need to. Kahneman states that, 'Memory was not designed to measure ongoing happiness, or total suffering. For survival, you really don't need to put a lot of weight on duration of experiences.

It is how bad they are and whether they end well, that is really the information you need as an organism.'

How often in our own lives has something been sullied by the final part of the experience? Indeed, think of films you've seen that were really enjoyable but for the last 5–10 minutes or so. How different was your perception of the film based on those last few minutes? Equally, if you've ever seen a film that was average but the last quarter of the film was exceptional, how much more positively did you remember the movie? Similarly, how often do short weekends away seem to be packed with lots of experiences, to the extent that as you are returning home you share with your partner the thought that you can't believe you have only been away for a few days. It appears that when we assess an experience, we tend to forget or ignore its length. Instead, we seem to rate the experience based on two key moments: essentially, the best and the worst moment known as the peak and the ending. What's certain is that when we assess our experiences, we don't average our minute-by-minute sensations.

It appears that we can use the peak–end rule to our benefit. For example, research has found that if they end an exercise or gym session at a lower intensity, people are more likely to feel positive about the experience and, therefore, far more likely to look forward to future sessions. The same thinking applies to losing weight. Research has found that people tend to remember small portions of their favourite dishes as fondly as eating a larger portion.

I SEE YOU EVERYWHERE

Let's pretend you have decided to purchase a brand-new car. Maybe you feel that most of the cars on the market look similar and you are looking for something a bit different; the type of car that will stand out from the crowd. You visit several showrooms and eventually you make a decision on the car and colour you want. Within minutes of making this decision, which you have deliberated about for days, does it seem that, suddenly, the car you have chosen is everywhere? In fact, the exact same type of car is parked down the road from your home. You see two of them next to you in traffic on your way home. As well as this, a colleague of yours has recently purchased the very same car as well, and in the colour you want it in as well! In reality, there are no more of this particular car this week than there were last week. Your work colleague didn't rush out and buy this particular car just to gaslight you. So, what exactly is happening here? How did this car, which you had seldom noticed before, start to dominate your awareness?

Well, welcome to the Baader–Meinhof phenomenon, otherwise known as the frequency illusion or the recency illusion. This phenomenon occurs when the thing you've just noticed, experienced or been told about suddenly crops up constantly. It gives you the illusion that out of nowhere, pretty much everyone is talking about a particular subject, or that something you purchased is now just about everywhere. It can begin to feel like this thing you are now noticing is a lot more prevalent than before. In reality, however, because this thing is in your conscious awareness you are just noticing it more. Naturally this confirmation bias can distort our perceptions and therefore our beliefs.

A couple of things happen when the Baader–Meinhof phenomenon occurs. Think of all you're exposed to in a single day. It's simply not possible to process everything in detail. Your brain has the job of deciding which things require your attention and focus and which can be filtered out. Your brain can easily ignore information that doesn't seem vital in the moment, and it does so every day.

When you are exposed to brand-new information, especially if you find it interesting, your brain takes notice. It excites you. It's relevant to your life at that particular time. These details are potentially destined for the permanent file so they're going to be front and centre for a while in your limited attention.

Similarly, have you have ever thought of a film only to turn on the TV and, hey presto, there it is? Or thought of a friend whom you hadn't thought of for a while and then had them call you on the phone? We tend not to associate meaning with the times we think of someone and they don't call us or the times when we think of a movie and don't see it anywhere – we tend to attach meaning to what we think of and see rather than what we think of and don't see. After all, we have between 60,000 and 80,000 thoughts a day – some of these will inevitably be of things that don't suddenly and miraculously appear in our lives! So once you're looking for something, you find it, and confirmation bias occurs after seeing it even once or twice. In other words, you start agreeing with yourself that you are positively seeing it more frequently.

Normally, with any new discovery in the field of psychology, the name of the phenomenon is sensibly derived from the name of the individual or group of individuals who first uncovered it. Oddly, that is not the case with this discovery. Baader–Meinhof was in fact a militant West German terrorist group active in the 1970s. The origin of its name was a St. Paul, Minnesota, Pioneer Press online commenting board. In 1994, a commenter dubbed the frequency illusion the 'Baader–Meinhof phenomenon' after randomly hearing two references to Baader–Meinhof within 24 hours. The phenomenon has nothing to do with the terrorist group.

Why then is the Baader–Meinhof phenomenon so relevant to what we are discussing here in this book? Take a moment to think about people you have met in your life, for whom everything seems to go wrong. Not just for a brief period, as we all encounter, but literally week after week and month after month some tragedy is happening in their lives, be it at home, at work or even travelling between the two. Literally everything in that individual's life seems to be tainted with some kind of melodrama. Of course, we all experience times in our lives that are challenging: the loss of a loved one, financial troubles, relationship issues, etc. But these people seem to slide from one drama to the next. Could it be that they are only noticing the experiences and events in their lives when there is a negative outcome, and ignoring any possible positive events or outcomes? Ignoring completely what has become to be known as the 'Nova Effect'.

The Nova Effect highlights that every adversity we experience in life can in fact turn out to be of benefit to us. With this in mind, it is impossible to establish if the outcome of any situation will be good or bad until the future has fully come to pass.

Similarly, as philosopher Alan Watts states, 'Maybe the whole process of nature is an integrated process of immense complexity, and it is really impossible to tell whether anything that happens in it is good or bad because you never know what the consequences of the misfortune or you will be never know what the consequences of good fortune will be'.

Now, take another moment to think about what it would be like if you looked at your life with the mindset that you can achieve whatever you truly want. That every day is truly unique and special. Feeling gratitude for the opportunities that you are presented with each and every day, and grateful for the challenges that you are presented with also, for it is just those challenges that drive us and shape us to achieve more. The Nova Effect also establishes the importance of being optimistic, particularly in the face of adversity – holding in our thoughts the belief that no matter how difficult or challenging an experience may be, and no matter how much perceived 'bad luck' we may be encountering, the long-term benefit may be positive – like a child who wishes for sweets but is given fruit by his parent or carer. In life, we often get not what we want but what is best for us. Indeed, if an experience outwardly appears to be bad fortune, it might actually be profoundly good luck, which might change the very course of our life. As the Dalai Lama asserted, 'Remember that not getting what you want is sometimes a wonderful stroke of luck'.

Always hoping for the best outcome and always looking for the positive in others and in our circumstances can be a challenge. But if we view every moment of life as an opportunity to grow and find happiness; if we hold the belief that all of the unpredictable, complex and random events in our life may be not only teaching us something valuable but nudging us into something great, the benefit of which we may only detect when it has long since vanished from the rear-view mirror of life, then we may perceive the challenges that face us each day from a fresh perspective. As

Walt Disney once poignantly said, 'All the adversity I've had in my life, all my troubles and obstacles, have strengthened me... You may not realize it when it happens, but a kick in the teeth may be the best thing in the world for you.'

Finally, before we close this look at perception and beliefs, bring back to your memory the painting we examined at the beginning of this chapter. If I tell you that this work was painted by Adolf Hitler, does that change how you feel about the work? Indeed, if you were to look at it again could you ever feel the same about it? Has your impression of the work been tarnished forever? Also, did you find that you used an availability heuristic to establish the nationality of the artist? Did you believe the artist to be British or French perhaps? If you did, what made you come to that conclusion? Was it the use of mustard gas?

As I mentioned previously, once we change our beliefs about something, it can often be almost impossible to return to our original beliefs. Indeed, once we view something differently, it is unlikely we can ever view it in the same way again. More about how we challenge and change our beliefs later in this book. Prepare to have the way you think about and view the world challenged and changed forever.

SUMMARY

Is the world more dangerous now than it has ever been, or are we just perceiving it that way? It's important to know that often in our lives we are deceived by our self-limiting beliefs. This chapter looked at detail into the peak–end rule – how we remember things based on how they end, rather than on an average of their minute-by-minute play, the purpose of this being to give our brains the opportunity to stop devoting more brain capacity to something than it needs to. This makes it easier for it to process the 60–80,000 thoughts we have a day. The chapter also discussed the frequency or recency illusion, which is your conscious awareness noticing things more often after you first become aware of them – think of an actor you saw in a TV show on Monday, then Wednesday, then again on Thursday. The question we must ask ourselves after finishing this chapter is: can the bad things that happen to us actually turn out to be positive?

CHAPTER SEVENTEEN

TIME TO TAKE A 'CIRCUIT BREAKER'

If you want to forget all your other troubles,
wear too tight shoes!
– ANON.

Most mornings, one of the first things I do is grab a fluffy towel, head downstairs and tiptoe barefoot outside to my garage. Like most garages in the UK, it's not used for the purpose it was designed for, namely, to house a car (according to the RAC only 24% or garages in the UK are actually used for that purpose!). Mine, like many others, is now home to a small gym/meditation studio. Here, I begin my day by undertaking a breathing technique devised by the 26-world record holder Wim Hof, more popularly known as the 'Ice Man'. This simple, yet incredibly powerful technique takes around 13 minutes, and consists of 3 sets of 30 deep breaths, through the nose, and then out through the mouth, culminating in a 1 minute and 30 seconds breath hold at the end of each set. The deep breathing can often make your body feel tingly, as well as quite lightheaded momentarily; fortunately, it's quite a pleasant feeling.

Following the breathwork, I either do a short workout or some yoga. Next, a 10-minute meditation session (more about meditation later in this book). Finally, my favourite activity of the day. In my garage/gym I have a black chest freezer that is three-quarters full of water. Not just any water though. This water is kept just above freezing. Often there is ice floating on its surface. I set my timer for 5 minutes, check again the freezer is not plugged into the mains and I begin to lower myself in. Some days I do it gradually, putting my legs in first, others I think to myself,

'Just get in it, ya wuss', and immerse myself immediately up to my chest. This is usually followed briefly by some choice words, which I hope my lovely neighbours can't hear!

For 3 minutes, my body is immersed, with me finally putting my arms in for the last 2 minutes. I have a projector and screen on the wall, and I will project something interesting and inspirational to watch, the idea being that it takes my mind off the discomfort I will be experiencing for the next 5 minutes.

When I emerge, I dry myself off and proceed to my house to make the best-tasting coffee of the day. It's a warm cup of heaven. If time permits, I will get some comfortable clothes on and begin to warm myself up naturally. If not, I will take a lovely, hot shower and get ready for my day. For the next few hours, I will experience a sense of euphoria brought on by the endorphin release of the cold immersion. It is this exact neurochemical release that makes the brief discomfort more than worth it.

After a few weeks, the cold sessions are actually quite addictive – to the extent that if I don't have any cold immersion on a particularly busy day, I feel like I have missed out on something great for that day. No matter what your day holds you know it is unlikely that it will make you feel as uncomfortable as the ice-cold water does. You have a strange sense of achievement. You are ready to take on whatever the day brings.

I think of the ice bath as a form of meditation. While I am immersed in the freezing cold water, I do not think about anything else, other than that I can't wait to get out of it! Not surprisingly, I can also experience a form of time distortion. Some days those 5 minutes seem like less than 5 minutes, whilst on other days the same time feels like 10, or even 20, minutes! It is as if the second hand on my timer has ceased marking the movement of time. Seldom can I accurately guess the passing of time. Frequently, I will glance at the timer I have placed next to the freezer and think how inaccurate our estimation of time is as human beings.

There is now some very strong evidence to suggest that cold immersion is not only great for your immune system, but also for your general well-being. In addition, cold exposure is also incredible at reducing inflammation. Despite these fantastic benefits, that is not the primary reason I have recommended it to just about every client I have worked with in the past few years. Of course, I don't expect clients to rush out and purchase a chest freezer for this purpose. Cold showers more than suffice. It's fine to have a hot shower and then turn it too cold for the last minute or so. The reason I write about it is to introduce what I call the 'Circuit Breaker technique'. In essence the Circuit Breaker technique is about building into your day several opportunities to shift your thought patterns. In NLP (neuro-linguistic programming) parlance, it is like a pattern interrupt. Think of it as like playing one note, over and over again on a piano. Even if you take your finger off the key the note will remain playing for quite a while, particularly in a room with a lot of reverberations. You then take your fingers away from the keyboard for a short period. When you return you choose a different note to play, until you take you hand off the keyboard again. That is the essence of the Circuit Breaker: your hand is off the keyboard for a short period.

Think of a repeating soundwave pattern. It repeats until it either stops or is interrupted. In music, a repeating wave or tone will only change if you play and hold another note, with that new note then being the repeated soundwave. Our thoughts can be very much like this. They can often remain until they are replaced by a new thought.

Think of a time when you have had a disagreement with someone. Afterwards you may have replayed the disagreement over and over in your head – thinking no doubt about the witty reply you wish you had delivered to your antagonist. You may have sat at home thinking of this quarrel, perhaps watching TV, but paying little attention to what was occurring on the screen. If you had then received a phone call informing you that a parent or loved one has been taken ill, instantly you would have been thrown into a new state of anxiety, desperately concerned for your loved one's welfare. At that point, would you have given any consideration to the disagreement you had earlier in the day? I would wager a bet that you wouldn't. It would have been superseded by a new, more pressing concern. Similarly, if you had received a call to let you know you had won a particular award, then, once again, you would have given little or no consideration to the your earlier dispute. Basically, you have interrupted the pattern of what you were thinking about prior to the phone call. Having a mental reprieve, even for a brief time, can make a massive difference to our levels of anxiety, as well as feelings of low mood or depression. That is what cold therapy, as well as a host of other methods we will examine shortly, will achieve for you.

In 2016, BBC One aired the programme *The Doctor Who Gave Up Drugs*. Dr Chris van Tulleken worked with Sarah, a 24-year-old who had been taking antidepressants since the age of 17. Sarah was introduced to cold-water swimming, and after a few weeks of undertaking it regularly, reported that the depression she had been experiencing since her teens had dramatically improved.

In addition to this, a study by Charles University, Prague in 2000 showed that the immersion of the body in cold water can increase the levels of dopamine (the neurotransmitter that is strongly associated with pleasure and reward) by 530%. In another 2008 study, molecular biologist Nikolai Shevchuk discovered that it also increased the number of feel-good chemicals beta-endorphin and norepinephrine in our brains.

I am not suggesting that you have to take up cold-water swimming or even have cold showers, unless of course you want to. If you do, always do so under the supervision of your healthcare professional. What I am proposing is much easier and can be done almost anywhere: it is what I call the 'Circuit Breaker technique'. Actively partaking in this technique at least twice a day will break the potential ruminating over negative and unhelpful thoughts. Often it can be these thoughts that add to our limiting beliefs, making us feel powerless and somewhat out of control in our lives.

Here are just some of the things you can do for a 5-minute Circuit Breaker.

- Do some deep breathing (ideally in through the nose and out through the mouth).
- Walk in nature, or tend to a plant.
- Meditate.
- Brush your teeth with your non-dominant hand.
- Cold immersion – take a cold shower first thing in the morning.
- Take time to reflect on all of the things you are grateful for in your life.
- Carry out a random act of kindness.
- Call or message a friend or family member.
- Eat something mindfully, such as a piece of fruit.
- Write in a journal.
- Go for a swim, in the sea or a lake if possible.
- Listen to a piece of music you love, preferably with headphones on.
- Use a Hypnosis or Meditation app for a midday nap.
- Exercise (use an app like the 7-minute workout).
- Play with your kids mindfully, and really listen to them.
- Listen to 10 minutes or so of an audiobook.
- Write a children's story.
- Leave a message for your family on a service such as 'Keylu. Visit them at https://keylu.com/
- Read or watch something inspirational and motivational.
- Reflect on the beliefs you may hold, in particular your auto-limiting thoughts.
- Do some box breathing.
- Do some drawing or colouring.
- Close your eyes and really listen to as many things as you can identify.
- Look around you and name three things you can hear, then two things you can see, and finally one sensation that you feel.

Often, when I leave my garage shivering from my cold immersion and head back to my house, I am reminded of one of the beliefs my lovely mum imparted to me as a child. In fact, this belief it seems has been taught to just about every adult I have spoken to whilst writing and researching this book: 'Don't go outside with wet hair or you will catch a cold!'

I always smile and think of my mum as I walk along the path to my house. What would she say to me if she saw how red my body was from the cold? I am pretty confident she would think, 'You need locking up, you do!' More significantly, she would believe that I would now, without any shadow of a doubt, get pneumonia or a bad cold at the very least! Goodness knows what she would think if she ever saw me do it in the evening! She'd probably call an ambulance, or worse, the mental asylum, as she used to call it!

For me, the revelation that you can't actually get pneumonia from being out in the cold was like finding out that weeing in a swimming pool doesn't actually make it turn blue, or even red, as American parents told their offspring! Disgustingly, on the 'blue swimming pool' note, a study at the University of Alberta concluded that an Olympic-sized swimming pool was likely to contain about 225 litres of urine. I guess the saying 'Come on in, the water's fine' doesn't always apply! Perhaps some beliefs are still worth propagating in our offspring.

SUMMARY

Chapter 17 looked at introducing Circuit Breakers into your day-to-day life. It took inspiration from Wim Hof, the Ice Man. His Circuit Breaker of choice is immersion in freezing cold water. This has the proven effects of releasing endorphins, improving your well-being and immune system, and also reducing feelings of depression. Although bathing in ice-cold water is an extreme example of a Circuit Breaker, there are many different examples that the chapter investigates – all designed with the purpose of breaking your rumination pattern and giving your brain a much-needed rest. In the words of author Russell Eric Dobda, 'Taking a break can lead to breakthroughs'.

STAGE THREE

INSIGHT

CHAPTER EIGHTEEN

LOOKING FOR WHAT WE WANT TO BELIEVE

There are three classes of people: those who see, those who see when they are shown, those who do not see.
– LEONARDO DA VINCI

In April 1965, the BBC broadcast an interview with a professor who had developed an amazing new ground-breaking technology. This new invention was called 'Smell-o-vision' and it allowed the transmission of smells over the airwaves. Viewers from around the world would now be able to smell aromas produced in the television studio in the comfort of their own homes. The professor went on to describe how a special machine broke scents down into their component molecules, which were then transmitted through the screen. In addition, he went on to demonstrate this new innovative technology by placing some coffee beans and onions into the Smell-o-vision machine. He then asked viewers to report whether they had smelt anything. Numerous viewers called in from across the country reporting that they had distinctly experienced these scents. Some even claimed that the onions made their eyes water!

Of course, there was no 'Smell-o-vision' at this time (the Japanese have actually invented something similar since!): it was an elaborate April Fools' Day joke by the BBC. But with today's easy access to smartphones, how many of us would have experienced the smells, and relayed that experience to the creators of the programme?

This chapter is about believing what we want to believe and looking for the evidence that supports those beliefs. There is a vast library of reports attesting to the fact that we often experience what we believe we will experience from a medical treatment. For example, in one particular study, professor of physiology and neuroscience at the University of Turin, Fabrizio Benedetti, examined the impact of expectation in patients with severe Parkinson's disease. Six patients with the debilitating disease were implanted with stimulating electrodes. When the electrodes were turned on, Benedetti discovered that these patients underwent a dramatic improvement in their ability to move. When the electrodes were turned off, they once again froze up. But, after several weeks of stimulator treatment, simply the thought that the stimulator had been turned on or off had almost as much impact on movement as the stimulation itself. Perhaps unsurprisingly, when the patients were told that the stimulator had been turned off, their motor velocity decreased even though the stimulator had remained on. This is a textbook example of what is understood as the 'nocebo effect'. Unlike the placebo effect, where patients believe a treatment will have a positive effect on their health, the nocebo is an effect where a patient is given or told something that should make no difference whatsoever to their health but it ends up causing a negative side effect – usually because of what they believe about the thing they are taking or that is being done to them.

The placebo effect doesn't just apply to drugs and medical procedures. It appears that the key to placebo is the notion of expectation. Induce a placebo response, and an individual will experience what they believe they will experience. For example, people who believe (incorrectly) that alcohol increases sexual arousal report an increase in sexual arousal when they consume either real or placebo alcohol. Likewise, the extent to which people believe that alcohol will induce intoxication or result in problems with coordination determines the degree to which they, in fact, experience these effects. In essence, if you believe you will get drunk from a substance, then chances are you will experience the effects associated with that particular beverage.

In another study, participants who were told that they had consumed caffeinated coffee reported greater alertness than those who were inaccurately told that the coffee was decaffeinated. Amazingly, the group who believed that they had drunk the caffeinated coffee also showed an increase in diastolic blood pressure and an improvement in reaction time, which was not seen in the control group.

Similarly, when patients with asthma inhaled an innocuous substance that they were told was an allergen, their airways constricted; when they inhaled an innocuous substance that they were told was a bronchodilator, they then began to breathe more easily again.

In one of the few studies that have observed the specific influence of expectation on the results of a clinical trial, a large number of depressed patients were treated with either a placebo, St John's Wort or the antidepressant sertraline. What the team discovered was that patients improved to the same extent with all three of the treatments. But what was surprising was that when the patients were asked to guess which treatment they had been assigned, those who thought they had been assigned a placebo showed little clinical improvement irrespective of what they had actually received. Amazingly, those who guessed that they had been given St John's Wort showed uniformly large improvement irrespective of what they actually received, including the placebo.

In addition, those who believed that they had received sertraline showed large improvements whether they actually received it or had just taken a placebo. The researchers concluded that, 'Patient beliefs regarding treatment may have a stronger association with clinical outcome than the actual medication received'. Consistent with these findings, depressed patients who expected an experimental antidepressant to be highly effective were far more likely to respond positively to the treatment. Some 90% claimed it was effective, as opposed to those who anticipated that the same antidepressant would only be somewhat effective: a much smaller 33% claimed its efficacy.

In another study published in *The Lancet Psychiatry*, patients with either mild to severe depressive symptoms, or anxiety, or a mix of both, were selected from some 179 GP surgeries in the UK and enrolled on the trial. In each instance, the GPs involved were not informed as to whether they were administering sertraline or a placebo.

After 6 weeks, the patients taking sertraline reported a 21% improvement in their anxiety symptoms, compared to the control group taking the placebo dummy pill. After 12 weeks, the gap had grown to 23%.

After 6 weeks, there was little evidence of the drug reducing depressive symptoms, such as poor concentration, low mood and lack of enjoyment, and only a marginal improvement of 13% after 12 weeks.

Nonetheless, the group taking antidepressants were twice as likely as the other trial participants to say their mental health felt better overall. The leader of the study, author Dr Gemma Lewis from UCL, reported that, 'It appears that people taking the drug are feeling less anxious, so they feel better overall, even if their depressive symptoms were less affected'.

We can perhaps conclude that the less anxious we are, the less likely we are to experience the symptoms of depression. Whilst anxiety and depression are very much bedfellows, often co-occurring, there are distinct differences. First, anxiety is generally considered a high-energy state, whilst depression is a low-energy state. In many ways, sufferers are trapped in a continuous cycle. When you get anxious, you tend to have more pervasive negative thoughts about a worry or problem, and you can feel helpless. Often when you feel like you've failed, you can move to depression.

The chance of experiencing depression is much higher when an anxiety disorder already exists: nearly half of those with major depression also suffer from severe and persistent anxiety. People who are depressed often feel anxious and worried. One can easily trigger the other, with anxiety often preceding depression. Similarly, individuals with post-traumatic stress disorder (PTSD) are especially prone to developing depression. There is also a widely held belief that there is a biological predisposition for both of these conditions. This seems to be true with anxiety disorders even more so than with depression.

Did the patients in the sertraline study improve because it lowered their anxiety, and therefore improved their depression? Clearly, our beliefs about the medicines we are taking can have a profound effect on their efficacy.

BAD MEDICINE

In a fascinating story from Australia, drug giant Reckitt Benckiser received a court order to stop the selling some of its popular Nurofen painkiller brands after it was discovered that some of the tablets marketed for specific complaints such as back pain and migraines contained exactly the same active ingredient.

The Australian federal court ruled that the British-based multinational had made misleading claims to its customers when selling its Nurofen Period Pain, Nurofen Back Pain, Nurofen Migraine Pain and Nurofen Tension Headache products.

The court found that these products were individually marketed as formulated to treat a specific type of pain and cost about double the price of standard Nurofen. However, tablets from the so-called Nurofen Specific Pain range were all found to contain the same active ingredient, some 342 mg of ibuprofen lysine, which is equivalent to 200 mg of ibuprofen.

The court ordered that the products should be removed from shops within 3 months of the hearing. As consumers, we are all shocked when we discover what the makers of these products have done, and how they have deceived us. But with what we now know about the effects of placebo, one must consider if, at some level, believing a particular product is targeted for your particular issue will make the benefit of that product that much greater. I would say that it is more effective combined with the inflated cost of the product. When we have a migraine or a headache, is our suffering worthy of a 69p tablet or a £4.99 one in a nice, shiny box? Strange as it may seem, despite containing the same ingredients, the £4.99 tablet will most likely be more effective in easing our discomfort.

Next, we are going to examine two cognitive biases. The first of these is what is known as confirmation bias. Confirmation bias is an implicit tendency to notice information that happens to coincide with our pre-existing beliefs and ignore information that doesn't. The second is motivated reasoning, which is a tendency to willingly accept the information that agrees with our worldview and critically analyse that which doesn't.

These biases can tend to degrade our judgements when our initial beliefs are wrong because we might fail to discover what is really happening until it is too late. Let's look at some stories that highlight these biases.

TWO TRIBES

Do you believe that in questioning your beliefs you can change your world? What about the world around you? What about saving the world? To one Russian engineer, challenging his beliefs one summer's night saved the world, and I mean that quite literally. The gentleman's name was Stanislav Petrov, a well-respected lieutenant colonel in the Soviet Air Defence Forces. Shortly before midnight on 25 September 1983, Petrov was seated at his station when the word 'launch' flashed up in front of him on a gigantic 30-m display, combined with an ear-piercing siren. Petrov knew only too well what this alarm meant: the thing he and the rest of the USSR had feared the most had finally materialised. Immediately, he knew that this night would push his decision-making skills to their max. One wrong judgement and it could mean the end of the world.

Satellites had detected the launch of an American nuclear weapon aimed at the USSR, and an impending nuclear strike was imminent. The 'Oko' missile defence early warning satellite system could detect the launch of an enemy warhead around 10 minutes earlier than traditional radar surveillance, giving the Russians a much sought-after heads-up on a potential nuclear missile strike. The USSR could then respond with a devastating counterattack. Deep in the Serpukhov-15 control centre, the eyes of 200 employees fixated on Colonel Petrov. Despite the panic, Petrov remained calm. He rose from his desk so every one of his subordinates could see him and shouted, 'Sit down! Keep working!'

At that moment, the fate of not just the USSR, but indeed mankind, lay in the balance. If Petrov launched an attack, it would very likely result in an estimated 750 million deaths and around 340 million wounded worldwide. It is unlikely that, in the history of the world, the outcome of a single decision has ever had so much resting on it.

At that moment, Petrov thought neither of the millions of possible victims of a nuclear conflict, nor of his family, but he thought of teaspoons. Nobody spoons water into a bucket with a teaspoon, he thought to himself. The USA would never fire individual missiles at the USSR. His training told him that a nuclear attack would come with the destructive power of hundreds of missiles at once, not just one solitary missile. Petrov was puzzled. On one hand, he had a set of beliefs gleaned from his training, and on the other was common sense. He had just a few minutes to make his unbiased decision and risked being killed in the impending attack and most likely losing the opportunity to instigate a retaliatory counterstrike. It's impossible to imagine how he must have felt for those few minutes.

Colonel Petrov's family had no idea where he worked, and that he had the responsibility to either start, or prevent, the Third World War. On that day the lives of millions hung in the balance.

Earlier that morning Petrov had said goodbye to his wife Raisa, his son Dmitri and daughter Yelena as he went about his routine shift, little knowing that the decision to commence the apocalypse, and most likely the end of mankind, lay in his hands a few hours later. The Cold War logic of the USSR at that time was that the enemy should die sooner.

Although he was an officer, Petrov was himself a civilian, a trained engineer. 'The world can be happy that I was in command that night – and not a dull military,' Petrov commented later. Perhaps a military man would have reacted differently, very likely in accordance with the strict regulations. Had Soviet leader Yuri Andropov, who at the time had been ruling the USSR from his sickbed, been less incapacitated he would most probably have pressed the 'red button'. And, in doing so, would have without doubt provoked an actual nuclear strike by the Americans, a war that no one could ever have possibly won.

At the time, it seemed not only possible, but highly probable, that a nuclear attack would take place. Russian spies had recently learnt of a planned major NATO manoeuvre – 'Able Archer 83' was earmarked to start at the end of November, and simulate a nuclear war. The tense leaders in Moscow saw this as evidence of an imminent Western attack. In addition, the shooting down of passenger airline Korean Airlines Flight 007, which had accidentally flown into Russian airspace in early September, showed how nervous were the fingers on the trigger. Cold War tensions were running at an all-time high. Moscow did not hesitate and gave the combat pilots the order to attack. Some 269 people died, placing the world on high alert for a potential, almost inevitable, conflict.

Petrov, on the other hand, trusted his feelings and his intuition, and we can be thankful that he did. He assessed the situation with clarity and, at that moment, did not allow his thinking to be clouded by the beliefs that no doubt his superiors had imposed on him. He did not allow his appraisal of the situation to be swayed by any bias that he may have had against the Americans or NATO, or by the tense situation in the world at that period in history. Thank goodness he didn't, and as a result we are all alive and able to read of his heroism and good decision making on that September night. Later we will consider the factors that perhaps played a part in shaping Petrov's decision that night and allowed him to make the judicious decision he did.

LOST IN FRANCE

The year is 1894, and a torn-up piece of paper is found in a wastepaper basket in France. But this wasn't just any piece of paper. On it were military secrets that had been sent to Germany. This outwardly innocuous piece of paper launched one of the largest political scandals of the 19th century. Suspicions quickly converged on an artillery officer: a captain named Alfred Dreyfus. Dreyfus was interrogated. Officials believed his handwriting to be a perfect match for the handwriting on the torn memo. They searched his apartment and went through his files as well as questioning his teachers. At the end of this search, they found nothing, and, ironically, this lack of anything tangible convinced the officials even more that they had found their man. After all, only a spy would hide everything in his apartment; only a spy would have studied foreign languages at school. Combine this with the fact that his teachers had informed officials that Dreyfus had a very good memory, and their beliefs were even further cemented. Only a spy would hide all of the evidence and only a spy would have need for such a good memory – Dreyfus was definitely their man.

Alfred Dreyfus

The case went to trial and Dreyfus was found guilty. In a ritualistic ceremony, they tore the insignia from his uniform and broke his sword in half. For his high treason, he was sentenced to life imprisonment in a penal colony off the coast of French Guiana in South America, infamously known as Devil's Island (made famous by the 1973 film and book of the same name). Here, Dreyfus spent 1517 days and he regularly wrote to his wife and successive presidents asking for justice.

Eventually, evidence was disclosed that implicated French major Ferdinand Esterhazy as the guilty party. The army attempted to suppress this information, but a national uproar ensued, and the military had no choice but to put Esterhazy on trial. A court martial was held in January 1898 and Esterhazy was acquitted within an hour. Doubts about his innocence began to grow, but it wasn't until a lieutenant colonel by the name of George Picquart looked into the allegation that evidence was found that Esterhazy was in fact engaged in espionage and it was actually his handwriting that had been found on the letter. Combined with the fact that the spying had continued even after Dreyfus was imprisoned, Picquart knew that Dreyfus had been wrongly convicted. It took 10 years for Colonel Picquart to prove Dreyfus's innocence and during that time he himself was imprisoned as it was believed he was being disloyal to the army. Dreyfus was eventually exonerated for the crime, but it wasn't until 1995 that Dreyfus was publicly declared innocent.

This whole terrible incident is a perfect example of 'motivated reasoning'. As the name suggests, the French authorities used emotionally based reasoning to produce justifications or make decisions that were most desired rather than those that accurately reflected the evidence.

Our judgement is strongly influenced unconsciously by which side we want to win, and by our fears and our desires. It is pervasive in shaping how we think about our health and our relationships as well as deciding how to vote. For me, the remarkable thing about the decisions we make is how unconscious they are. Regardless of how objective and fair-minded we believe we are being, we still end up making decisions based on our own belief systems.

Think of a referee in a sport and how motivated you are when he finds a foul made by a member of the opposing team, but how silent you fall when a member of your own team is called for making a foul. Or if something you support is found to be not effective, such as the use of imprisonment for criminals, then you will look for evidence to support the idea that the research is somehow flawed – again, because you need to believe in something, and moving too far out of the comfort zone of your beliefs can feel uncomfortable and even something to be feared.

Finally, perhaps if there is hero of this story, then it must surely be Colonel Picquart, who, despite being anti-Semitic himself, sought to find the truth regardless of his own biased beliefs.

TURNING JAPANESE

Hiroo Onoda

Another fascinating example of an individual demonstrating a cognitive bias is that of a World War II soldier in the Imperial Japanese Army, Hiroo Onoda. Japan surrendered on 15 August 1945, but incredibly Lieutenant Onoda did not surrender on this date. In fact, he didn't surrender for another 30 years! Onoda's commitment to his orders allowed him to miss world events such as the Moon landing, the Korean War, the entire career of The

Beatles, the Cuban Missile Crisis, the assassinations of John F. Kennedy and Martin Luther King, the 1964 Tokyo Olympics, the building of the Berlin Wall and most of the Vietnam War. If he had held on just a little longer, he might have managed to miss Justin Bieber as well!

Loyal to a military code that taught that death was preferable to surrender, Hiroo Onoda remained at his jungle post on the island of Lubang, some 93 miles southwest of Manila in the Philippines, for 29 years – refusing to believe that World War II was over. Onoda believed that the emperor was a deity and that the war was a sacred mission. Building bamboo huts and surviving on a diet mostly consisting of bananas and coconuts, Onoda and three other soldiers pilfered rice and other food from a village and killed cows for meat. He was tormented by the tropical heat, rats and mosquitoes, and he patched up his uniform and kept his rifle in good working order.

After Japan surrendered, thousands of Japanese soldiers were scattered across China, Southeast Asia and the western Pacific. Many stragglers were captured or went home, while, despite leaflet drops and radio announcements, many hundreds went into hiding. Many more died of starvation or sickness or committed suicide rather than surrender to the enemy.

Onoda continued his operation as a Japanese intelligence officer, with his three fellow soldiers. During his stay, Onoda and his companions carried out guerrilla activities and engaged in several shootouts with the local police.

The first time he saw a leaflet announcing that Japan had surrendered was in October 1945; another cell had killed a cow and found a leaflet left behind by islanders that read: 'The war ended on 15th August. Come down from the mountains!' However, they didn't believe the leaflet, but instead believed that it was Allied propaganda. Understandably, they also believed that they would not have been fired on if the war had indeed been over. Towards the end of 1945, leaflets were dropped by air with a surrender order printed on them from General Tomoyuki Yamashita of the Fourteenth Area Army. After being in hiding for over 6 months, this leaflet was the only evidence they had that the war was over. Onoda's group studied the leaflet closely to determine whether it was genuine, and decided it was not.

In September 1949, one of the four soldiers left the others and, after 6 months on his own, surrendered to Philippine forces in 1950. This seemed like a security problem to the others, and they understandably became even more cautious. In 1952, letters and family pictures were dropped from an aircraft pressing them to surrender, but the three remaining soldiers decided that they were not genuine. On 7 May 1954, another one of the soldiers was killed by a shot from a search party looking for the men. On 19 October 1972 the final man remaining was sadly killed by two shots fired by local police, while he and Onoda, as part of their guerrilla activities, were burning rice that had been collected by farmers. Onoda was now on his own.

On 20 February 1974, Onoda met a Japanese man, Norio Suzuki. Suzuki found Onoda after 4 days of searching. He and Suzuki became friends, but Onoda still refused to surrender, saying that he was waiting for orders from a superior officer. Suzuki returned to Japan with photographs of himself and Onoda as proof of their encounter, and the Japanese government located Onoda's commanding officer, Major Yoshimi Taniguchi. Taniguchi was flown to Lubang Island, and on 9 March 1974 he finally met with Onoda and fulfilled a promise he had made back in 1944: 'Whatever happens, we'll come back for you'. The ragged soldier saluted and wept. Taniguchi then ordered Onoda to stand down.

Onoda was thus properly relieved of duty, and he surrendered. He turned over his sword, a functioning Arisaka Type 99 rifle, 500 rounds of ammunition and several hand grenades, as well as the dagger his mother had given him in 1944 to kill himself with if he was captured. Only Private Teruo Nakamura, arrested on 18 December 1974 in Indonesia, held out longer.

Mr Onoda surrendered to the Philippine president in March 1974. He saluted the Japanese flag and handed over his Samurai sword while still wearing a tattered army uniform. The president pardoned him for crimes committed while he thought he was at war.

Despite being greeted as a hero at his homecoming, he felt that the Japan he had now returned to was too far removed from the Japan he had left behind all those years ago.

In 1975, he moved to a Japanese colony in São Paulo, Brazil, where he raised cattle. The following year, he married Machie Onuku, a Japanese tea-ceremony teacher. In 1984, the couple returned to Japan where they founded the Onoda Nature School – a survival-skills youth camp. In 1996, Onoda revisited Lubang, the site of his long holdout and gave $10,000 to a school there. In recent years, he lived in Japan and Brazil, where he was made an honorary citizen in 2010.

Onoda's story is one of incredible loyalty and determination, and, despite all evidence to the contrary, he believed that any attempt to get him to surrender was a plot concocted by the pro-US government in Tokyo. By the time he surrendered he had been on the island since 1944, 2 years after he had been drafted into the Japanese Imperial Army. Like many of us who demonstrate a cognitive bias in our beliefs, he believed all evidence to the contrary was designed to be against him, to fool him and catch him out. His beliefs were so strong that it wasn't until his superior flew to Lubang and relieved him of his duty that he felt he could stand down. In other words, only when he witnessed overwhelming evidence to the contrary did he change his beliefs.

How many of us do that daily with the beliefs we hold about things in our lives?

SUMMARY

All of our brains work with cognitive biases that sway our decisions or beliefs, regardless of how unbiased or objective we believe we are being. This can be shown through the 'nocebo' effect, which is similar to the placebo effect but makes us feel that something is having a negative effect on us even if it makes no difference to our health at all. You may be able to recognise it in yourself in instances when you believe something will happen and then it does. Have you ever paid more for a painkiller designed specifically to tackle a headache, and found that it has done just that? In truth, the ingredients are the same as a generic painkiller, but because of the belief that it is specifically targeting your headache, it seems to do just that. The chapter also looked into motivated reasoning, which explains how we make decisions off the back of our own belief systems, and confirmation bias, which is how we can ignore evidence that is contrary to our beliefs.

CHAPTER NINETEEN
A WORD TO THE WISE

Thinking is difficult. Therefore,
let the herd pronounce judgement.
– CARL JUNG

The Judgement of Solomon

How many of us, when others have needed our help, have offered a sympathetic ear and a steady shoulder to lean on? The wisdom that we impart at these times would impress a guru, or perhaps, even Yoda. We are the voice of reason when it comes to giving good, solid advice to others. We are all experts when it comes to solving other people's problems. Indeed, when a friend is starting a business, we suddenly become marketing gurus, offering advice on all aspects of the business as if we had just completed an MBA in marketing. Bizarrely though, when it comes to our own issues, we seem to falter somehow. With regard to problems in our own life, we are suddenly met with confusion. It appears that people often reason more wisely about other people's dilemmas and problems than about their own. This is what has come to be known as Solomon's Paradox, based on the tale of wise King

Solomon, and first coined by psychological scientist Igor Grossmann from Ontario's University of Waterloo.

Throughout history King Solomon (970–931 BCE), who was the third leader of the Jewish Kingdom, has been regarded as a paragon of wisdom and wise judgement. It is said that during his long reign people would travel great distances to seek his sage counsel. Despite this incredible insight that allowed him to assist others, his personal life was a cataclysm of bad decisions and uncontrolled passions. He kept hundreds of pagan wives and concubines, and loved money, often boasting of his great riches. Sadly, he neglected to instruct his only son, who grew up to be an inept tyrant. Indeed, it was alleged that it was these oversights and misjudgements that contributed to the eventual demise of his once splendid kingdom. It seems incredible that someone could have the insight to be able to assist so many but lack the same insight to help themselves.

To test Solomon's Paradox, Grossmann first wanted to establish if it is indeed a common pattern in all of us. He recruited volunteers and had them imagine that they had been cheated on, and another group to imagine that their best friend's partner had cheated on their friend. Grossmann then asked all the volunteers to reason about how their relationship, or their friend's, would unfold in the future. Afterwards, the volunteers took an assessment used to measure aspects of 'wise reasoning', such as recognising the limits of what they know, empathy and seeking compromise. The assessment included questions such as: Do you need more information and context to really understand this situation? Is it important to you to look for a compromise? How much do you consider other people's perspectives on the event? How many different futures can you imagine? And so forth.

In support of Solomon's Paradox, as Grossmann predicted, subjects demonstrated greater wisdom when reasoning about their friend's situation than when reasoning about their own. This assumption was based on the belief that they would have more psychological distance from the cheating and betrayal. In other words, it's not so much that some people possess wisdom and others lack it, but that our ability to reason wisely depends on a variety of external factors.

Grossmann then conducted a second study and posed the same cheating dilemma to a new set of participants. This time, Grossmann had the participants either take a first-person or third-person perspective when reflecting on their own, or their friend's, dilemma. What he found was that the participants reflecting from a third-person perspective scored higher on the wise reasoning assessment than those that took a first-person perspective – therefore demonstrating that those who distanced themselves from the problem were able to reason much better than those who didn't.

The main take away from Grossmann's study is that, in order to solve our own problems effectively, we need to psychologically distance ourselves from them as, when we are trying to make an effective judgement on how to solve them from a first-person perspective, we seem to lack sufficient cognitive reasoning to do so effectively.

Perhaps we need to think of our problems as if they were being experienced by someone else. Maybe then we would be able to reason more effectively and sagaciously.

Fascinatingly, older subjects were just as vulnerable to Solomon's paradoxical reasoning and were just as likely to become wiser if they practised self-distancing. The obvious implication of this is that wisdom does not necessarily accompany years of experience, but appears to remain malleable, even in older age.

Research has consistently shown that when we actively self-reflect, in other words, when we deliberately pay attention to our own thoughts, emotions, decisions and behaviours, we are more likely to experience lower levels of depression. Conversely, when we practise self-rumination – a form of negative, chronic and persistent self-focus that is motivated by perceived threats, losses or injustices – then we are far more likely to experience bouts of depression and anxiety. The problem here perhaps is that when we brood and ruminate about a particular problem it causes us to become somewhat myopic about its solution. To solve a complex issue we often need to look at it from various perspectives. Frustratingly, when we attempt this practice, we can sometimes get further and further away from understanding a particular difficulty, whereas someone on the outside could consider the dilemma and easily offer up some useful and insightful advice as to its potential resolution, much like King Solomon did for his loyal subjects. To the individual with the issue, it can feel like they are trying to wade through mental mud – the answer to their problem is so far outside their comprehension. Often, as a psychotherapist, I have listened to a client describe a particular issue, the resolution of which seems so perfectly clear to any lay person that it seems almost awkward to suggest it. Clearly, we don't all 'see' our 'own stuff' as easily as others close to us are able to. Often it can take another to help us see the wood for the proverbial trees. The Alfred Technique is very much about taking this third-person perspective on our thoughts. It seems that when we take this stance we can challenge our thoughts more effectively, much like King Solomon. As Robert Trivers, author of the brilliant book Deceit and Self-Deception, writes, 'The great sage Thales once put the general matter succinctly "Oh master," he was asked, "what is the most difficult thing to do?" "To know thyself", he replied. "And the easiest?" "To give advice to others."'

BLINDED BY THE LIGHT

Somewhere between the 1950s and the 1970s, the following cautionary tale appeared: if you were to put a frog in boiling water it would jump out quickly – if it could! However, if you were to place a frog in cold water and let the water gradually boil, the frog would just sink into a stupor and eventually die. The notion behind this metaphor was that, as humans, sometimes we don't take action if the circumstances surrounding a particular issue change too gradually for us to notice.

As it turns out, behind the scenes, so to speak, there has been much debate as to whether or not the frog would actually exit the water. During the 19th century, several experiments were performed to observe the reaction of frogs to slowly heated water. In 1869, while doing experiments searching for the location of the soul, German physiologist Friedrich Goltz revealed that a frog that has had its brain removed will remain in slowly heated water, but an intact frog would attempt to escape the water when it reached around 25°C.

Other 19th-century experiments purported to show that frogs did not in fact attempt to escape the gradually heated water. One 1872 experiment by Heinzmann was said to show that a frog would not attempt to escape if the water was heated slowly enough. His work was later corroborated in 1875 by Fratscher. Whilst these experiments did indeed show that the frog remained in the water, in 1888 William Thompson Sedgwick claimed that the apparent contradiction between the results of these experiments was a consequence of the different heating rates used. Slow heating did not cause the instinctive reflex movements that would be produced in the normal frog. One thing is for sure, a lot of frogs were getting boiled in the 19th century for little reason.

Whilst there are some contradictions as to whether this would actually happen, the message it presents is quite clear. We as humans often don't act upon things that can be potentially harmful to us. Some would describe this as being akin to an ostrich, with our heads buried firmly in the sand. Which, ironically, also happens not to be true! It appears that ostriches don't bury their heads in the sand, as they simply wouldn't be able to breathe! What they do, however, is dig holes in the dirt as nests for their eggs. In fact, they do this several times a day to turn the eggs. I did say this book would ask you to question the beliefs you have held for so long! To examine this phenomenon, let's once again examine the act of smoking.

Imagine the following scenario. Picture that we live in a world where cigarettes are not harmful anymore, except for one packet in every 18,250 packets. This packet has some dynamite in it that, once lit, will explode and kill the smoker instantly, making a horrible mess for everyone present to witness. Obviously in this scenario, cigarettes would be instantly banned outright without question. After all, if 30 million packs of cigarettes are sold each day, then an average of 1600 people per day would be expected to die in a rather unpleasant way. What about if, instead of a pack of cigarettes, there was a gun with 18,250 empty chambers in it? But in one of the chambers there was a bullet. Much like Russian roulette, the lethal bullet could be in the first chamber, or it could be in the 18,250th chamber. Would you still risk firing it?

Surprisingly, the total expected loss of life from smoking using the dynamite-laden, but otherwise harmless, cigarettes over 40 years would not be as great as with ordinary filtered cigarettes. But what about the perception? Vernon Howard sums it up skilfully when he writes, 'We are enslaved by anything we do not consciously see. We are freed by conscious perception.'

Perhaps not surprisingly, ego can play a huge role in how we assess risk. We all have the tendency to believe we are somehow special – although, of course you are, as you have purchased this book! Our psychological self-protection can lead us to draw consistently wrong conclusions. As a rule, we tend to overestimate the possibility of bad things happening to others, but not to ourselves. However, we still go to incredible lengths to minimise perceived risks to ourselves. This may be to do with our self-esteem or not wanting to feel vulnerable or out of control within a situation. People have a tendency to believe they will live a longer life than the average person – a phenomenon that has come to be known as 'illusory superiority'.

As it turns out, however, thinking and believing we're above average, even though statistically only half of us can possibly be above average, is actually rather beneficial for us. People who experience depression usually show what has come to be known as 'depressive realism'. In other words, they actually see themselves more accurately than the rest of us do. Think of the drunk driver who believes he or she will never get caught. Similarly, despite the fact that more than 90% of crashes involve human error, almost three-quarters, some 73%, of American drivers consider themselves better-than-average drivers!

In an insightful study by Ross and Sicoly, husbands and wives were asked separately how much work they believed they contributed to a variety of household chores, such as cleaning or making breakfast for the kids. Specifically, the researchers asked each person to estimate what percentage they believed they were personally responsible for. They then took each of those figures and added them together. Of course, the logically combined sum of the two figures should not exceed 100%. Perhaps unsurprisingly, that wasn't the case. As University of Chicago psychologist Nicholas Epley writes in his 2015 book Mindwise: 'If I claim that I make breakfast 80 percent of the time and my wife claims that she makes breakfast 60 percent of the time, then our kids are apparently eating breakfast 140 percent of the time. Not possible.' Remarkably, this is indeed what the researchers found again and again – the sums consistently exceeded 100%.

What's especially interesting here is that this disparity didn't just happen when couples were quizzed about the helpful household activities, like chores. The researchers also asked couples to estimate how often they did annoying stuff around the house, such as picking fights or making messes. Here, too, the combined estimates consistently exceeded 100%.

It appears that these overexaggerated claims are not just about making us appear better. Instead, it's an example of how egocentric we all can be. Perhaps you can bring to mind times when you cleaned a room in your house more readily than you can remember the times your partner did, so you just assume you've done more housework than you actually have done. This distortion doesn't just happen at home, it can happen at work as well, as Epley and his colleagues observed when they turned an eye to their own field of psychology research. When they asked co-authors of academic papers to estimate what percentage they believed they had contributed to the final result, they came up with similarly farcical figures – totals that once again far exceeded 100%. It's not exactly that we believe our work is superior to that of others, but it appears that other individuals and their contributions to a piece of work don't even cross our minds when we make judgements such as these.

Similarly, we tend to overestimate how long we will live, how healthy we will be, how good our marriages will be and how few wrinkles we have compared to our peers. In one study, three out of four baby boomers (those born between 1946 and 1964) think they look younger than their peers and four out of five believe they have fewer wrinkles than other people of that age – an obvious statistical impossibility.

According to anthropologist Melvin Connor, author of Why the Reckless Survive, our poor judgement about potential risk may well be the legacy of evolution. Our hunter-gatherer ancestors' lives were at constant risk from accidents, diseases and predators. Basically, they died young. In evolutionary terms 'winning' meant not necessarily longevity, but simply living long enough to pass on your genes to the next generation. Taking risk was therefore a winning strategy – especially if it meant you had a chance to mate before dying. Besides, decisions had to be made rapidly. If searching for a meal of fresh ripe berries meant risking an attack from a sabre-tooth tiger, you took that risk. For a half-starved cave dweller this was a no-brainer.

I BELIEVE

Beliefs have different origins. They can, for example, be formed through direct experience, or by accepting information from a trusted or authoritative source. Beliefs vary in terms of the level of evidence and support they command. Some beliefs have high levels of evidence, while others appear to be accepted without requiring much evidential support. Beliefs can be said to be 'held' at different levels of awareness. Some beliefs may involve considerable conscious preoccupation and rumination, whereas others can be readily accepted when we are susceptible and running on unconscious autopilot. Other beliefs, however, may appear implicit, unconscious and only evident by inference from our behaviours.

Beliefs vary in their degree of personal reference. A belief can be limited to the specific individual holding the belief, e.g. 'I am unique'. Beliefs can be held with different levels of conviction or degrees of confidence. This can range from firmly held to relatively uncertainty. In some instances, this conviction may even fluctuate over time or across different contexts.

Beliefs vary in their resistance to change in response to counterevidence and social pressure. While related to conviction, people can also vary in how open they are to disconfirming evidence towards their belief, and to considering alternative points of view. Beliefs can vary in their impact on cognition and behaviour. This may likewise be influenced by degree of conviction. Where people may act on one belief, they may fail to act on another that they verbally endorse.

Beliefs can produce different emotional consequences. Whereas some beliefs may be relatively innocuous or even self-serving, other may cause considerable distress.

Beliefs vary in the degree to which they are shared by other people. Some are very common; others may be comparatively unusual, such as in the case of some delusions.

ANOTHER BRICK IN THE WALL

Many years ago, I was a schoolteacher in a rather 'challenging', as Ofsted would label it, inner city secondary school. I would ask the pupils to line up and enter the classroom one by one, where I would then greet the pupils individually and ask how they were doing. Most of the greetings to me would be in the form of 'Hi Sir' as they entered the classroom. But within every class would be a pupil or two who would inform me that they have something that prevented them from doing any work in my class on that particular day. Pupils would acknowledge me with, 'I can't do any work today because I am dyslexic, Sir', or 'I have ADHD, Sir, so I can't do no work today', or sometimes a pupil would proudly proclaim they couldn't do any work because they are 'fick' (thick) or words to that effect, almost as if it were a badge of honour.

My response to them was always the same, 'Not in here, you don't', and with few exceptions, I treated them accordingly. In other words, the limiting beliefs they had about themselves, or more importantly that had been placed upon them by the education system, did not exist in the four walls of my classroom. You might be thinking, 'Gosh what an inspirational, forward-thinking teacher', but to be honest, I adopted this tactic because it was easier on me as a teacher. If the pupils behaved and did the work I expected of them, my life was easier, and they did better! It was a win–win situation! The not-so-strange outcome of my non-altruistic method was that for an hour or so the pupils did not have those limiting beliefs, and I would remind them of that fact when they left my classroom. Little did I know then that many years later I would be working in the field of personal transformation as a hypnotherapist and trainer. One of the areas that frustrated me as a teacher was the way pupils' self-worth and self-esteem were built in the modern education system.

This belief system surrounding what pupils can achieve is beautifully documented in the work of Rosenthal and Jacobson (1968) in what is known as the 'Pygmalion effect'. The study was named after the Greek myth of Pygmalion – the king and sculptor who fell in love with a female statue he had himself carved, which he eventually ended up marrying after it came to life. If that had happened in the UK, it would definitely feature on daytime TV!

The two researchers started by administering intelligence tests on a number of elementary school students. Rosenthal and Jacobson then informed the teachers of the names of the 20% of pupils who had demonstrated 'unusual potential for intellectual growth' and who would bloom academically within the year. Unknown to the classroom teachers, the students who were chosen were not actually chosen for their potential intellectual abilities, but in fact were chosen completely at random. The amazing outcome to this experiment came when, 8 months later, these randomly chosen pupils were tested again and it was discovered that this cohort did indeed score significantly higher on the follow-up test. Rosenthal insisted that the Pygmalion effect also applies to higher education, the military and sports teams as well as the workplace.

Rosenthal defined it as 'the phenomenon whereby one person's expectation for another person's behaviour comes to serve as a self-fulfilling prophecy' (American Psychologist, November 2003). The work of Rosenthal, Jacobson and others has clearly displayed that teacher expectations can influence students' performance. Indeed, he went on to say, 'When we expect certain behaviour of others, we are more likely to act in ways that make the expected behaviour more likely to occur' (Rosenthal and Babad, 1985).

He boiled down the massive change that occurred when teachers reacted to those chosen students in the following four ways:

1. Warm and friendly behaviour towards these exceptional students (including non-verbal language, vocal tone, facial expressions, posture and gestures).
2. Devoting more time, effort and energy to the chosen students.
3. Choosing the highlighted students to answer questions more often in class.
4. Giving the special students more precise feedback and more helpful responses.

As the French philosopher and mathematician Blaise Pascal stated, 'Treat a human being as they are, and they will remain the same. Treat them as what they can become, and they will become what they can become.'

So, without realising it, I had initiated my own Pygmalion effect as a teacher. What this effect has shown me as an adult is that we should endeavour, whenever possible, to surround ourselves with people who will make us grow. Not necessarily people who feed our self-esteem, but friends who genuinely want to see us succeed – whether that success be in the form of happiness, achieving a personal goal or just reaching our full potential. Myself and my business partner have often referred to people we have met over the years as either 'drains' or 'radiators'. In other words, does that individual help you grow and achieve a state of happiness (radiator), or does that person take away from you (drain)? Some people you spend time with inspire, motivate and make you feel bliss and contentment, whilst others seem to almost drain you of your life force, questioning every decision you make with 'Why would you do that? That's not going to work in a million years!'

They say that if you add up the earnings of the people you count as your friends, chances are your earnings will be right slap bang in the middle of this group – the median of the assembly, if you will. Perhaps it's the same with positivity. Whilst I am not advocating removing people from your life – not always easy if they are family members! – try, when possible, to think of yourself as having a protective coat of influence when you meet with them. In other words, picture yourself as having a 'negativity' force field. Indeed, use that negative energy to remember why you never want to think and behave the way they do, remembering to always focus instead on gratitude and being as complaint-free as you possibly can. As Will Bowen, author of the brilliant book *A Complaint Free World*, wrote, 'Hurt People, Hurt People'. He goes on to write, 'Misery not only loves company; it derives validation from it'.

I perhaps didn't realise it at the time, but there was always something that troubled me as a teacher. It was not that positive learning wasn't taking place, it was that we seemed to be educating a generation of children whose sole purpose in life was to be the best and to be famous. Failure was frowned upon, and the children's self-esteem was built with a very unstable foundation. This way of living was also propagated by the media with shows such as *Pop Stars* and, much later on, *The X Factor*. Why would a child need to work hard at school when in a few years they would be 'discovered' and signed up for a life of stardom and financial abundance? I often found myself playing motivational audio from speakers such as Anthony Robbins, Zig Ziglar and Jim Ron, as well as the legendary Les Brown. I feared for the future mental health of these pupils, as I knew the statistical likelihood of them getting 'discovered' as the next big musical or acting talent was, sadly, pretty remote. In education at that time, the focus was often on building a fragile sense of self-worth in the children in our care. With around 7% of children attempted suicide by the time they reach their 17th birthday, and a shocking one in four saying that they have self-harmed in the past year, the fears I had previously had for the children I taught, and the children after them, seemed to be sadly well-founded. In my own experience, at no point in a child's education were they taught how to manage their thinking. Similarly, at no stage was a child given the tools to understand the workings of their mind, particularly the formidable subconscious mind.

Dr Bernadka Dubicka, chair of the Royal College of Psychiatrists' child and adolescent mental health faculty, has described these findings as part of a 'really concerning trend' that they had been witnessing for a long time. She went on to add that the data have shown there to have been an increase almost every year in the number of teenagers injuring themselves intentionally, and that 'There is definitely a need to provide more, better, and earlier support for young people to prevent their mental health difficulties from getting so severe, but equally we really need to think about why young people today are struggling so much'.

Let's hope the past does not represent the future when it comes to teaching our children about the workings of the mind, and how they can use it effectively to overcome any adversity. Let's hope that developing a mindset and working on building resilience become just as important as maths and English are in school curriculums of the future.

SUMMARY

This chapter began by looking at the old and wise King Solomon. Although able to give brilliant advice to others, King Solomon was renowned for being awful at following it himself. In this same way, we often cannot solve our own problems with the advice that we can easily give to others. It sometimes takes someone else, an outsider, to come along and point out something that would be very obvious to spot if it were happening to someone else. So it may be best to take this stance on our own problems: to step back from our problems and look at them from someone else's perspective. We can be, like a frog in hot water, unable to notice changes in our surrounding circumstances if they happen too slowly.

The chapter also explored the idea of illusory superiority – where we tend to think we are better than the average person at a given task – and the Pygmalion effect – how other people's expectations of our behaviour will inevitably lead to a self-fulfilling prophecy.

CHAPTER TWENTY

DEVELOPING A GROWTH MINDSET – GROWTH NEGLIGENCE

The whole problem with the world is that fools and fanatics are always so certain of themselves, and wiser people are so full of doubts.
– Bertrand Russell

One day a monk went to ask the abbot at the monastery the following: he asked, 'Is it okay if I smoke during prayers?' Without hesitation the abbot said, 'Of course not, my son! The very suggestion borders on sacrilege!'

A few weeks later the same monk asked the abbot, 'Is it okay to pray when I am smoking?', to which the abbot replied, 'Of course. God wants to hear from us at any time.'

This charming yarn is a lovely example of how we can reframe something to our advantage. The outcome is the same for the monk, but the way he cleverly reframed the request made it more palatable for the apprehensive abbot.

We tend to think of framing our requests for others, but of course we can reframe suggestions to ourselves to achieve something we want. For example, if we have perhaps struggled to learn a particular subject area, then rather than holding the belief that we will never be good at it, we can think of our learning achievement as 'not yet' – implying that, with time and effort, we may be able to learn it in the future. Think of the vast swathes of us who have failed in a particular subject in our own education. To us, that subject is almost a no-go area for the rest of our lives – to the extent that we have almost mentally ringfenced it as something not to be considered ever again. But what if we labelled our achievement of it as 'not yet'? Then, the door is still open to tackling it. This 'not yet' framing has been successfully adopted by education authorities both in Scandinavia and in parts of the United States and is proving to be enormously successful with students. In addition, some schools here in the UK are now adopting the concept, which is fantastic news.

Much of the work around what has come to be known as a 'growth or fixed mindset' has been carried out by the inspirational author and psychologist Carol Dweck. In her TED Talk, Dweck refers to an experiment where two groups of students are given an easy test, which they are all successful at. One group of students is praised for the way that they have carried out the work, whilst the other group is told that they must have succeeded because they are naturally clever at this type of work.

Students were then given a task of a similar difficulty level to the first task and the results showed that the group who were praised for being clever did much *worse* than they did the first time. However, the group praised for the way they worked tried much harder and did even better. The group praised for being clever appeared to be developing what is thought of as a fixed mindset, and the other group, a growth mindset. As American chess player Josh Waitzkin once stated, 'The moment we believe that success is determined by an ingrained level of ability, we will be brittle in the face of adversity'.

So, what is the key to achieving the goals and success we want in life? Most would likely say that it is hard work, focus and persistence. Research, however, has shown that these attributes are the byproduct of something even more powerful: a growth mindset. If you have this powerful mindset in one area of your life, then, with effort, you can apply the same thinking to other areas, and achieve great success.

With a fixed mindset, we tend to believe our abilities, intelligence and talents are just fixed, immovable attributes. We have a certain amount and that's pretty much it. Our goal then becomes trying to look smart all the time and never to look silly or stupid. With the opposite, a growth mindset, we understand that our talents and abilities can be developed through time, effort, persistence and perhaps a good teacher. In modest terms, with a growth mindset, we don't necessarily believe everyone can be Einstein, but we do believe everyone can gain more skills and knowledge if they work at it.

Initially the benefits of a growth mindset might seem particularly obvious, but most of us are guilty of having the opposite in certain situations. Predictably, holding a fixed mindset can often prevent skill development and growth – important areas that can sabotage your happiness and health in your passage through life.

For example, if you say, 'I'm not a maths person' or 'My sister is the sporty one, not me', then those beliefs can act as an easy defence to avoid those particular areas. In the same vein, holding a fixed mindset can mean you can miss out on things that may become pleasurable, or even a passion for you. In the short term, holding a fixed mindset may mean that you fail at very few things, but in the long run, it may hinder your ability to learn, grow and develop new skills.

An individual with a growth mindset would be willing to try to find a solution to a maths problem, for example, or try to learn a new language even if they had failed at first. They see failure and setbacks as an indication that they should continue developing their skills, rather than a signal that indicates they will never be good at a particular activity. As an obvious result, people who have a growth mindset are more likely to maximise their potential. They tend to take on board any criticism, and use it to springboard their learning, rather than ignoring it. Similarly, they tend not to see criticism as an attack on their ego.

We all have areas of ourselves we need to work on. Maintaining the 'not yet' attitude to learning can help us grow as individuals, and perhaps experience new things.

Dweck's research raises an important question about the connection between what you believe and what you do. As writer

Debbie Millman says, 'If you imagine less, then you deserve what you get'. As Dweck goes on to write in her work, 'For twenty years, my research has shown that the view you adopt for yourself profoundly affects the way you lead your life. It can determine whether you become the person you want to be and whether you accomplish the things you value. How does this happen? How can a simple belief have the power to transform your psychology and, as a result, your life?'

If you believe you are not creative, or that you are a procrastinator, then your belief systems will channel you into those boundaries. Similarly, if you believe that it's hard to lose weight, and that you are not a natural athlete, then those are the beliefs you will make true.

When working with clients, I have often observed some subtle red flags when it comes to observing a fixed mindset. These observations are certainly not set in stone, but act as a fairly good benchmark. First, holding particularly strong opinions about things that don't necessarily call for such rigidity; for example, strongly disliking something such as a film or a particular actor or musician, or frequently using words such as 'hate' and similar derivatives such as 'I can't stand' and 'I loathe'. Another red flag can be a client frequently repeating back a solution to an issue we may have been discussing, as if the answer were obvious the whole time – an obvious protective mechanism to protect the fragile ego. Again, these are not set in stone, and, as we have discussed above, we can have a growth mindset in many areas of our lives but a fixed mindset in others. I have a colleague who calls people with fixed mindsets 'Ask Holes', as they frequently tell you what they know they need to do, often asking for your advice, but seldom, if ever, actually act on either.

So how can we shift from having a fixed mindset to having a growth mindset? What can you do about this? How can we change the beliefs we have about ourselves and actually achieve our goals?

As Dweck's work shed light on, much of what we think we understand of our personality comes from our mindset. We develop these at an early age, so, as with any beliefs that we have held for a substantial amount of time, they will require time, effort and insight to change. In addition, we must be willing to change. As previously discussed, self-esteem writer Nathaniel Branden states, 'The first step toward change is awareness. The second step is acceptance.' In this context acceptance does not mean settling for less, but adopting an attitude that can be somewhat empowering.

As we have discussed earlier in this book, your beliefs can unconsciously drive you to sabotage your behaviour. Believing that your qualities are carved in stone can create an urgency to prove yourself over and over. If you believe your intelligence, skills and talents are fixed, anything that forces you beyond them can make you feel apprehensive. Consequently, it can be easier to sabotage yourself rather than face the alternative. Knowing and believing you are right, and proving it repeatedly, is the safety net for your fragile ego. When it comes to understanding what makes the growth mindset so engaging, Dweck says, 'It creates a passion for learning, rather than a hunger for approval. Its hallmark is the conviction that human qualities, like intelligence and creativity, and even relational capacities like love and friendship, can be cultivated through effort and deliberate practice. Not only are people with this mindset not discouraged by failure, but they don't actually see themselves as failing in those situations – they see themselves as learning.'

Here are just some of the ways we can cultivate a growth mindset:

1. It's important to incorporate 'not yet' into our vocabulary, as it signals that despite any struggles, we can overcome anything. Acknowledge and embrace imperfections. Replace the word 'failing' with the word 'learning', and stop assuming that 'room for improvement' translates into failure.
2. Cultivate grit and resilience. View challenges as opportunities. Grit gives us that internal push to keep moving forwards and fulfil our commitments when we are met with adversity. According to Carol Dweck, 'In one

world, effort is a bad thing. It, like failure, means you're not smart or talented. If you were, you wouldn't need effort. In the other world, effort is what makes you smart or talented.'
3. Take time to acknowledge, reflect and embrace all your failures. Stop seeking approval and try not to be ego-driven in the results you are looking for, as it can limit your successes. Stop comparing yourself to others and remember that we all share the same weaknesses.
4. Take on challenges and try different learning ways of learning. Part of developing a growth mindset is shattering the negative perception of a challenge. How many self-limiting beliefs do you have around what you are capable of? Always try and take risks in the company of others.
5. Write your goals down. Growth mindset individuals are aware that once a goal is committed to paper it has a much greater chance of being realised. Likewise, set aside regular opportunities for reflection.
6. Try and find your purpose and try and value the process over the end result.

Finally, as philosopher and writer Elbert Hubbard once said, 'The greatest mistake you can make in life is to be continually fearing you will make a mistake'

SUMMARY

Are you in a fixed mindset, or a growth mindset? Do you see any shortfalls as failures, or as learning opportunities? This chapter will help you to acknowledge where you may fall in this respect, and help you to alter your mindset, so that your talents and abilities can keep improving with some time and effort. You may not be there now, but that doesn't have to be permanent – just not yet.

CHAPTER TWENTY-ONE

SELF-ESTEEM, SOCIAL ANXIETY AND SELF-SABOTAGE

When you've had a life of overthinking, you have the same reaction time and time again. Shyness becomes habitual. When you're put in an unfamiliar situation, all you want to do is retreat and hide by default. You watch but don't participate. You listen but don't respond. You read, but rarely comment. You take a photo, but you rarely post. You write, but you rarely publish. All of this is because your overthinking mind cannot stop thinking about how you will be perceived by the outside world.
– JOEL ANNESLEY

I have anxiety, I've always had anxiety, both in the light-hearted 'I'm anxious about this' kind of thing, and I've been to the depths of the darker end of the spectrum, which is not fun.

So, who could have spoken the second quotation above? In fact, it could have been any one of us. The vast majority of us have had times in our lives when we are filled with anxiety; when our self-esteem is not as high as it should be.

In this chapter, we are going to examine the belief systems that, perhaps, have the most devastating effect on us as humans. As a psychotherapist, I am aware that low self-esteem is at the root of virtually every problem of every client we meet at our practice. Fundamentally, low self-esteem is a thinking disorder in which an individual views him/herself as inadequate, unlovable and/or incompetent. Once formed, this negative view permeates every thought, producing faulty assumptions and ongoing self-defeating, self-sabotaging behaviour. Almost all of our self-esteem beliefs are formed in the first 6 years of life as the result of interactions we have with our primary caregivers, almost always our parents.

First, let's classify what we mean by self-esteem. In Latin, esteem actually means 'to estimate', so self-esteem is often defined as how you estimate yourself. Self-esteem refers to a person's overall sense of his or her value or worth. Self-esteem is often used to describe an individual's self-perception of his or her abilities, skills and overall qualities – qualities that guide and motivate specific behaviours. In short, the better we feel about ourselves, the more motivated and happier we tend to be in life. People with low self-esteem, on the other hand, tend to compare their situation to others.

Often self-esteem can be confused with self-confidence. Self-confidence is more about your trust in yourself and your ability to deal with challenges, solve problems and engage successfully with the world. Self-confidence is based more on external measures of success and value than the internal measures that contribute to self-esteem. In other words, you can have high self-confidence, particularly in a certain area or field, but still lack a healthy sense of self-esteem.

But how pervasive is low self-esteem? Well, the statistics are both frightening and reassuring – reassuring because if you are experiencing low self-esteem at this time in your life, then you are certainly not alone.

According to research by the World Health Organization (WHO), low self-esteem has been linked to violent behaviour, school dropout rates, teenage pregnancy, suicide and low academic achievement. It reports that, sadly, more deaths are caused by suicide every year than by homicide or war.

One doctor suggests that up to 85% of the world's population experience low self-esteem at some time in their lives. According to new research, an estimated 61% of 10- to 17-year-old girls in the UK have low self-esteem, and around 20% of teens will experience depression before they reach adulthood. In addition, it is estimated that a staggering 75% of girls with low self-esteem reported engaging in negative activities such as self-harming, bullying others, smoking, drinking or disordered eating. This compares to 25% of girls with high self-esteem.

Boys are not exempt either when it comes to body issues, with 40% of teenage boys reported to be exercising regularly to increase muscle mass.

Sadly, suicide in young people aged 15–24 is the third leading cause of death in this age group. In addition, it is estimated that some 50% of mental health disorders are established by the age of 14, while 75% are established by age 24.

A study carried out by toiletry manufacturer Dove reported that only 4% of women around the world consider themselves beautiful (up from 2% in 2004). In addition, more than half of women globally, 54%, agree that when it comes to how they look, they are their own worst beauty critic.

In simple terms, with high self-esteem we are far more likely to persevere in the face of difficulties. With low self-esteem, we are more likely to give up or go through the motions of trying without really giving our finest effort. Research has demonstrated that individuals with high-self-esteem will persist at a task significantly longer than individuals with low self-esteem. The idea being that if I persist, the likelihood is that I will succeed more often than I fail. If I don't, the likelihood is that I will fail more often than I succeed. Either way, an individual's self-image will be reinforced. The problem lies, however, in the fact that with low self-esteem, if we do succeed at something, then our self-image doesn't match up to the facts. When this occurs, we can begin to feel as if something isn't quite right, and we can experience cognitive dissonance – holding two opposing beliefs at the same time. When this happens, we can feel a compulsion to remove the discomfort by getting rid of the success. This then is the basic pattern of self-sabotage, and often we can self-sabotage at the height of our success.

The level of our self-esteem has profound consequences for every aspect of our existence: how we operate in the workplace, how we deal with people as well as how much we are likely to achieve in our lives. Similarly, it can impact on whom we are likely to fall in love with, how we interact with our spouse, children and friends, and what level of personal happiness we attain.

The higher our self-esteem, the more motivated to achieve success and happiness in our lives we tend to be. Not necessarily in our careers or in financial terms, but in relation to what we hope to experience in our lives. The lower our self-esteem, the less we aspire to achieve and the less we are likely to achieve. Either path tends to be self-reinforcing and self-perpetuating.

Let's briefly consider the connection between our self-esteem and our self-concept. Essentially, self-esteem refers to the judgements and evaluations we make about our self-concept. While self-concept is a broad description of the self, self-esteem is more specifically an evaluation of the self.

Self-concept was defined by Baumeister (1999) as a person's understanding or beliefs about their personal attributes. These beliefs can affect how they interact with the outside world. An individual's levels of self-confidence, as well as other attributes such as self-love, self-respect and self-worth, are impacted by how intact our self-concept is. At its core, an impaired self-concept can adversely interfere with a person's ability to find true happiness.

In American psychologist Abraham Maslow's hierarchy of needs (1943), he places self-actualisation at the pinnacle of his five-tier model. He believes that to achieve this position one must achieve one's full potential, to accomplish everything that one can, to become the most that one can be. Below self-actualisation are our esteem needs.

Maslow classified these into two categories: esteem for oneself (dignity, achievement, mastery, independence) and the desire for reputation or respect from others (e.g. status, prestige).

[Pyramid diagram showing Maslow's hierarchy of needs, from bottom to top: Physiological needs; Safety & security; Love & belonging; Self-esteem; Self-actualize]

Maslow noted that when self-confidence is driven by notoriety from outside sources it will be fragile. However, when the feeling is cultivated from within, it will feel more deserving, and thus, be regarded by the 'self' as of higher value. Perhaps this is why so many of the celebrities we enjoy watching and following seem to have breakdowns, often experiencing the anxieties linked to 'imposter syndrome'. Sadly, many individuals in the public eye and under public scrutiny can self-medicate with drugs and or alcohol as they struggle to find their worth in the world, whilst those of us not in the spotlight can struggle to believe how an individual, so glamorous, so adored, so talented and loved can be struggling with self-esteem-related issues.

Perhaps one of the most pertinent lessons on how we can observe the lives of others comes from author Henry B. Eyring. Eyring insightfully proclaims that, 'when you meet someone, treat them as if they were in serious trouble, and you will be right more than half the time'.

So who said the quotation at the beginning of this chapter? It may surprise you to know it was actor Ryan Reynolds. Like many of us, Reynolds has battled with depression and anxiety. The quotation at the beginning of this chapter is from an interview he gave with *The New York Times*. Other actors such as Brad Pitt have experienced similar emotions. Indeed, the turning point for Pitt's depression was a trip to Casablanca, where he witnessed extreme poverty. Pitt claims that the shock of what he observed forced him to gain perspective on his own issues. In an interview with *The Hollywood Reporter*, Pitt said, 'I got really sick of myself... I was hiding out from the celebrity thing; I was smoking way too much dope; I was sitting on the couch and just turning into a doughnut. I got to: "What's the point? I know better than this."'

OH, HAPPY DAY

With the recent onset of Covid-19, anxiety and feelings of hopelessness have become commonplace across the globe. For many, the lockdown and physical isolation have intensified feelings of loneliness and disconnection. Anxiety generated by both fear of Covid-19 and loneliness has potentially led to alarming depressive symptoms. However, psychologists believe that what is termed as the anxiety-buffer hypothesis can act as a shield against possible anxiety symptoms. In other words, the higher an individual's self-esteem, the more of an 'anxiety buffer' they are likely to have. The benefit of this buffer is the ability to deal effectively with the fear and loneliness produced by the lockdown. In essence, the higher your self-esteem, the more resilient and adaptive to change you can be, thus hampering any anxiety and depressive symptoms.

It is worth remembering that, with few exceptions, our low self-esteem is established in our formative years, from our childhood experiences and relationships. Our teachers, friends, siblings, parents and even the media can and do shape how we feel about ourselves, and our place in the world. The message that you are not good enough can remain with you to adulthood.

Whilst stress and difficult life events, such as serious illness or the loss of a loved one, can have a negative effect on self-esteem, with higher self-esteem we are more likely to have the resilience to 'bounce back' from these challenging experiences.

Personality can also play a part in how we feel about ourselves. If we have grown up having one or both parents who are 'black-and-white' or 'catastrophic' thinkers, then the way we process our own experiences will very likely be with the same 'tarnished' perception as our caregivers. We may be more prone to negative thoughts and limiting beliefs. Similarly, if we have some learned helplessness then we can feel overwhelmed and believe that we are unable to challenge and change how we feel about ourselves. If an individual sets unrealistic expectation for themselves, which are unattainable, then they can also react with depression and anxiety.

Over the years as a psychotherapist, I have met many individuals who seem to 'have it all' but deep-down feel very unhappy within themselves. One client I had the pleasure of meeting recently seemed to have it all on the surface. He was handsome, warm and friendly with a great sense of humour and a successful business. The sort of male most other men would love to emulate. He was, however, very unhappy and had been for many years; often feeling not good enough and experiencing some social anxiety and lack of motivation for life. He serves as a good reminder for us all about how often we make the assumption that how somebody looks and acts is a marker of how they feel inside. We are all prone to using the heuristic; to assessing someone's level of perceived happiness based on how we as individuals view them. Our quick-thinking System 1 processing makes the judgement rather than our slower and more rational System 2 processing.

Again, his unhappiness and lack of motivation for life were very much based on childhood experiences. For me, he serves as a good reminder that our beliefs and our belief systems about ourselves are not real. They are our perceptions.

> *I am not who you think I am; I am not who I think I am;*
> *I am who I think you think I am.*
> – THOMAS COOLEY

THE WAY YOU LOOK TONIGHT

In one classic study by Professor Thomas Gilovich and two of his graduate students, researchers asked college students to wear a Barry Manilow t-shirt (viewed as extremely uncool at the time) and then walk into a room of strangers facing the entrance. The researchers predicted that the students would assume that more people had seen their t-shirt than was actually the case.

When the students were surveyed as to how many of the strangers they believed had seen the t-shirt, the students assumed that about 50% would have noticed it. In reality it was about 20%. Participants allowed their own focus on the embarrassing t-shirt to distort their assessment of the degree to which others noticed it. This effect has come to be called the 'spotlight effect'.

The spotlight effect reflects our tendency to believe that the spotlight shines more brightly on us than it actually does. When it comes to social anxiety, what is interesting is the belief that individuals have that they are being observed and judged far more than they actually are. Many social anxiety sufferers know all too well that feeling of being stared at and noticed by others. The great news is that studies like this one confirm for us that this feeling is most likely exaggerated. We may believe we can read the minds of others, but more often than not we are wrong in our assumptions.

What we believe to be true regarding our public appearance is often not the case. At the heart of social anxiety, otherwise referred to as social phobia, is the fear of being judged by others. Of course, most of us have a certain amount of social anxiety, but it is when it becomes all-consuming and prevents one from leading a full life that it becomes an issue. A person with a higher than normal level of social anxiety feels symptoms of anxiety or fear in virtually all social scenarios. Situations such as meeting new people, dating, interviews, answering a question in class, answering the phone and having to talk to a shop assistant can all cause anxiety. Other everyday things such as eating or drinking in front of others or using a public toilet can also cause anxiety or fear. At its root, the individual is afraid that he or she will be humiliated, judged and rejected.

To someone with extreme social anxiety challenging the belief that, most of the time, people are just not that interested in our appearance or performance can have a profound effect on relieving the symptoms of anxiety. Regardless of how much social anxiety you experience, it's always worth keeping this in mind the next time you feel yourself the centre of attention in a public space. If an uncool and awkwardly worn Barry Manilow t-shirt is noticed by only about 20% of people in a situation designed to draw attention to it, your worst gaffe or blunder can hardly do more.

Whilst there is some limited evidence that anxiety disorders such as severe social anxiety tend to run in families, assessing such assertions can be fraught with difficulty. Therefore, it is virtually impossible to assess accurately how much of a person's behaviour may be due to genetics and how much is due to modelling of a parent or guardian. For example, if a parent is socially anxious, and experiences a lot of anxiety symptoms, and we model their behaviour, are we experiencing the actual anxiety, or are we just modelling the observed behaviour?

One of the most likely causes, and something I have personally witnessed hundreds of times whilst taking clients through therapy, is that the social anxiety we feel is rooted in experiences in childhood – usually caused by events where an individual felt overwhelming embarrassment, shame and often guilt. This could be one single experience or several experiences where the individual felt very much on the spot and wanted the ground to open up and swallow them.

Often such experiences can easily be recalled by the client before therapy, but more often than not they are repressed to the extent that they are hidden from view from the client's immediate memory. These embarrassing experiences are often, to adult eyes, almost trivial. But to the young, developing child they can seem overwhelming.

Who among us cannot remember a child in our class having 'an accident' in a school assembly, for example? Few of us can get through childhood without a gamut of similar embarrassing experiences.

Once the emotion of the experience has been recalled, the social anxiety of the client tends to dissipate quite readily, to the extent that they are then the person they would have been had the experience never happened in the first instance. Again, social anxiety at its root is about the anxious feelings generated by being judged and scrutinised by others.

GREAT BALLS OF FIRE

Imagine for a moment that you are playing in the World Cup, and you are about to take a penalty shot. The entire stadium is holding their collective breath. Across the world millions are poised in front of their TV sets inspecting your every move. The next few moments could either bring elation for you and your team or misery. You stare at the goal ahead and plan your kick. The question is: do you kick to the left or the right? Or do you risk a shot to the middle?

This footballer's dilemma was discussed in detail in the 2014 book *Think Like a Freak* by authors Stephen J. Dubner and Steven Levitt. The authors reviewed the raw stats on penalty taking. Their conclusion was that a penalty kick towards the centre of a goal is 7% more likely to succeed than a kick to the corner. Every penalty that has been hit down the middle in a World Cup shoot-out has resulted in a goal. Despite this, only 17% of penalties are aimed towards the centre.

This dilemma was the focus of a 2002 study by Chiappori et al., who looked at data from 459 penalties from the French and Italian Leagues between 1997 and 2000. They found that penalties aimed to the middle of the goal, despite being rare (only 17%), have a statistically significantly higher probability of success than penalties aimed at either side of the goal, some 81.0%. Compare that to 70.1% for shots aimed at the right side and 76.7% for the left.

So why, given the higher success rate of penalties aimed at the middle of the goal, are there so few of them? The thinking behind this rationale is perhaps quite simple. If you aim to the left or the right and you either miss the shot or the ball is caught by the goalie, you are just unlucky. If, however, you aim in the middle and the goalie snatches the ball, you could possibly appear to be not only the worst footballer in history but, depending on the match, the worst human who ever existed. Put simply, the fear of being judged, humiliated and perhaps ultimately ostracised from their tribe forces the player, even unconsciously, to minimise this risk when taking the shot.

Similarly, a survey of professional goalkeepers confirms that goalkeepers would feel worse about conceding a goal after standing in the middle than after diving to either side. Diving and missing, even if you dive the wrong way, at least shows you made an effort. Not moving looks suspiciously like not trying your best. Goalkeepers it seems adopt a strategy that compromises their effectiveness in order to maintain a perception that they are doing their best. Those among us who have faked looking busy when the boss walks by may recognise this familiar behaviour pattern.

I BELIEVE I CAN FLY

When working with clients with moderate to extreme social anxiety, I often refer to a painting believed to be by the Dutch artist Pieter Bruegel entitled 'Landscape with the Fall of Icarus'. The painting depicts the demise of Icarus. In Greek mythology, Icarus was the son of the master craftsman Daedalus. Icarus and Daedalus had been locked in a high tower on the island of Crete. To escape this tower, Daedalus cunningly constructed wings for them both fashioned from feathers and wax. Daedalus cautiously instructed Icarus to not fly too close to the Sun for fear that the wax would melt away. Icarus ignored the warning and determinedly flew too near the Sun. The wax holding his wings together melted and he plunged into the sea where he drowned.

What is extraordinary about this painting is that when you examine it, the only visible sign of the unfortunate Icarus is his legs as he drowns. They are miniscule compared to the other features of the work. Indeed, they are completely dwarfed by the rump of the workhorse that is afforded centre stage. It appears that what Bruegel is saying with his beautifully detailed painting is that life goes on, regardless of what tragedy sadly besets others. The ploughman ploughs; the majestic trading vessels go about their commercial business. Life goes on. The death of an unlucky aviator is of no more importance than the fall of a sparrow, even if we attempt to delude ourselves into thinking otherwise.

Bruegel's extraordinary work is a gentle reminder to us all that often we can be so consumed with ourselves and our own lives that we tend not to afford the level of attention to others that they may believe we are. As American writer David Foster Wallace brilliantly states, 'You will become way less concerned with what other people think of you when you realise how seldom they do'.

As humans we are all, to a certain degree, rather self-centred. In many ways, we are all somewhat narcissistic and that is perfectly healthy and normal. Author John Koenig, in his compendium of invented words entitled *The Dictionary of Obscure Sorrows*, puts it perfectly when he calls this type of human behaviour 'Sonder'. Sonder is the realisation that each random passer-by is living a life as vivid and complex as your own and that everyone has a story. In your story, you are the main character, the protagonist if you will; the hero at the centre of your own unfolding tale, and your friends and family are your supporting cast. Others in our self-narrative are our network of acquaintances and the random passers-by each living their own lives. Each one of these individual lives a life as vivid and complex as our own. Each one carries the accumulated weight of their own dreams and ambitions. Each one shrouded in their own worries, their own mistakes and triumphs, and their individual inherited irrationality.

It makes perfect sense that we are all the centre of our own universe. The positive takeaway from this, like the painting depicting Icarus, is that we really don't need to be so concerned with what others think of us for the simple reason that others rarely *do* think of us. That does not mean that others are uncaring or uninterested in our lives but, put simply, the vast majority of us are living so much in 'our own heads' and absorbed by our own neuroses and anxieties that we fail to notice the mistakes or possible faux pas of our fellow humans. We are all so preoccupied with our own fears about potential social slip-ups and the ridicule that this may create that we most likely experience 'inattentional blindness' when it comes to others, as shown in the Barry Manilow T-shirt example.

To some degree, having a manageable level of social anxiety is healthy. It makes us more aware of the feelings of others in relation to ourselves. We are social beings; we fear isolation. Indeed, the fear of isolation and being ostracised by our 'tribe' is hardwired into us from our hunter-gatherer ancestors. If we were rejected by the other members of our community then we would very likely meet with an unpleasant end. The fact that we are alive today means that our ancestors were not ostracised from their group and survived to reproduce.

The feelings of being judged by others that are at the root of social anxiety are at their core generated by our belief systems. In other words, they are not real; they are just our perceptions, created by our experiences and what we have learnt along the way on our journey through life. These beliefs often have their origin in our formative years in our early childhood experiences. They are then cemented through the years by how we manage our thinking. In other words, if our behaviours are driven by the fear of being judged by others, then we can often avoid activities and situations that may bring those uncomfortable emotions to the surface. They are learnt ways of thinking and feeling and, as such, can be unlearnt and reprogrammed in our subconscious minds.

Use the Alfred Technique to learn to manage your thinking and assess your beliefs around your social anxiety. Picture the Bruegel painting to obtain some perspective on your social fears and remember the Manilow experiment. When possible, place yourself in situations that previously you may have avoided due to the belief that they may have made you feel uncomfortable feelings. Remember, the more we avoid something, the more we buy into the belief that it will be difficult and challenging. Essentially, what we resist persists. Perhaps writer and actor Woody Allen says it best when he says, 'Ninety percent of success in life is just showing up'.

The freedom gained from being free of high levels of social anxiety can be profound and life enhancing.

I have tried to avoid quizzes in this book as there are lots of websites you can visit to assess your personality and how you feel about yourself. However, self-esteem is so fundamental to how someone thinks and feels about themselves, it is perhaps the single most important determinant for success and happiness in life. Here are just a handful of statements for you to consider to give you a flavour of how you may be feeling about yourself right now. Of course, as we have established, self-esteem can fluctuate and change; perhaps review these statements every few weeks. Do notice any changes that have occurred in your thinking as your self-esteem will without doubt change as you follow what we discuss in this book.

1: The vast majority of the time, I like myself as I am.

- Agree strongly
- Agree
- Neither agree nor disagree
- Disagree
- Strongly disagree

2: I feel that other people enjoy having me in their lives.

- Agree strongly
- Agree
- Neither agree nor disagree
- Disagree
- Strongly disagree

3: If I didn't know me, I'd think I was okay.

- Agree strongly
- Agree
- Neither agree nor disagree

- Disagree
- Strongly disagree

4: As I grew up, I felt loved and valued.

- Agree strongly
- Agree
- Neither agree nor disagree
- Disagree
- Strongly disagree

5: Other people value my opinion and my viewpoint.

- Agree strongly
- Agree
- Neither agree nor disagree
- Disagree
- Strongly disagree

6: Often I feel sensitive to criticism.

- Agree strongly
- Agree
- Neither agree nor disagree
- Disagree
- Strongly disagree

7: I often avoid social situations that might make me feel uncomfortable.

- Agree strongly
- Agree
- Neither agree nor disagree
- Disagree
- Strongly disagree

8: I frequently have negative thoughts about myself and my abilities.

- Agree strongly
- Agree
- Neither agree nor disagree
- Disagree
- Strongly disagree

9: I sometimes find eye contact with others difficult.

- Agree strongly
- Agree
- Neither agree nor disagree
- Disagree
- Strongly disagree

10: I often find it difficult to challenge and assert myself.

- Agree strongly
- Agree
- Neither agree nor disagree
- Disagree
- Strongly disagree

If you find that you answered closer to the 'disagree' and 'strongly disagree' end of the spectrum on the majority of statements in this assessment, then your self-esteem and levels of social anxiety may not be where you want them to be at this moment in time. Sometimes anxiety is not really anxiety: sometimes it is just a very well-disguised and well-entrenched habit of disliking who we are. But, like any habit, it mostly originates from our habitual subconscious mind, and therefore with repetition can be changed.

SUMMARY

Chapter 21 examined the concept of self-esteem and how it has an effect on our lives. It is estimated 85% of us will experience low self-esteem at some point in our lives, and this can affect how persistent one is with a task, and to what extent someone believes they will achieve something. If an individual has low self-esteem, they are more likely to think that they will not succeed at a particular task, and therefore either avoid doing it, or give up a lot more quickly. Someone with a higher level of self-esteem has a much stronger buffer between themselves and anxiety, making them a lot more resilient and able to complete a task without constant worry of failure.

Low self-esteem can also play a large part in social anxiety. When we think we aren't capable of something, or that we aren't good enough, we begin to assume that others must also think this. However, a large majority of the time, we think things we feel anxious or embarrassed about are more obvious than they are, and most of the time the people we feel anxious about judging us don't even notice. This is known in the psychology field as the spotlight effect.

References

CHAPTER TWENTY-TWO

THE SKY IS FALLING

*Instead of complaining that the rose bush is full of thorns,
be happy the thorn bush has roses.*
– PROVERB

One morning, while eating her breakfast, a lady looked out of her window and saw that her neighbour had hung her washing out on the line to dry. She noted how dirty and dingy it was, and disgustedly commented to her husband that 'our neighbour obviously doesn't know how to wash her clothes and can't be using a detergent; they are so dirty!' Week after week, she would gaze out of the window at the dirty clothes on the neighbour's line and comment to her husband on just how dirty the laundry was. One morning, when she started making breakfast, she looked out of the window and saw that the clothes were clean and bright! She called to her husband to come and look, as she could not believe what she was seeing. She exclaimed, 'At last, she has finally learned how to wash her clothes; I wonder what happened?'

At this, her husband turned to her and with a wry smile said, 'Honey, I got up early this morning and cleaned our windows!'

I HEARD IT THROUGH THE GRAPEVINE

One of the most powerful and life-enhancing ways to bring about massive change in our lives and the lives of those around us is to notice how much we complain and gossip about others. In this brief chapter, we are going to look at the potentially harmful psychological effects of complaining and gossiping.

You might be thinking right now, 'I could never do this', or 'I love it when the girls (or boys) get together and put the world to rights!', or 'A good moan makes me feel better!' Well, of course, you may be right. However, over time, complaining, criticising and gossiping can have a negative effect on your self-esteem and how you feel. Complaining can create a cognitive bias in how you see your life and your experiences. In other words, complaining often can potentially distort how you see the world, by allowing you to focus on the negative events that happen in your life rather than the positive ones. Not only that, but it can impact how others see you. If others see you as someone who is a complainer, then how they treat you can change and have an effect on your own self-esteem and self-worth (remember the 'but' and the 'wow' personality traits from earlier in this book?). Be seen as a 'wow' person rather than a 'but'. I often think of the magnificent quote by motivational speaker Zig Ziglar, he writes, 'There has never been a statue erected to honour a critic'.

I first began to notice the link between success and how much and how often we complain several years ago with one of our weight loss apps. I began to witness that the more individuals seemed to complain, the greater the chance of them not successfully losing weight seemed to be. Whilst this was just an observation not an empirical study, it inspired Sue and me to create a new app to help people. The end result was called 'Your Positive Mindfulness Coach' app. The app went on to be a best seller and help many thousands of individuals to manage their thinking and become more positive and empowered. The app focused on four key areas: negative thinking, self-criticism, complaining and self-limiting beliefs. A large part of the app encouraged users to focus on managing their thinking for 3-, 7- and 14-day periods. These challenges encouraged users to be the observer of how much negativity there was in their lives and begin to challenge and change it.

Think of complaining as a signal that you are managing your life badly! No one wants to do that! We all complain. Even if you argue that you are the happiest person in the world, you still complain sometimes. This challenge is to manage it, and ideally, over time, reduce it. This is not to suggest that you should pretend there's nothing wrong when a challenge arises, but there's a big difference between complaining and making an authentic observation. When we complain, we can often play the victim role, and in doing so buy into feelings of powerlessness.

RUMOUR HAS IT

Remember when your mum used to say, 'If you don't have anything good to say...?' Well, it turns out that was really great advice. Not only because it stopped family quarrels, but because there is, in fact, strong scientific evidence behind why we shouldn't. When it comes to gossiping there is some good news and some bad. First, let's look at why we have a tendency to gossip about others.

Researchers have estimated that in our conversations about other people, anywhere from 65–80% of conversations are based on gossip, both positive and negative. As social creatures, we focus a lot of our attention on other people and that comes through in what we talk about. Psychologists believe that talking about others is a habit that likely evolved as a safety mechanism. The survival of our hunter-gatherer ancestors depended on them knowing whom they could trust and whom they should avoid. Similarly, this form of communication, an early form of gossip, helped people keep tabs on who was the most likely to betray members of the group. In addition, it allowed our ancestors to know who was the most dependable and whose families were the healthiest and best to reproduce with.

Now, here's the bad news: spontaneous trait transference. First demonstrated in clinical trials by Skowronski et al. (1998), spontaneous trait transference refers to people associating what comes out of your mouth with you as an individual, regardless of your intentions, be it gossip or seeking to damage another person's reputation, as if you the gossiper yourself possess those negative qualities. In other words, just like a boomerang, when you talk about someone, in either a positive or negative way, those traits are now associated with you in the mind of the individual you are choosing to share your gossip with. If you express that someone is untrustworthy and insincere, the person listening will subconsciously assign those traits to you as well.

In addition, researchers noted that the effects of such trait transference can persist over time. As actress and humanitarian Audrey Hepburn once said, 'You can tell more about a person by what he says about others than you can by what others say about him'.

GOOD VIBRATIONS

Think about how often you answer the question 'How are you today?' with 'not bad', even when you've had an amazing day. Perhaps the next time someone asks how you are you could try answering with, 'I'm great thanks!' or 'Really good thanks!' or my personal favourite, 'Outstanding but I am improving', and see how good it makes you feel!

So why can complaining, and particularly catastrophising, have such a negative impact on us? Well, it's mostly down to a thing called Hebb's rule. 'Hebbian associative learning', as it was originally known, originated from the work of Donald Hebb back in 1949. The law states that 'Neurons that fire together, wire together', meaning if you continually have the same thought patterns or do the same activity over and over, then the neurons in your brain tend to strengthen that learning, becoming what we know as a habit. Basically, every time this electrical charge is triggered, the synapses grow closer together in order to decrease the distance the electrical charge has to cross carrying the relevant information you're thinking about. The brain is rewiring its own circuitry, physically changing itself, to make it easier and more likely that the proper synapses will share the chemical link and thus spark together – in essence, making it easier for the thought to trigger. Imagine that you have two pairs of people throwing a ball back and forth. One pair stands 6 feet apart and the other at a distance of 20 feet. One person from each team throws their ball to their respective partners at the exact same moment at the exact same speed. The first team to catch the ball gets to dictate your personal decision and mental state of mind. That is in essence what our brains are doing when our thoughts are creating new neural pathways. Of course, when you don't repeat a behaviour or thought you get the inverse, namely 'Neurons that fire apart, wire apart'.

The more we do an activity, the more 'habitual' the learning will become. For example, consider driving a car or riding a bike. When you first start to drive a car or ride a bike, you will be very conscious about ensuring you are focusing on the activity at hand, thinking intently about each aspect of the activity. It all feels very unfamiliar to you; indeed little about it feels natural. After a period of time, you tend to get into the car, or sit on your bike, and although you still carry out the usual safety checks, you soon go into autopilot. Your focus is now entirely on the road and on the other drivers rather than the activity of driving or riding. You really don't think consciously about it! Similarly, how often have you had to go back and check your front door as you can't remember locking it? I would wager a bet that when you first moved into your new house you locked the door consciously, perhaps noticing every new aspect of locking up your new abode safely.

FREE YOUR MIND AND YOUR ASS WILL FOLLOW

Picture a desert scene. Within the malleable, sandy surface, there are thousands of shallow channels and several deeper channels. Our brain is just like this desert landscape, and our thoughts the etched channels cut into it. If we keep repeating thoughts and actions, then the channels get deeper – hence Hebb's rule. The desert, like our brains, is highly pliable. New channels can be created, and old ones can be superseded easily, particularly if the sand is moved to new channels on its surface. The more we repeat a thought, the deeper the channel, or the positive or negative thought. The desert cares not what type of thought it is; it just creates a new channel for it. If a thought is catastrophic in nature, then the channel is that much deeper. Picture a gardener using a trowel or a shovel to create the individual channels. In addition, if that catastrophic thought is repeatedly spoken out loud, then a team of builders will rock up and reinforce its walls with cement. But why does our brain do this so easily? Well, here's the rub. Because your brain is calorically ravenous, it takes up in the region of 20% of the energy usage of the entire body. So, to be energy efficient, if you are repeating a thought, activity or behaviour, then it will create neural pathways for that thought, much like the grooves in the desert analogy above. The stronger the neural pathways we have for a particular thought, the less energy we need to continue that thought. So, if you are rehearsing failure and catastrophic outcomes frequently, with thoughts such as 'I'm never going to make a success of anything' or 'Why does everything seem to go wrong for me all the time?' or maybe even 'I am such a failure', your brain will recognise that it needs to hardwire the anxiety response you are feeling right now to prepare for future threatening scenarios.

Neuroscientists call this thinking style 'negativity bias'. It appears that this particular bias is an adaptive trait of human psychology that appeared to serve us well when we were hunting with spears on the savannah 120,000 years ago. Perhaps though it's not required as much in our modern world, where for many of us the most dangerous thing we face each day is a harsh email or an unexpected bill.

I've discussed before in this book that the average person has between 60 and 80,000 thoughts per day. Unsurprisingly then, if the majority of those thoughts are negative, individuals can experience the symptoms of depression and anxiety. It's also worth noting that 95% of the thoughts an individual has on a daily basis are the same as the day before, and the day before that. Only when you begin to challenge those thoughts can your personality change and you can become the person you were destined to be. Through changing your thoughts, you can literally change the structure of your brain – in effect getting Hebb's rule to work for you rather than against you.

Many years ago, Sue and I undertook a 21-day challenge to stop complaining. It took us numerous attempts to last the 21 days, starting again when we found ourselves complaining. Eventually, we managed to complete the challenge, and I've done the challenge several times since. When you develop the habit of not complaining you literally rewire your brain, so the default setting is not to complain anymore. In fact, it becomes considerably easier to grasp the positive in just about any situation. I noticed a profound effect it had on my life, and I have since encouraged many others to undertake the challenge as well. Initially just try for half a day, then expand to a full day and develop from there.

In a similar vein to the Baader–Meinhof phenomenon discussed in Chapter 16 of this book, once you begin to notice others complain, you witness how often it happens. Chances are you may begin to notice how much complaining there is in the modern world. Not just with other friends and colleagues but with the media; in particular social media. In fact, you may find it quite shocking how, for many individuals, the default setting is to complain. You may also find that you are surprised how often you have complained in the past. This is a helpful thing, because only when you become the observer can you become the modifier of a behaviour. It is better to be the observer and not the participant. Like focusing on red cars, pretty soon, you'll see red cars all over the place. You'll begin to notice that complaining much less makes you feel more empowered, more in control and happier!

Research has shown how our brains are in fact hardwired to focus on the negative. Think of a time when an employer or teacher praised your work multiple times on a project, but suggested one or two areas of improvement? You clearly did a terrific job, but it's likely all your brain could do was zero in on the negative part of the interaction. This negativity bias is an innate human reaction and is believed to be an evolutionary survival method that kept our ancestors safe in a threat-filled world. Put simply, those who expected the worst were more likely to survive, and, in doing so, were far more likely to pass those crucial pessimistic genes down. If our hunter-gatherer ancestors were more focused on how great the sunset looked one particular evening rather than a predator waiting behind the tree then, chances are, you and I would never have been born. Our ancestors had to be on guard for giant hyenas, cave bears and lions. They had to watch out for eagles, snakes, wolves, sabre-toothed cats, false sabre-toothed cats and even, down under, giant, predatory kangaroos. So basically, you really had to have your wits about you.

Unfortunately, that primitive inclination can hold us back in many aspects of our modern-day lives. What happens in our highly developed brains is that we tend to focus on something we *perceive* to be a threat, rather than something that actually is one. We may worry about future 'what ifs', like losing our job or a relationship issue with a spouse, going over and over the thoughts like a broken record until, like the grooves in the sand, they are burnt into our brains. Similarly, negative bias can also explain why a bad first impression can be so difficult to overcome, and why past traumas can, without therapy, have such a long and lingering effect on us. Likewise, in almost any interaction, we are more likely to register any negative aspect of it and remember those parts more vividly.

This negativity bias explains why we can think about negative experiences more frequently than positive ones, and also why we tend to remember traumatic experiences over more positive ones. Why also we can easily recall insults more readily than the times we have been complimented. Who among us has not had the experience of having a great day at work sullied by an offhand comment from a co-worker? The result being we brooded and ruminated over the experience for hours, or even days, after the event occurred. When we returned home from work on the day of the disagreement and our partners asked us how our day was, did we talk about the positive events of the day or zone in on the one negative incident?

The effect of sustained negative bias can in the long term impact our health. Indeed, researchers from the Institute of Psychiatry, Psychology and Neuroscience at King's College London have suggested that repetitive negative thinking, what they refer to as RNT, can be a common symptom of many psychological disorders and may in fact increase the risk of developing Alzheimer's disease.

Until recently, research into Alzheimer's disease had very much focused on how physical factors are linked to the onset of symptoms. However, this latest research has suggested that there are indeed psychological factors that make a person more vulnerable to this most devastating of diseases. These factors occur before any physical indicators of the disease can emerge.

In an article published in the *Journal of Alzheimer's Disease*, the researcher Natalie Marchant argued that a habit of negative thinking over a prolonged period of time can indeed have a devastating effect on our brain's capacity to think, reason and form memories. To once again quote Zig Ziglar, 'We all need a daily check up from the neck up to avoid stinkin' thinkin' which ultimately leads to hardening of the attitudes'.

BAD HABITS

So now for the good news. With patience and continued practice, Hebb's rule can work in the opposite direction, and in our favour. We can train our brains to start 'firing and wiring' together in more positive thought, and in doing so, actually create new neural pathways. Even better, and perhaps unexpectedly, this doesn't just create a mental shift, as head of the Mind & Body Lab at Stanford University Alia Crum has shown: 'Our mindsets are not inconsequential, but instead play a dramatic role in determining our health and well-being'.

So perhaps next time you're with your friends, family or co-workers and they are engaged in complaining, speak up or quiet down. Depending on the crowd, either speak up to stop the complaining and change the subject to something sunnier, or simply be quiet and don't complain yourself. Maybe stop for a minute and think of all the great positive things and people in your life. Really focus on encouraging others and be the positive change you wish to see in the world. The whole area of complaining is perhaps best summed up by Maya Angelou when she writes, 'What you're supposed to do when you don't like a thing is change it. If you can't change it, change the way you think about it. Don't complain.'

SUMMARY

This chapter asked us to look at ourselves and realise how often we complain. It may be easy to notice the negativity coming from someone else, but not so easy to recognise when we ourselves are constantly moaning about something. Persistent complaining about something can lead us to feel helpless and powerless in our own lives and can lower our self-esteem. Due to spontaneous trait transference, it can also mean that other people in our lives associate us as people with complaining. When looking at changing something about ourselves and our thinking patterns or habits, it is perhaps best to think about Hebb's rule: neurons that fire together, wire together. Put simply, when we do something over and over, it becomes more strongly formed in our brains and then takes less energy for that to be the chosen action next time it is needed. Therefore, in order to become a sunnier person with a more positive outlook on life, we need to start behaving this way from the outset – we need to become the observers of our own thoughts in order to change them into better ones. After all, if 95% of our thoughts today are the same as they were yesterday, then unchallenged thoughts can easily become engrained in us.

CHAPTER TWENTY-THREE

FATE, LUCK AND CHANCE

Life is what happens to us while we are making other plans.
– ALLEN SAUNDERS

In the summer of 1947, renowned behavioural psychologist B.F. Skinner published his study on a group of pigeons who demonstrated that even animals are susceptible to the human conditioning we think of as superstition.

Regarded as the father of the process of operant conditioning – a method of learning that employs rewards and punishments for behaviour – Skinner conducted his research on a group of hungry pigeons. For a few minutes each day, a mechanism fed the birds at regular intervals. The birds would receive food when they tapped a switch. The switch was then removed, and Skinner's team changed to providing the pigeons with food at random intervals. What Skinner discovered was astonishing. The pigeons had, in fact, developed what could only be explained as superstitious type behaviours: believing that by acting in a particular way, or by committing a certain action, they would be rewarded with food.

Incredibly, by the end of the study, three-quarters of the birds had demonstrated superstitious behaviours. For example, one pigeon, in pursuit of food, believed that by turning around in the cage two or three times more food would magically materialise.

On the surface, it could be easy to dismiss such behaviour as normal – a bird in a cage might be expected to exercise a little. But the majority of the other birds developed unique ritualistic behaviours in an attempt to obtain a meal as well. Other behaviours observed by Skinner and his team included what they described as a 'pendulum' movement of the head and a regular nodding movement in another bird.

Birds are certainly not alone in associating the attainment of a reward with a superstitious ritual. Not long after the end of World War II, anthropologists discovered a curious religion that had developed among the islanders of the South Pacific. It was oriented around the concept of *cargo*, which the islanders perceived as the source of the wealth and power of the Europeans and Americans. During World War II, vast amounts of military equipment and supplies from both sides of the conflict in that region had been airdropped to troops on these islands. Clothing, medicine, canned food, tents, weapons and other goods arrived in vast quantities for the soldiers. These supplies were often shared with the islanders, who were their guides and hosts.

As a result of these airdrops, islanders believed that if they carried out particular rituals and ceremonies, shipments of riches would be sent from some heavenly place. To the islanders, this was a perfectly logical assumption. The islanders saw that they worked hard but were poor, whereas the Europeans and Americans did not work, instead wrote things down on paper, and in due course a shipment of wonderful things would arrive from the sky. The islanders, who later became known as the Cargo Cult, painstakingly constructed replicas of airports and aeroplanes out of twigs and branches and made the sounds associated with aeroplanes to try to activate the shipment of cargo.

At some level, the islanders had formed the same belief in superstitions that the pigeons had years later in B.F. Skinner's ground-breaking experiments: believing that if they were to carry out a particular ritual they would be rewarded for it.

Skinner's pigeon experiment revealed that even birds can be conditioned to develop superstitious behaviours in the belief that they will be rewarded. This begs the question: how many of us develop superstitious rituals we feel a compulsion to observe? Would not adhering to them create some anxiety within us? Perhaps some cognitive dissonance? After all, who among us doesn't feel compelled to say 'Bless you' when someone sneezes, even if that person is a complete stranger? Do we say the words out of politeness, habit or just in case the devil should decide to steal their soul (as our ancestors thought)? We do this often, despite knowing on some level that they cannot be true, perhaps thinking to ourselves, 'Better safe than sorry'.

So, let's look at what a superstition actually is. The Merriam–Webster dictionary defines superstition as 'a belief or practice resulting from ignorance, fear of the unknown, trust in magic or chance, or a false conception of causation'.

According to a survey conducted by psychologist Professor Richard Wiseman at the University of Herefordshire, a whopping 77% of people in the UK indicated that they were at least a little superstitious and/or carried out some form of superstitious behaviour, with almost half of the people surveyed indicating that they were very/somewhat superstitious.

The two most common luck-based superstitions in the UK are touching wood and crossing fingers, followed by not walking under ladders and not breaking a mirror. Next is carrying a lucky charm and having superstitious beliefs about the number 13. Of course, superstitions can vary massively across the world and from culture to culture. For example, in some countries, a black cat crossing your path is seen as lucky, whilst in others it is viewed as unlucky. Intriguingly, research has shown that women tend to be more superstitious than men, and that young people are more superstitious than the generation before them.

Superstitions tend to have two main causes: cultural tradition and individual experiences. If an individual grew up in a culture or religion steeped in superstitions, then chances are they may carry these beliefs forward, even subconsciously. For many people, engaging with superstitious behaviours can provide a sense of perceived short-term control and reduced anxiety, which is why research has shown that levels of superstitious behaviours tend to increase at times of stress and worry.

I SHOULD BE SO LUCKY

With regard to superstitions, the crucial question is this: is maintaining superstitious beliefs harmful to our mental well-being? Well, it would appear so. Research has demonstrated that individuals who are superstitious tend to worry more about life and have a strong need for control and certainty. It would also appear that when there is economic and political uncertainty in the world, there tends to be a significant increase in superstition, perhaps due to people desiring a feeling of control over the unknown at these unpredictable times. This is especially true of people with a high need for control, for example, during wars and conflicts. Interestingly, researchers have observed how in Germany, between 1918 and 1940, measures of economic threat correlated directly with an increase in superstitions.

Individuals who report worrying about life more than the average tend to be far more superstitious. An estimated 50% of people who claimed to worry excessively confessed to being very, or somewhat, superstitious. This is compared with just 24% of non-worriers. People who had a strong need for control in their lives reported that they were far more superstitious than others – 42% of people indicating high need for control were very/somewhat superstitious, compared with just 22% of people indicating low need for control. Also, individuals who had a low tolerance for ambiguity tended to be more superstitious than those with a high tolerance – 38% of those with low tolerance were very/somewhat superstitious compared with just 30% of those with high tolerance.

Whilst there is some evidence indicating that there may be benefits to maintaining superstitious beliefs, particularly in certain areas such as sports and examinations (such as a coach not changing his underwear for a season!), research in this field points to the fact the outcome experienced by those sportspeople tends to be down to the placebo effect of believing the result will be positive. With this in mind, it seems natural to conclude that superstitions actually help those who hold these beliefs to deal with pressure and to overcome mental and physical obstacles. Unfortunately, though, there is very little research in this area.

References

Often, holding onto superstitions can give us the Illusion of control. This illusion is the tendency for us to believe we can control, or at least influence, outcomes that we have no influence over. It is the perceived illusion of control that can have a negative effect on individuals who hold certainty in the power of superstitions. Having a strong desire for control can mean that an individual feels very much out of control in their life. If a person holds the belief that outside factors have an influence on their life, then chances are they are less likely to feel 'in control' in their own life. In essence, the more a person believes in fate, luck and chance, the less likely they are to exert control over their own life. Superstitions represent people's attempts to control and enhance this most elusive of factors.

For many centuries, people have searched for an effective way of improving the good fortune in their lives. Talismans, lucky charms and amulets have been found in virtually every civilisation throughout recorded history. 'Knocking on wood' dates back to pagan rituals that were designed to elicit the help of formidable tree gods. The number 13 is believed to be unlucky due to there being 13 people at Christ's Last Supper. When a ladder is propped up against a wall it forms a natural triangle, which used to be seen as a symbol of the Holy Trinity. To be brave enough to walk under the ladder would break the Trinity, and therefore bring bad luck.

As well as the perceived anxiety reduction and feeling of control that maintaining superstitious beliefs can enable, many believe that superstitions can bring about good luck and good fortune. For many, this is the main drive in maintaining superstitious acts: good luck is essentially success or failure apparently brought by chance rather than through one's own actions.

After working with hundreds of exceptionally lucky, and unlucky, people over a 10-year period, Professor Richard Wiseman identified four principles for achieving good fortune in your life. He documented his work in his ground-breaking book *The Luck Factor*. He believes that to improve your chance of luck and good fortune, four simple principles need to be observed. These are:

1. *Maximise chance opportunities.* Lucky people are skilled at creating, noticing and acting upon chance opportunities. They do this in various ways, including networking, adopting a relaxed attitude to life and being open to new experiences.

2. *Listen to lucky hunches.* Lucky people make effective decisions by observing their intuition and gut feelings. In addition, they take steps to actively boost their intuitive abilities by, for example, meditating regularly.

3. *Expect good fortune.* Lucky people have a more positive outlook. They hold a belief that the future is going to be full of good fortune. These expectations become self-fulfilling prophecies as they help lucky people persist in the face of adversity. These beliefs also shape their interactions with others in a more positive way.

4. *Turn bad luck to good.* Lucky people tend to employ a variety of psychological techniques to cope with, and often even thrive upon, the ill fortune that comes their way. For example, they spontaneously imagine how things could have been worse, do not dwell on ill fortune and take control of the situation.

The last principle, in essence, refers to resilience and what is viewed as a 'sense of coherence'. A sense of coherence refers to a person's ability to use existing and potential resources to combat stress and promote health. More about this in the next chapter.

According to the American Psychological Association, many people are outwardly aware that their superstitious rituals or beliefs are disconnected from reality. However, that doesn't mean that they're ready to let go of them. One study in 2016 strongly suggests that superstitions are powerful intuitions that our brains don't want to correct – belief systems we feel we need to hold on to, if you will. While the logical part of us may know that our superstitious behaviours have no actual effect on outcomes, holding on to them is a way of 'playing it safe'.

Often, one may consider a positive outcome to an event as a result of good luck, resulting from maintaining a particular superstitious ritual or carrying some type of lucky charm. Rarely do we consider that the outcome to an event is more likely down to the heuristic known as the law of parsimony, otherwise known as Occam's razor. According to Occam's razor, if you can have an adequate explanation without assuming some mysterious intervention (such as the hand of fate or devil cats), then don't assume that the mysterious intervention exists. In other words, a team may have been victorious because they played particularly well rather than because of the particular jersey a fan wore. Or one hopeful individual may have got a job because they were perfectly suited to the position, rather than the lucky necklace they wore.

Sometimes partaking in more religious or superstitious beliefs can be down to being unaware of the particular origin of the superstition or the origin of a word. For example, the original meaning of the commonly used word 'enthusiasm', translates as 'possessed by God's essence'. The origin of the superstition around breaking a mirror is believed to come from Ancient Greece where it was common for people to consult 'mirror seers', who told their fortunes by analysing their reflections. This was called catoptromancy. The mirror was dipped into water and a sick individual was asked to gaze into the glass. If his image appeared distorted, then they were very likely to die; if clear, then they would live.

Intriguingly researchers estimate that at least 10% of the US population experience some anxiety around of the number 13, and the specific fear around Friday the 13th, known as 'paraskevidekatriaphobia'. These fears result in financial losses in excess of $800 million annually, as people avoid marrying, travelling or, in the most severe cases, even working on this feared day.

Not surprisingly, however, Friday the 13th doesn't have the same macabre connotations everywhere. In Spanish-speaking countries, it's Tuesday the 13th that's unlucky, and in Italy it's Friday the 17th, because there the number 13 is considered lucky. 'To do 13' in Italian (*fare tredici*) is to hit the jackpot. However, due to Americanisation, young people in Italy consider Friday the 13th unlucky as well.

In one interesting study, 13% of people surveyed indicated that staying on the 13th floor of a hotel would bother them, and 9% said they would ask for a different room. On top of this, some airlines such as Air France and Lufthansa do not have a 13th row. Lufthansa also has no 17th row because, as mentioned above, in some countries – such as Italy and Brazil – the typical unlucky number is 17 and not 13.

The superstitious beliefs that surround the number 13 can thrive on confirmation bias. Once you have a belief and your mind is set on this idea, it can be hard to challenge that belief. It's made even harder because subconsciously we look for evidence and memories that support the beliefs rather than those that refute them: days where bad things happen are just unfortunate but, if something were to happen on the 13th day, it would be entirely down to the unlucky number. Individuals with particularly strong superstitious beliefs would most likely claim that if it weren't for the association with 13 the bad thing wouldn't have happened at all. However, considering what we have discussed previously regarding luck, is it possible that we are more likely to have bad luck or misfortune if we are anticipating that it may occur?

POKER FACE

Before we close this chapter, lets briefly return again to luck, and in particular the idea of attending to our 'lucky hunches' – sometimes thought of as intuition or a feeling in our gut about something. In a fascinating study examining the role emotions can play in our decision making, named the Iowa Gambling Task, researchers Damasio et al. presented participants with four decks of cards and instructed them to choose a card from any of the decks. Each time they chose a card they would either win or lose some money based on what card was drawn. The 'trick' to the task, unknown to the participants, was that two of the decks had small rewards and penalties but, over the long term, led to a gain of money, whereas the other two decks had large rewards but

References

also large penalties, and over the long term led to a net loss. Remarkably perhaps, participants ended up exclusively selecting cards from the money-winning decks, usually within 40 or 50 trials.

Damasio argues that our decisions are guided by what he refers to as 'somatic markers' – essentially feelings in the body that are associated with emotions. Examples include the association of rapid heartbeat with anxiety or nausea with disgust, even before participants are consciously aware of which decks are 'good' or 'bad'.

While people played, their palms were connected to a galvanic skin response machine (GSR), similar to a polygraph. The GSR was able to detect tiny changes in the electrical conductance of the skin, a type of micro sweating. The responses it showed reflected the flickers of emotion that the participants were not consciously aware of. During the task, players were also interrupted occasionally and asked to say what they thought was going on.

During the experiment, subjects soon reached a hunch stage. According to Dr Damasio, participants said things such as, 'I don't know what's going on here, but there may be some kind of hidden rule or spacing of cards'. He found that, after turning about 50 cards, most of the participants reached the conclusion that two decks were good and two were bad.

But their actions anticipated the conclusions that they voiced later. At the hunch stage, normal players were already making more selections from the good decks than from the bad decks, and their bodies reflected some of the unconscious perceptions. Early in the game, every time they reached for a card in a 'bad deck', their palms sweated, as if they already expected excess punishment from the bad decks. 'They are playing advantageously before they know what is happening', Dr Damasio added.

The findings of the Iowa Gambling Task suggest that the emotional system, essentially feelings in the body that are associated with emotions, guided participants towards the money-winning decks even before they were consciously aware of it. These gut feelings may act subconsciously, steering us towards advantageous options even in the absence of a conscious understanding of the benefits or consequences of a choice. Perhaps then we should listen to our intuition or gut feelings even more, and permit our subconscious to do its job – a job that it has done amazingly for thousands of years, keeping us alive and safe from harm.

When it comes to some of the more magical mystical beliefs we may have, Isaac Asimov perhaps sums it up best when he states, 'Humanity has the stars in its future, and that future is too important to be lost under the burden of juvenile folly and ignorant superstition'.

As a final word on the subject, perhaps the best summing up of superstitions comes from a joke my friend Big Dave often regales people with. He states, 'I don't believe in star signs … but that's a typical Gemini!'

SUMMARY

This chapter looked at the behaviours we adopt that we think are written in the stars, or perhaps lead us to think we will be luckier. Originally looked at by Skinner in pigeons, it was found that animals, as well as people, will adopt specific behaviours if they think it will bring them closer to their desired outcome – in Skinner's experiment, food. This was also observed in the Cargo Cult in World War II. The chapter also asked us if we see ourselves as superstitious. If you answered yes, you are not alone. In fact, you are among a massive 77% of Britons. Whether you cross your fingers, touch wood or wear lucky pants, your superstition can be a result of your culture or your experiences. It may also be down to the level of control you wish to have over your life and the things that happen to you. Whether or not these behaviours actually help us to bring good luck, or in fact avoid bad luck, is yet to be seen. However, many believers will conclude that they are helpful to them purely because of confirmation bias and the illusion of control.

References

CHAPTER TWENTY-FOUR

CONTROL AND RESILIENCE

For many years now I have often called on my favourite quote by inspirational author Napoleon Hill when faced with a challenge in my own life, or similarly when a friend or client is experiencing a challenge in their life. To date I have found its sage wisdom to be powerfully true. The quote declares the following:

> *Every adversity, every failure, every heartache carries with it the seed of an equal or greater benefit.*

If you hold onto this belief, no matter what challenges you will face in life, I assure you at some stage in the future (near or distant) whatever adversity you are facing will indeed carry with it the seed of something that is of the equivalent or greater benefit. In many ways there is something quite powerful in this belief. For me it is resonant of the extremely powerful book by Holocaust survivor and psychotherapist Viktor Frankl *Man's Search for Meaning* (1946) – not that I am asserting in any way that the adversities any of us will face are comparable with what Dr Frankl experienced in Auschwitz and the other concentration camps he was interned in.

When asked about those who survived the horrific experiences of the Nazi extermination camps, Dr Frankl observed that many of the prisoners who survived the horrific experiences had a purpose bigger than themselves. He noted the following, 'He who has a why can bear any how'. Frankl witnessed that the prisoners who survived found a way to endure. He believed that excruciating endurance was made possible because they always had a greater purpose, and it was that purpose that carried them onwards through the most nightmarish of conditions. For some it was a child who was sheltered away in some distant country and who was waiting for them upon liberation. For others it was a spouse or family member. For others it was an unfinished task or creative work that required their unique contribution.

Dr Frankl went on to write, 'The prisoner who had lost faith in the future – his future – was doomed. With his loss of belief in the future he also lost his spiritual hold; he let himself decline and become subject to mental and physical decay.' Whilst working in a camp hospital, Frankl noticed the death rate spiked in the week between Christmas and New Year's in 1944. He credited the dramatic increase to the number of prisoners who had been optimistically holding out hope for liberation before Christmas. As the end of the year drew closer, and it became clear that their situation was unchanged, they lost courage and hope. This in turn impacted their power of defiance and their previously unwavering ability to survive.

Whilst hopefully none of us will ever experience anything remotely close to what Dr Frankl endured during his time in the concentration camps, it's still good practice to try and foster a resilient thinking style. Resilience is not just about 'bouncing back' from a major life challenge. Resilience is more about learning to effectively manage the daily stressors of life, such as a difficult day at work, a tough conversation with a friend, or a failure or setback with your career. Resilience is about the ability to capitalise on opportunity – to take calculated risks because we are not afraid of failure. Only then, can we truly flourish, be the best version of ourselves and reach our potential.

WHEN THE GOING GETS TOUGH, THE TOUGH GET GOING

In Lucy Hone's brilliant 2020 TED Talk she identifies what she calls the 'three secrets of resilient people'. Lucy, the director of the New Zealand Institute of Wellbeing & Resilience, states that without exception we will all face some adversity in our life, regardless of who we are. As she puts it, 'Adversity doesn't discriminate'. Indeed, if you are alive today, then without doubt you will have to deal with some tough times in your life. In recent times, never more so than with the 2020 Covid-19 lockdown.

Lucy shares the following three areas that she believes people can use to become more resilient. First, she believes that resilient people accept that 'shit' happens to us all – to the extent that we must accept that suffering is part of all of our lives. The obvious benefit of adopting this stance is that it stops resilient people from feeling discriminated against. As Hone states, 'We seem to live in an age where we're entitled to a perfect life, where shiny, happy photos on Instagram are the norm, when actually, the very opposite is true'. In psychological terms this approach is very much about benefit finding. Indeed, it is the antithesis of what Ross's character from the TV series *Friends* once declared when he cried, 'Why do bad things happen to good people?!'

Second, resilient people are particularly good at choosing where they place their attention. 'They typically manage to focus on the things that they can change, and somehow accept the things that they can't', Hone says. As we have discussed previously in this book, we are hardwired to focus on the negative in order to protect us from danger. In simple terms the fact that we are alive today is solely down to the fact that our hunter-gatherer ancestors focused on what potential threat there might be as opposed to how breath-taking the sunset is. Hone states that we now live in an era where we are continually bombarded by threats all day long, 'and our poor brains treat every single one of those threats as though they were a tiger'. Hone goes on to say that 'Our stress response is permanently dialled up', and that resilient people don't diminish the negative, but they have also figured out how to tune in the good.

Third, resilient people ask themselves the following key question: 'Is what I'm doing helping or harming me?' According to Hone this act alone has the most significant impact on an individual who has experienced some form of challenge in their life. Hone states that whether you're ruminating over the past, or scrolling through social media, ask yourself whether what you're doing – the way you're thinking, and the way you're acting – is helping or harming you. Doing so very much puts you back in the driving seat and feeling more in control of the decisions you are making.

SOMETHING INSIDE SO STRONG

In 1954, psychologist Julian Rotter suggested the concept of what he calls a locus of control. A locus of control is a construct that is said to be part of our personality. Imagine a straight line, at one end of which is what is called a strong external locus of control and at the other end what has come to be known as a strong internal locus of control.

The basic concept behind a locus of control is that it is a way of describing the extent to which an individual feels that they are in control of what happens to them in their life and, in addition, the extent to which they, as an individual, can affect their own life.

If a person has an internal locus of control, usually that person attributes success to his or her own efforts and abilities. A person who expects to succeed will be more motivated, more persistent and more likely to learn. A person with an external locus of control will most likely attribute his or her success to fate, luck or chance, and will be less likely to make the effort needed to learn. People with an external locus of control are also more likely to experience anxiety and depression in their lives, since they can often hold the belief that they are not in control of life events. Having a strong internal locus of control describes someone who believes they are in control of what happens to them in their life.

As an example, picture a student taking a driving test. Sadly, the student fails the test on this occasion. Now the student may say that it is because they just didn't practise their driving skills enough and hadn't spent enough time learning the Highway Code. This individual would be viewed as having an internal locus of control because they see themselves as to blame for the examination failure. Conversely, an individual could say that they had failed due to poor driving conditions, or another driver on the road. Similarly, they could blame it on an unfair instructor. Someone with this perspective on the test would be seen as possessing an external locus of control.

When you are dealing with a challenge in your life, do you feel that you have control over the outcome, or do you believe that you are at the mercy of outside forces? In one fascinating study that looked at the potential health effects of the locus of control, researchers discovered that of more than 7500 British adults followed since birth, those who had shown the traits of an internal locus of control at the age of 10 were less likely to be overweight at age 30. Similarly, they were less likely to describe their health as poor or show high levels of psychological stress. The possible explanation for these findings was that children with a more internal locus of control behave more healthily as adults because they have greater confidence in their ability to influence outcomes through their own actions. Similarly, it appears they are far more likely to have higher self-esteem and self-efficacy.

Oher studies into the locus of control include Garber (1980), who concluded that indicators of good psychological well-being come from participants reporting lower cases of stress and depression, linking this to a high internal locus of control. Grob (2000) also reported that having an external locus of control is often linked to stress and feeling powerless in a given situation. According to Emmons and Diener (1989), individuals who are low in self-esteem are more likely to believe outcomes are not under their own influence and control. Indeed, our locus of control can influence not only how we respond to the events that happen in our lives, but also how motivated we are to take action to bring about a potential change in the outcome. If you believe that you hold the keys to your fate, you are more likely to take action to change your situation when needed. If on the other hand, you believe that the outcome is out of your hands, that it perhaps is predetermined, you may be less likely to work towards change.

It is important to note that a locus of control is a continuum. No one has a 100% external or internal locus of control. Instead, most people lie somewhere on the continuum between the two extremes. Indeed, we can have a very strong internal locus in one area of our life but be very external in another.

These are the characteristics of people with a dominant internal or external locus of control.

Individuals with a strong internal locus of control:

- are far more likely to take responsibility for their own actions;
- tend to be less influenced by the opinions of others;
- can often do better at tasks when they are allowed to work at their own pace;
- usually have a strong sense of self-efficacy;
- tend to work hard to achieve the things they want;
- feel confident when faced with a new challenge;
- tend to be physically healthier;
- report being happier and more independent;
- tend to experience less depression and anxiety;
- often succeed in the workplace.

Individuals with a strong external locus of control:

- tend to blame outside forces for their circumstances;
- often credit luck or chance for any successes;
- don't believe that they can change their situation through their own efforts;
- frequently feel hopeless or powerless in the face of difficult situations;
- are more prone to experiencing learned helplessness;
- tend to be more negative and give up easily on tasks;
- feels victimised by illness and stress.

LOSS OF CONTROL

Often in life we believe that we have more control over certain events than we actually do: what psychologist now refer to as the illusion of control. 'The illusion of control' was first coined by Harvard psychologist Ellen Langer. Langer conducted a series of experiments to see where and when this bias would appear. In each experiment, participants had to take part in some sort of game that was governed by chance, including cutting cards and entering a lottery. What Langer discovered was that people's confidence in their chances of winning was influenced by a host of different factors, none of which actually had anything to do with their chances of winning.

The Illusion of control is essentially a cognitive bias where we believe we can control or at least influence outcomes that we demonstrably have no influence over. Langer discovered for example that gamblers often believe they can control chance events. She showed that people think they have more control over the outcome of a dice game if they throw the dice themselves, as opposed to someone else taking the throw. Langer refers to this illusion that the participant has more perceived control than they actually have as 'skill cues'. These 'skill cues' are properties more normally associated with the exercise of skill, in particular the exercise of choice, competition, familiarity with the stimulus and involvement in decisions. Similarly, people greatly prefer to choose the numbers for a lottery ticket themselves rather than have someone else choose the 'lucky' numbers. This thinking can lead us to pin our hopes on superstition and magical thinking, when the reality is that these things aren't going to change our situation.

In another study carried out by Langer, participants cut cards against a competitor, the winner being the participant with the highest card. In one study the competitor dressed poorly and appeared nervous; in the other condition, the competitor dressed rather smartly and looked relaxed and confident. Even though the appearance of the competitor has no obvious influence on the outcome of the game, participants staked more money when playing against the more poorly outfitted and more nervous competitor than when playing against the more composed challenger.

Any time we are encouraged to feel like we have more control over an event than we actually do, we're at risk of making bad decisions. This thinking can contribute to a number of potentially harmful behaviours; for example, individuals who frequently gamble even after they have lost large amounts of money. Often they have the underlying false belief that on some level they have special skills or knowledge that will help them eventually win big, and that big win is just around the corner.

Research also shows that depressed individuals are less susceptible to the illusion of control than non-depressed individuals – the rationale perhaps being that the depressed have a clear, unmuddied mind enabling them to make a 'good' decision where the outcome could mean a win or a loss. As we have discussed previously, we all have a considerable aversion to loss. In one such study researchers informed participants that pressing a button may, or may not, turn on a green light. In reality however the light turning on was prearranged – the button pressing actually having no effect. The surprising results of the study showed that non-depressed individuals thought they were more responsible for the light turning on than depressed individuals, especially when their actions brought about desired outcomes, for example gaining $0.25 as opposed to losing $0.25.

Of course, we like to think of ourselves as rational decision makers, carefully making choices based on logic and the data at hand. The illusion of control is one of many cognitive biases that throw a wrench into this idea. Understandably, every day, we aim to control our lives. The greater our internal locus of control, the more we believe and feel we have control in our lives. Perhaps unsurprisingly, the more we have a desire for control, the more we feel somewhat out of control in our lives. Oftentimes individuals who are constantly looking to exert control over every aspect of their life, what we can sometimes refer to as a 'control freak', can feel very much out of control. The control freak has the distorted belief that having a hypervigilant and 'constantly on' attention to control will enable them to feel very much in control. Sadly, the opposite is more often than not the undesired outcome of this concentrated effort.

We try to avoid poor decisions and aim to make positive things happen for ourselves and others. While we know that we can never fully control what happens to us, we understandably feel safer when we believe we can. We feel safer when we believe that the choices and decisions we make are fully ours and not someone else's. The illusion of control is that very belief that we can influence outcomes that are, in fact, beyond our ability to control.

A number of our daily behaviours, especially those involving superstitions, are motivated by the illusion of control. We keep lucky trinkets, perform ritualistic ceremonies and maintain traditions because we believe these things will give us more control over random events. Equally, we believe that not doing then may bring about an unfortunate turn in our luck. More often than not, these behaviours are harmless. However, when they do lead to harm, such as is the case with gambling, it may be time to look for a way to get comfortable with our lack of control.

At times like this it may be better to focus on what psychologist Albert Bandura describes as self-efficacy. Self-efficacy is not self-image, self-worth or any other similar construct. Although it is often assigned the same meaning as these, along with confidence, self-esteem or optimism, it is slightly different to these related concepts. Self-efficacy is the belief we have in our own abilities – specifically our ability to meet the challenges ahead of us and complete a task successfully. In simple terms self-efficacy is the belief that you can succeed in a specific area of your life, and a locus of control is how much control you feel that you have over a situation.

SUMMARY

Chapter 24 looked into the true definition of what it is to be resilient; more than bouncing back from a tough time, it is the ability to take hardships and find opportunities from them. It is about taking risks, without the fear of failure holding us back. There are three main suggestions for how we can become more resilient: accepting suffering as part of everyone's lives, choosing to focus on things we can change rather than those that we can't and asking ourselves frequently whether what we're doing is helping or harming us. The chapter then explained the concept of a locus of control – meaning to what extent you view yourself to be in control of your life, and what you believe is down to other external factors.

CHAPTER TWENTY-FIVE

IF ONLY BANANAS WERE LONGER!

Reject your sense of injury and the injury itself disappears.
– MARCUS AURELIUS, MEDITATIONS

In the brilliant children's book *Alexander and the Terrible, Horrible, No Good, Very Bad Day* by Judith Viorst, young Alex has a day where just about everything goes wrong for him – to the extent that he wants to move to Australia, as he believes nothing bad ever happens there. At the end of the day, his mum reassures him that some days are just like that, even in Australia! Of course, what Alex doesn't think about on his 'very bad day' is the fact that he lives in a nice home, with nice caring parents, has food to eat, friends to play with and a nice bed to sleep in at night. The book is very much about what psychologists' term 'black-and-white thinking'. For Alex, everything is just bad; there is no perceived shade of grey in his 'black' day. From getting out of bed in the morning on his bad day, Alex 'knew' everything would go wrong for him. Even if something did go his way, he would probably have followed it up with phrases such as 'Well, it won't last', and 'About time I had some flipping luck go my way!' We all know someone just like Alex, and maybe that someone is us sometimes.

In this section, we are going to consider the possible negative effects of this 'black-and-white' thinking style as well as, and perhaps more importantly, how it can easily become magnified and influence its bedfellow – catastrophic thinking. Consider for a moment if you have ever used any of the following phrases, or know someone who regularly does:

- My head is killing me!
- The traffic was a nightmare!
- I'm absolutely starving!
- I've told you a hundred times!
- What a nightmare!
- It was absolutely horrific!
- I'm dreading the meeting!
- My life is over!
- I could have been killed!
- You could have broken my neck!
- The weather at the weekend is going to be absolutely horrific!
- It's the end of the world!
- That's disgusting!
- Oh, what a day it's been!

Or do you ever use words such as terrible, awful, atrocious, appalling, fiasco, hate, disastrous, horrible, horrendous or revolting? Get the idea?

Do you sometimes consider the worst-case scenario first? Do you tend always to blow things out of proportion? Do you sometimes react in an over-the-top and dramatic way? Similarly, do you sometimes find that you can have extremes of emotions in seconds? Do you perceive things as terrible or awful? And can you sometimes be accused of making a mountain out of a mole hill?

When it comes to relaying a story do you sometimes embellish or colour it? Do you make an experience more dramatic than it actually was? Do you on occasions overelaborate something for dramatic effect?

The Oxford English Dictionary's definition of catastrophise is to 'view or present a situation as considerably worse than it actually is'. Essentially, catastrophic thinking is when we react to a small incident as if it is a major incident. People who catastrophise tend to emotionally magnify, exaggerate or blow out of proportion a perceived threat or concern. They can frequently use very strong and exaggerated language.

Many of us are prone to catastrophising at times, but continually using catastrophic language and having catastrophic thoughts can lead to an individual quickly losing perspective in many situations. Whilst for a catastrophiser, catastrophic language can sometimes feel like it is relieving stress and anxiety, sadly the opposite can be the case. Many times, this unhelpful thinking system can be the foundation of 'black-and-white' thinking – a tendency to think in extremes. Though it's normal from time to time to use catastrophic language, developing a continuing habit of dichotomous language and thinking can interfere with an individual's health, relationships and career. Being hypervigilant to any perceived threat – real or imagined – can be exhausting, as the sympathetic nervous system is constantly on high alert to this perceived danger. This unhelpful thinking system can also be associated with anxiety and depression.

Our brains are hardwired to pay more consideration to the negative than the positive. It makes sense from an evolutionary standpoint. You and I are here today because our hunter-gatherer ancestors paid more attention to the possibility of a sabre-toothed cat lurking in the undergrowth than the pretty flower on the side of the path. Our minds favour the negative because it keeps us safe. Faced with the unknown, it's safer to assume the worse than to hope for the best. In our modern world though, rarely, if ever, do we need to be this hypervigilant to danger.

TRAGEDY

Research has shown that acting and using language in a catastrophic way can negatively affect psychological and physical well-being. This is because when we think, react and speak in a catastrophic manner, our body reacts as if the situation or event has actually happened, causing unnecessary anxiety and stress. One of the effects of catastrophising is that it can lead to a style of thinking known as 'cognitive distortion'. In simple terms, our mind convinces us of something that isn't actually true but feels true. In simple terms our minds don't know the difference between something that is real and something that is imagined. A person who catastrophises also often ruminates about an unfavourable outcome to an event – the rationale being that if such an unfortunate event does occur, then the results will be a disaster. This hypervigilance to perceived danger can force the catastrophiser into a continual state of flight or fight. Of course, catastrophic thinking bears little resemblance to reality, but it can have a real effect on the catastrophic thinker's life. When we catastrophise, we take a potentially small problem and build it into a disaster of epic proportions. That kind of sustained thinking is incredibly toxic to your emotional climate. In many ways catastrophic thinking can be thought of as the arch-rival of resilience.

It's perhaps worth reminding ourselves of something we examined earlier in this book – that our modern brains are energy hogs. Whilst the human brain accounts for just 2% of our body weight, the average adult brain, even in resting state, consumes about 20% of our body's energy. If we assume an average resting metabolic rate of 1300 calories per day, then the brain consumes 260 of those calories just to keep things in order. That's 10.8 calories every hour or 0.18 calories each minute. Perhaps unsurprisingly then, during acute mental stress, the energy supply to the human brain increases by 12%. Experiencing stress can cause a chain reaction. When we experience a stressful event, the amygdala – an area of the brain that contributes to emotional processing – sends a distress signal to the hypothalamus. This area of the brain functions like a command centre, communicating with the rest of the body through the nervous system so that the individual has the energy to fight or flee from the perceived threat.

This 'fight or flight' response is responsible for the apparent physical reactions most people associate with stress. These reactions include increased heart rate, heightened senses, a deeper intake of oxygen and the rush of adrenaline. Finally, a hormone called cortisol is released, which helps restore the energy lost in the response. When the stressful event is over, cortisol levels fall, and the body returns to stasis. But these continued fight or flight reactions can have an effect on the individual over time. The side effects can include memory loss, sleep problems, fatigue, weight gain, a weakened immune system and a greater risk of mental illness.

The waste of energy associated with being anxious about what the future holds is summed up beautifully by author and Anglican priest William Ralph Inge when he writes, 'Worry is interest paid on trouble before it comes due'. In other words, spending time, effort and energy worrying about and imagining potential disasters that may never occur robs us of the joy of the present moment and borrows with interest from your future. Inge was known as the 'Gloomy Dean' for his pessimistic views, so he seemed to know a lot about how not to think – not something you want on your epitaph.

Of course, reducing your stress levels can be a challenge. Around 25% of Americans state that they deal with high levels of stress daily, and another 50% say their stress is moderate. But learning to manage your thinking and minimising the effects of catastrophic and black-and-white thinking can have a profound effect on reducing your stress response.

Use the Alfred Technique to be mindful of your internal language and begin to notice how often your thoughts and your external language are potentially catastrophic in nature. Using catastrophic language continually can result in reinforced limiting beliefs. For example, 'If I fail this test, I will be a total failure in life', or 'Just my luck, I knew I wouldn't be able to do it – I make a mess of everything I touch'.

Also, use the Alfred Technique to start to observe when you are having repeated catastrophic thoughts, and how much worry, stress or anxiety these are causing you.

Begin to recognise that you're not your best when under stress. Challenge the beliefs you have around your thoughts and make a plan to shift to a more positive and more grounded emotion. Use this book to break your thought patterns, and to halt, even momentarily, any obsessive or ruminating thoughts.

References

I highly recommend the Wim Hof breathing technique if you are at any time feeling anxious. Alternatively try the following traffic light breathing technique:

1. Take a big diaphragmatic breath in and count 1. Think red. Release it.
2. Take another big diaphragmatic breath in and count 2. Think amber. Release it.
3. Again, take a big diaphragmatic breath in and count 3. Think green. Release it.
4. On the exhale, completely let go of thinking anything for a moment. Release it.
5. Repeat as many times as you need until you think just green for all three breaths.

Finally, address the problem once your thinking is clearer. Focus on the areas where you do have control. Indeed, take time to remind yourself how much control you actually do have in your life. Remember doing something like taking a shower, exercising or going for a walk can allow your subconscious to find a solution to a problem. Indeed, you may surprise yourself with a novel, creative solution.

For additional help, take time to look at the 'Army Resilience Directorate' – a programme established to help people cope with adversity, adapt to change and overcome challenges. The programme can help turn catastrophic thinking into purposeful action.

HERE COMES THE RAIN AGAIN

When it comes to catastrophising, here's the rub according to psychoanalyst Donald Winnicott: 'The catastrophe you fear will happen has already happened'. Winnicott also went on to state that the catastrophe has also been forgotten, and that is what is making us so full of worry and anxiety. To move forward in our lives, we need to remember the catastrophe and locate it where it really belongs: safely but also poignantly and tragically in the past. But how do we do this? Particularly if we have no conscious memory of the originating experience or experiences, i.e. if that traumatic experience is repressed and therefore veiled from our conscious awareness. In psychological terms, what we think of as repressed experience occurs when a thought, memory, feeling or even dream is too painful for an individual to process effectively. So the unconscious pushes the experience out of our consciousness, and we can become unaware of its existence, with our only awareness occurring when we begin to feel anxious or uncomfortable when undertaking an activity that would otherwise create little or no emotion in the vast majority of the population. For example, if you feel uncomfortable in a lift or when flying, the origin could be in an experience where you perceived you felt out of control.

Over the years, I have taken hundreds of clients through a particular type of psychotherapy known as hypnoanalysis. Hypnoanalysis is similar in structure to traditional psychoanalysis, the main difference being it is significantly shorter than tradition psychoanalysis, which can often proceed for years. The other difference is it uses a light state of hypnosis to allow the client to be relaxed and allow bottled-up emotions to be resolved, safely and effectively. For me, it is the best therapy I have come across during my years as a therapist for resolving unconscious anxieties – those anxieties that, more often than not, are rooted in childhood traumas.

I choose to think of experiences in our lives that have troubled us as being like bubbles. The size of the bubble is dependent on the magnitude of how a particular experience has impacted us. For example, a young child being told by their father that they are the reason for their parents' divorce would for most children be a highly charged, emotional and stressful experience. The effect of this could follow the child throughout their life, with the guilt of the experience perhaps even creating problems in their future relationships. If, however, their father was an alcoholic and abusive to their mother, then it may be the case that they actually wished for and wanted their father to leave, so, whilst there will be some obvious emotion here the type, and level, of emotion experienced may be quite different. The personality type of the child can also have a considerable bearing on how the experience is processed by the child. As the Roman Stoic philosopher Seneca stated, 'It does not matter what you bear, but how you bear it'.

Imagine, for a moment, holding an empty glass out in front of you. You could perhaps hold it for a fairly significant period of time – assuming you have that much free time for such a mundane task! If you then poured a small amount of water into the glass, would that then reduce the duration of time for which you could hold that glass? What about if that glass were full to the brim – how long would your arm manage to hold it in front of you then? Much less time than if it were empty I would bet. The analogy I am making here is to liken our bottled-up emotions to that glass. As the days go by, we are still holding the glass. Perhaps we find tricks and techniques to make the holding of it easier and less uncomfortable and unpleasant, but it is not until we finally drink from it that we finally feel at ease. Only then can we look back in the rear-view mirror of life and realise how heavy was the burden of the 'bottled-up' emotion that we carried for so long. It is perhaps of no great surprise that hypnoanalysis clients actually describe feeling lighter, as if some invisible weight has been lifted from them post-therapy.

FIX YOU

So, what exactly is a childhood trauma? Childhood trauma can occur when a child witnesses or experiences an overwhelming negative experience, such as abuse, neglect or violence. These types of traumas are more commonly known as interpersonal trauma. Children can also experience traumatic events such as accidents, natural disasters, war and civil unrest or medical procedures. Trauma can also occur with the death of a loved one or caregiver. Something thought of as a relatively small and insignificant event in a child's life can have an effect on how they grow up. Again, it's not the size of the event, but how it is interpreted and processed that can create an issue for the developing child. Let's consider for a moment an experience from my own childhood.

When I was at primary school, every morning for a 2-week period we were taken on a trip to our city's main swimming baths, the intention being that we learn to swim in this 2-week period. I can still remember now standing in the cold pool with our floats being asked to take turns swimming from one end to the other. I had never been swimming before so, like many others in my class, I wasn't particularly good at it. Not a nice experience by any stretch of the imagination, but not enough to cause any significant distress.

When we were instructed to leave the cold pool and head for the changing rooms, which were a similar temperature to the inside of a fridge, this is where the stress started to mount for the young me. We all went to changing rooms to get into our school uniform for our return to school. Our teacher yelled at us to get dried and dressed as soon as we could, as the fume-expelling bus was waiting to take us back to school. At this stage, most children would be feeling some anxiety as the clock was ticking, but what happened to me caused my young mind to feel tremendous pressure. The water had made the tie on my swimming trunks seemingly impossible to undo – I just could not get the two strings apart to be able to get my underpants and trousers on. No matter how hard I tried, the trunks would not come off! The teacher called out to the whole class repeatedly, telling us not to miss the bus. As time was not on my side, I was left with no alternative but to put my trousers on over my wet trunks. Annoyingly, drip-dry swimwear had not been invented yet, so my trunks felt like they had absorbed at least 10% of the water in the swimming pool. I managed to get on the bus but sat there in discomfort for what seemed like hours, even though the journey back to school was just a jaunty 20 minutes or so. The rest of a day is somewhat blurred from my memory, but I do remember the continued discomfort of the school day. If only the trip to the pool had been in the late afternoon! Upsettingly, my trousers remained wet until I was able to squelch my way home at the end of the school day.

Now, as an adult, if a similar experience had happened to you, you would feel annoyed and uncomfortable. You would probably also laugh about it to your friends down the pub, and they would call you names such as Aquaman, Soggyslacks or similar out of friendly banter. You would put it down as a bad day and make a promise to yourself to buy better-quality swimwear in the future. But, as a child, you can feel quite powerless. You couldn't ask the average 1970s PE teacher for help, as many of them had comparable levels of compassion for children as a Japanese officer held towards a POW. Similarly, you couldn't run home to your mum or dad. You just had to tolerate the discomfort and hope Mum had made you a nice tea for when you eventually got home. Basically, as an adult it wouldn't be a pleasant experience, but as a child it was traumatic. Do I remember any of the other trips to the city centre baths? No, I don't – the reason being that there was no significant emotion attached to them. Had something worse happened on another trip, such as nearly drowning, or a fall from the diving board, then chances are this would be stored in my memory.

Think now of your own childhood and the millions of memories and experiences you have had. Interestingly, scientists now believe that the human brain can store 1 petabyte[1] of memory – 10 times more than was originally believed. To put this in perspective, 1 petabyte is the same as 20 million four-drawer filing cabinets filled with text, or 13.3 years of HD-TV recordings. Or, seen another way, it's a whopping 4.7 billion books or 670 million web pages.

The likelihood is that you are only able to bring to mind the experiences with some significant emotion attached to them. For example, you probably remember your first day at school, but chances are not the second or third day. You probably can recall your first kiss, but not your fifth soggy smacker. Similarly, out of the hundreds of school assemblies you would have experienced in your life, you can most likely only recall the school assembly where either yourself or someone else wet themselves or had a similar embarrassing experience. If the level of emotion that is attached to that experience is overly significant and disturbing to the young, developing mind, then we tend to bottle up that experience. We can sometimes recall the experience but not the intense emotion of it, or we completely repress the experience altogether to the extent that we have no conscious awareness of it. It is as if it has been wiped from our memory. But of course, that is not the case – it's just hidden from us.

Often, we then tend to avoid situations that either consciously or subconsciously remind us of those uncomfortable experiences – refusing to go anywhere near those untouchable areas of anxiety. As psychotherapist Carl Jung states, 'That which you most need will be found where you least want to look'. But whenever we avoid these emotions, there can be a price to pay. Again, as Donald Winnicott brilliantly points out, 'The catastrophe you fear will happen has already happened'. In my case, whenever I felt pressured to be on time for something or was getting hurried, such as visiting the toilet before the start of a theatre show, I would feel a wave of anxiety come over me. It would feel like my whole body began to heat up. It was an unpleasant, unwelcome feeling. Of course, I never knew why I felt like that. It was just me; it was who I was. It felt like it was something outside of my control.

Do I have that feeling anymore? Well, that answer is fortunately a resounding no. As therapists, we have to be taken through hypnoanalysis ourselves by other, more experienced hypnoanalysts. I never gave this experience much thought when it came up in therapy – it was just a slightly uncomfortable memory, nothing major. There were no tears. But what I did notice was the feelings I used to have when pressured or rushed for something disappeared completely. Of course, the experience that (I assume) triggered this uncomfortable reaction was not a major experience, but because it occurred in my formative years, it did create some bottled-up emotion that produced an effect. The cause was anxiety about being put under pressure and the discomfort of the wet clothes. The effect was anxiety, which I felt I had no control over, every time I was put under pressure to meet a timed deadline – even if that deadline was visiting the toilet before a trip out. The whole reaction was unconscious, and I had no cognitive link when I experienced the anxiety to what I believe was the originating cause.

Initially it may seem strange that we might have forgotten the originating experience, but that's more often than not the pattern with trauma: it disappears from our conscious memory. It is too painful to be held in active consciousness, to be processed and verbalised, and it therefore gets pushed into the unnameable, unknown zones of the mind, where it can sometimes produce ongoing unconscious turmoil.

SHOOT THAT POISON ARROW

Spiritual traditions are big on parables. One of the most powerful comes from the *Sallatha Sutta* in the Buddhist traditional metaphor known as the second arrow.

> *When touched with a feeling of pain, the uninstructed*
> *run-of-the-mill person sorrows, grieves, and laments,*
> *beats his breast, becomes distraught. So, he feels two pains,*
> *physical and mental. Just as if they were to shoot a man with*
> *an arrow and, right afterward, were to shoot him with another*
> *one,*
> *so that he would feel the pains of two arrows.*
> – BUDDHA

The thought-provoking parable of the second arrow beautifully expresses how our reactions to events can, on occasion, brand the challenges we experience in our lives as being much more traumatic than perhaps they need to be. After telling the two-arrow parable, the Buddha said, 'In life, we cannot always control the first arrow. However, the second arrow is our reaction to the first. When shot by the arrow of physical pain, an unwise person makes matters worse by piling mental anguish on top of it, just as if he had been shot by two arrows. A wise person feels the sting of one arrow alone.'

It is true that our interpretation of events plays a large role in how we experience them. Let's say for example that you are driving to the shops and another car accidently pulls out in front of you. The driver waves to you in an apologetic manner, and you both drive on, slightly shaken, but otherwise fine. Driving perhaps with a bit more caution than before the altercation.

We could react in a number of ways to this unfortunate encounter. First, we could react with anger towards the other driver, perhaps in an over-the-top fashion, screaming profanities at them. We could choose to think that the driver who had pulled out was possibly, as many of us are, experiencing a lot of difficulty in their own life at present. Perhaps they have just lost their job, or perhaps they are caring for a sick parent or child, and as such were not giving the road their undivided attention. Indeed, we can all recall times in our own lives when we have unwittingly pulled out in front of another driver, knowing that the blame for this momentary lack of concentration rests entirely on our shoulders.

Perhaps also, this experience reminds us how we all make mistakes sometimes and that we should ourselves drive more carefully, in doing so perhaps avoiding a much more serious incident later that day.

We could also feel gratitude that we have the technology, financial capability and physical skills to be able to drive such incredible vehicles. If we had lived 100 years prior, we would either have been in a vehicle that was not as safe as what we drive nowadays, or, worse still, we could have been run over by a horse and cart, and that's more than enough to ruin anyone's shopping trip!

We could, however, decide to think that we are an idiot driver ourselves, giving over time to thinking thoughts such as, 'I knew I should've got up early and gone a different route. I'm such a loser for going shopping when I did. I knew it would be busy today.' We may also consider that we are always attracting misfortune, thinking, 'I'm so bloody clumsy. My life is one big accident waiting to happen!'

One thing we cannot be certain of is how the driver who first caused the potential collision reacts to the event (without pulling over and grilling them as to their interpretation of the event, which is not advisable, as they may react by calling the police!). Potentially, they could go through their day not giving any more thought to it. Alternatively, they could be beating themselves up with that painful, slower, second arrow by reminding themselves how stupid they are for driving so badly. They may even be reminding themselves how accident prone they are, and that they are so unlucky in life. Maybe even muttering to themselves, 'Just my luck I'd have an accident at the moment when I need it the least!'

In essence, the second arrow is about how we interpret events in our lives. More often than not the second arrows are underpinned by our belief systems and how we feel about ourselves on a day-to-day basis. They are very much entwined with our self-esteem. For example, if you have an argument with somebody at work, effectively, they shoot the first arrow. You could choose to reframe the experience and *not* ruminate about it long after the event has occurred, recapping it throughout the day with your internal 'self-talk', replaying it over and over and creating in your head a new alternative rebuttal to the other party.

In many ways, the lower our self-esteem is, the more likely we are to fire the second arrow at ourselves. Similarly, the more our limiting beliefs underpin who we believe we are, the more likely we are to shoot that second arrow based on what we think we deserve for ourselves.

Essentially, all the above, and many more permutations, are just different interpretations of the same somewhat unimportant event. It's how we see and interpret the world that really matters in the end. Those interpretations are seen through the filter of our belief systems. It is those very same belief systems that this book aims to change for the better, so that when we are hit with the first arrow, our first reaction is not to hit ourselves with the second, often more painful arrow.

We are all going to get hit with a few arrows over the course of our lives. Pain and suffering are sadly inevitable for all of us. But if we are mindful about it, we'll expend our vital energy getting back to a state of homeostasis as efficiently as possible.

BROKEN ARROW

Stop for a moment and think about this: what do you actually think about yourself?

Most of us have a shiny, confident exterior – the part of us that we show the world. But when you're alone with your thoughts, what do you say to yourself about who you really are? Does the 'real you' presented to the world reflect the authentic you? How would it feel if the world knew how you really felt about yourself? As a psychotherapist, I have often been astounded by how people really feel about themselves. Often, I would meet a new client and naively think, looking at their outward persona, they must have the world eating out of their hand. Outwardly, they seem to have it all: good looks, wealth, charm and generosity. However, rarely, if ever, does the exterior projection of the self match the internal beliefs.

In the philosophical words of psychotherapist and concentration camp survivor Viktor Frankl, 'A man who let himself decline because he could not see any future goal found himself occupied with retrospective thoughts. In a different connection, we have already spoken of the tendency there was to look into the past, to help make the present, with all its horrors, less real. But in robbing the present of its reality there lay a certain danger. It became easy to overlook the opportunities to make something positive of camp life, opportunities which really did exist.'

Finally, if you are ever unfortunate enough to meet someone who is unreasonably negative, and insists on complaining about just about everything, then you can terminate your conversation quite speedily with the words 'If only bananas were longer'. Try it! You can thank me for it personally one day.

[1] A petabyte (PB) is a unit of measurement in computers and similar electronic devices. One petabyte holds 1024 terabytes (TB) or 1,125,899,906,842,624 bytes.

SUMMARY

This chapter investigated our thought patterns, and how frequently we can catastrophise. This is often paired with a tendency to think in extremes: one small thing can feel like the end of the world and as if our whole life is bad. This style of thinking can have a big impact on our lives; our relationships, careers and mental health are all affected by catastrophising. Viewing seemingly minor or insignificant events as life-changing can constantly force our bodies into fight or flight mode – spiking our anxiety and wearing down our resilience.

The second half of the chapter made us look internally at how much we may be holding on to with regard to our emotions. Our minds can store away a traumatic event, so to save us from reliving and processing it over and over. Although seemingly a useful thing to do, this strategy in the long run can lead to further damage. If you have been holding a full cup of water for years, the weight will only decrease when you pour from it.

CHAPTER TWENTY-SIX

TRAUMA – HURT PEOPLE, HURT PEOPLE

Every man has reminiscences which he would not tell to everyone, but only to his friends. He has other matters in his mind which he would not reveal even to his friends, but only to himself, and that in secret. But there are other things which a man is afraid
to tell even to himself, and every decent man has a number of such things stored away in his mind. The more decent he is, the greater the number of such things in his mind.
– FYODOR DOSTOEVSKY

Imagine for a moment a sheet of standard, white, A4 paper. Scrunch part of it with your hand, and then let it go. Then go to another part and scrunch that. Keep doing that for about a minute, so that the whole piece of paper is scrunched up. What sort of shape is the piece of paper now? Can you fashion it back to how it originally looked and felt? Even if you manage to flatten it out again, assuming that you've not torn it, does it look the same as it did? I seriously doubt it. It's creased forever. Even if it had several heavy books on it for days, the 'scars' of the creasing would no doubt be clearly visible. This is how we are as children, growing up and experiencing events that shape us and, in many ways, change the person we were originally destined to be. Regardless of how much care and intervention received, those scars are always partially visible. Therapy helps of course, but at the end of the day those experiences stay with us and change how we see the world. As a result of our childhood, we tend to develop like a ship that permanently lists to one side. We tend to lean far too much in one direction or another. We are too shy or too assertive, too rigid or too accommodating, too focused on material success or excessively apathetic. We are dreamily naive or abruptly down to earth. What is almost certain is that these imbalances can come at a significant cost, rendering us less able to exploit our talents and opportunities, and less able to lead satisfying lives.

In this chapter we are going to consider how trauma, and in particular how the trauma we all experience in our childhoods, can impact our lives and our belief systems – particularly the beliefs surrounding self-esteem, social anxiety and how in control we feel in our lives, our self-efficacy and our locus of control. Often the emotionally charged experiences we encounter as children can seem somewhat inconsequential if we experience the same event as an adult, where we have the mental resilience to deal with them and process them effectively. If as a child your parents were arguing and your mother or father was going to leave, this may have threatened your basic need for love, nourishment and security. As an adult, however, the same events might be viewed as just Mum and Dad 'kicking off' again. It will blow over! As children such events can be of huge consequence and impact on a child's mental well-being. In essence, when a child suffers at the hands of an adult, the child almost invariably takes what happens to them as a reflection that something must be wrong with them. This becomes the foundation of a lack of self-love.

The traumas we experience as children can obviously vary in severity, the severity also being magnified or diminished depending on the personality type of the child involved. A child who is quite sensitive and internalises experiences more may have a good deal more anxiety as a result of an unpleasant experience than a child who is more robust and deflective in how they process experiences.

Similarly, as we grow into adults, we can live our lives hypervigilant to any potential damage to our ego or our self-identity. We avoid with great agility anything that can bring up uncomfortable feelings and emotions. The fundamental difference between the two is that feelings are experienced consciously, whereas emotions manifest either consciously or subconsciously. Many of us spend years, or even a lifetime, not understanding the depths of our emotions.

Picture a child who is always chosen last for a team in a sports lesson in school. When that child is chosen for a team, they are taken because there is no one else to pick. They literally are at the bottom of the barrel in terms of desirability. What message would any child, or indeed adult, glean from such an unpleasant scenario? Essentially that they are not wanted. The child is very unlikely to reason that their sporting skills are not desired, but if the class were selecting someone for drama, then of course 'I would be the first chosen!' No, instead, what they take from the experience is, 'I am not worth anything as a person. I am worthless.' Is an experience similar to this worse than being involved in say a car crash? Assuming no one was badly injured, I would suggest that perhaps it is. Indeed, this and other similar experiences can have a profound effect on a child's development that will follow them through the entirety of their adult life. The ramifications of this are potential feelings of inadequacy, never quite feeling good enough or worthy of love. Will this child as an adult place themselves in situations where the emotional response to this experience may be comparable? I doubt it. Will they grow up liking team sports? Unlikely I would say. Indeed, any situation involving an element of being chosen, say for example doing 'team building' activities at work, will potentially bring up, even unconsciously, possible feelings of anxiety. In this way we become hugely fragile. We also can begin to dissociate from our emotion – a cognitive process whereby we are able to disconnect from our thoughts, feelings, memories and our sense of identity. This is often the main strategy to deal with stressful and traumatic experiences.

Trauma can disrupt one's sense of identity, and one's self-identity can affect the way one perceives and recovers from the trauma. The trauma, however, can also become incorporated into one's identity. The fact that you have to face trauma and how you deal with that trauma can be life defining. In therapy when a client is recalling a traumatic experience, often the client recalls the experience as if they were a third-party observer, watching a film of the experience, and disconnecting themselves mentally from the memory. Only when the client feels comfortable and safe can they begin to re-experience the potentially traumatic event again first-hand, the way it was processed in their memory when it took place. Only in reliving traumatic experience with adult eyes – assuming the experience is from the client's childhood – can they process it effectively and disperse the bottled-up emotions that the incident generated.

WALKING ON BROKEN GLASS

At the tender age of 23 Princess Alexandra Amalie of Bavaria (1826–1875) was observed walking clumsily sideways down the corridors of her family's palace in Schloss Johannisburg in Franconia, Bavaria. She had previously also been seen tiptoeing down hallways carefully turning her body so that nothing would touch her. When questioned by her understandably concerned royal parents, the princess explained that she had just discovered something amazing. As a child, she had swallowed a full-sized grand piano made entirely of glass. It now existed inside her, wholly intact, and would she be jostled, the instrument inside her would no doubt shatter into thousands of pieces.

Prior to this encounter her relatives, who had previously observed that the princess only ever dressed in white, had noticed that she was acting even more strangely than usual.

The princess was not alone in this misbelief. Indeed, this peculiar glass delusion was common from the Middle Ages until about the 19th century. Prior to this period there had been reported cases of individuals believing that they were made of pottery. Bizarrely, accounts of earthenware men abound in earlier periods in history. The glass delusion, however, came much later, possibly because glass had become a highly prized, almost alchemic material. During that period in history, glass led the field as the obsession of the time. The fear of being too fragile for this world was believed to be especially common among the nobility and educated men of the time.

I find this true story fascinating as it's a brilliant example of how we can hold false beliefs for several reasons. At some level many of us can relate to the absurdity of the young girl's delusions, in so much as deep down we know we all believe in some things that others may consider a 'little peculiar' or possibly irrational. Princess Alexandra could have believed that since swallowing the grand piano she could make beautiful music when she walked around the palace. Similarly, she could have believed that beautiful music lived within her. Instead, due no doubt to some childhood trauma, her subconscious adopted the belief that harm would come to her if she were to come into contact with a hard object – emphasising perhaps the fragility she felt in her life. Much like the young child avoiding a sport where they may not get picked, Princess Alexandra lived her life avoiding anything that may cause her discomfort and, in her mind, possible mortality.

The glass princess tale is a wonderful reminder to all of us to take time to search out, challenge and replaced the distorted beliefs we all potentially hold on to – the beliefs we hold on to in the mistaken certainty that they are protecting us.

PUPPY LOVE

In 1955, researcher A.E. Fisher conducted a series of experiments with puppies. The focus of his study was to analyse their behaviour when faced with varying degrees of attention. The puppies were separated into three groups. The first group were embraced warmly and comforted whenever they approached the researchers. The second group were punished for approaching the researchers. The third and final group were treated either with kindness or punishment in a sporadic and unpredictable fashion.

What was remarkable about Fisher's study was that, at the end of it, he discovered that the third group, who had grown up in a world of uncertainty, had formed the strongest attachments to the researchers. In nature, animals can confront uncertainty by increasing their level of attachment to their real or surrogate parents, even when their parents are the cause of the uncertainty.

So how does this relate to abuse? How many of us have heard of or known personally people in abusive relationships? How often has it been hard if not virtually impossible for that individual to leave that abusive partner, with them citing things such as financial dependence, the shame of a broken family and supposed remorse from the abuser as their reasons to remain? Often they may mention another important reason – the love they feel for their abuser. As an outsider we can argue that the individuals in these relationships are not experiencing true love, as true love involves kindness, compassion, joy and equanimity. However, we cannot deny that what these individuals are experiencing is attachment, possibly perceived as love, much like the puppies in the third group.

Abusers are rarely if ever similar to the researchers and how they reacted to the second group of puppies, in that they are not consistently abusive. If they had been then chances are the fledgling relationship would never have taken flight. Instead, the relationships appear to be defined by seemingly random bouts of positive and negative interactions, more analogous to the behaviour of the third group's researchers.

From this fascinating experiment, Fisher concluded that, 'stress, including the mental stress of uncertainty, is an ingredient in attachment or love, and that perhaps even manifestations of hatred (its polar opposite) somehow enhance love'.

In another study by Harry Harlow on attachment in animals, baby monkeys were separated from their mothers at birth. The monkeys were then provided with two alternative mothers: a wire 'mother' that provided food, and a soft, cuddly 'mother' that did nothing. To test which of the two 'mothers' fostered greater attachment, the researchers introduced a frightening object to the monkeys to observe their reaction. The babies unanimously clung to the 'useless', soft mother. Even more surprisingly perhaps, when the monkeys were 'rejected' or pushed away by the soft mothers through the use of pressurised air, they clung even tighter.

DO YOU REALLY WANT TO HURT ME?

In 1911, a Swiss physician named Édouard Claparède published his observations of an amnesiac patient. A lady he had been working with had experienced brain damage and had seemingly lost the ability to create new memories. Despite repeated interactions with her, sometimes only minutes apart, Claparède had to reintroduce himself every time he re-entered the room; the patient never recognised him as someone she'd met before.

During one of their 'introductions', Claparède hid a pin in his palm and pricked the patient when they shook hands. Fascinatingly, on subsequent occasions when he entered the room and went to shake her hand, she refused to shake Claparède's hand, though she couldn't explain why since she had no conscious recall of having ever met the doctor before. It appears that her subconscious mind knew that there was some unpleasantness linked to doing so.

Nowadays, neuroscientists interpret the patient's reaction as proof that multiple memory systems are at work within the normal human brain. A subconscious memory system in the woman's brain had formed an association between shaking Claparède's hand and a painful experience. Therefore, despite the damage to her brain, the memory system that would normally have enabled her to consciously remember the event was still working, trying to keep her safe from harm. This demonstrates perhaps the level of importance the brain places on protecting us and keeping us free from harm. In many ways this is like trauma. Many times, we respond to something by instinct, without ever knowing why. A co-worker who frustrates you, your child's teacher who angers you or a shop assistant who feels the wrath of your misplaced anger – sometimes, a fairly innocuous experience seems to 'press a button' deep within us. As author Marian Keyes writes, 'The things we dislike most in others are the characteristics we like least in ourselves'.

Perhaps then we would do well to listen to and adopt the words of writer Steve Goodier: 'And here's the surprising truth: As you gaze at yourself in the mirror held by another, you will see far more than your flaws. You also will see the beauty that is uniquely you; beauty that others see clearly, and you may hardly know exists. That is also part of the truth about you.'

CRAZY LITTLE THING CALLED LOVE

Because we are reluctant historians of our emotional pasts, we easily assume that these imbalances aren't things we could ever change – it feels like they are somehow fundamentally innate. It's just how we were made, and who we are. Our imbalances of course are invariably responses to something that happened in our past. For example, when we suffer at the hands of an adult as children, we almost invariably take what happens to us as a reflection of something that must be very wrong with us. Similarly, because as children we cannot easily exit a difficult situation, we can begin to feel very powerless and out of control. No wonder then that many of us can maintain a strong desire for control in our adult lives.

Even small events can stay with us, and often we are able to recall them as adults for the simple reason they have a strong emotion attached to them. Most of us can remember instances such as wetting ourselves in class, a teacher telling us off or perhaps being told by a teacher we weren't very good at something. Likewise, most children would be able to recollect a time when their parents had an argument, or would remember if one parent had threatened to leave home. Similarly, we tend to remember the special unexpected toys we received at Christmas as well as the toys we didn't receive. Children of certain eras, me included, can perhaps remember having to do PE in our underwear because we had forgotten our PE kit!

As a child I can clearly remember dropping 10 pence down a drain by accident on my way home – money that was intended for the purchase and consumption of a bag of sweets from our local corner shop. In terms of an incident, it was a trivial event, a relatively small amount of money, but as a child it might as well have been the keys to a gold-plated Bugatti Veyron. The event, no matter how insignificant, was momentous to me as a child and therefore there was an emotion attached to it. This type of event is placed in the part of our brain where we are able to recall it, where it becomes a particular type of explicit memory known as an episodic memory – a memory we can recall if we put enough effort into doing so, or if it is triggered in some way. For example, it's impossible for me to now saunter down the street where I dropped the money without thinking about the incident. In my mind the event is linked to the street. Similarly, must of us can readily recall where we were and what we were doing on 11 September 2001, when we witnessed the 9/11 attacks. We link these experiences in our minds to where we were when the event occurred and how we felt about it.

Was it hugely traumatic? No, not really. Was it significant? Well, yes. Enough for an adult to be able to recall the event some 40 years later (I even can still remember which coin-devouring drain it was on the street!), particularly as I knew the likelihood of it being replaced with a shiny new 10-pence piece was slim to none, as it would have been for most children growing up in the 1970/80s.

Interestingly, it is believed that the amygdala stores the visual images of trauma as sensory fragments, which means the trauma memory is not always stored like a story; rather, our senses store the trauma at the time it was occurring. The memories are stored through fragments of visual images, smells, sounds, tastes and touch.

Now, had the 10-pence piece been given by a parent who had asked me to get something for them from the local shop, and had that parent had a predisposition to be particularly abusive, then the level of emotion would have been much more significant. Being frustrated at losing the coin would be replaced by the thought of a potential beating or worse. The anxiety surrounding the loss is radically changed by the potential outcome of the event.

It is these events and experiences that contribute to the type of person we become and the personality we ultimately shape and share with the world. Trauma and addictions expert Dr Gabor Maté once described personality in the following way: 'What we call the personality is often a jumble of genuine traits and adopted coping styles that do not reflect our true self at all but the loss of it'.

With regard to trauma, why are some people more resilient than others, and, perhaps more importantly, can that resilience be taught? Well, psychologists Richard Tedeschi and Lawrence Calhoun believe so. Post-traumatic growth (PTG) is a theory that explains this kind of transformation following trauma. It holds that people who endure psychological struggle following adversity can often see positive growth afterwards. As Tedeschi states, 'People develop new understandings of themselves, the world they live in, how to relate to other people, the kind of future they might have and a better understanding of how to live life'.

WAITING FOR THAT DAY

When we feel that we have no control as a child, we can react in several ways. We may grow up with a strong desire for control and certainty in our lives, or alternatively we may grow up with a certain amount of learnt helplessness. This helplessness is the belief that there is nothing that anyone can do to improve a bad situation, such as being diagnosed with an illness – essentially a belief that we have little or no control over the situation or its outcomes. The good news is that, like all beliefs, helplessness is learned not innate. Learned helplessness is very much analogous with the external locus of control we examined in Chapter 24. As with the external locus of control, individuals with learned helplessness often exhibit higher than normal levels of anxiety and depression.

The model of learned helplessness was first hypothesised in the 1960s by psychologist Martin Seligman and was first demonstrated in animals. Seligman discovered that an animal repeatedly exposed to a painful stimulus that it could not avoid would eventually stop attempting to escape – in many ways similar to the behaviour of the Indian elephant that we discussed in Chapter 9.

When applying this model to people, Seligman discovered that the motivation to react is restrained when the perceived control over a situation is lost, even when the situation changes so that control might be taken back. Naturally, learned helplessness can lead to the development of negative beliefs about one's abilities and a tendency to take on blame when things don't go according to plan. The condition often results from a lack of control, either real or perceived, over one's situation.

For example, a child who is repeatedly bullied at school by other children might begin to believe that there is no way out of the situation, and may just resign themselves to their fate rather than considering ways to stop it occurring. Similarly, children who experience a traumatic childhood may still feel powerless as adults, believing they cannot improve any situation in their lives. Essentially, once a person discovers that they cannot control events around them, they lose will and motivation. Even if an opportunity arises that allows the person to alter their circumstances, they do not take action. Perhaps not surprisingly, a person's experiences can increase their risk of developing learned helplessness. Typically learned helplessness begins after experiencing repeated traumatic events, such as childhood abuse or domestic violence. In addition, individuals experiencing learned helplessness are often less able to make decisions and are at much greater risk of experiencing depression. The good news is, though, not everyone who experiences these things develops learned helplessness.

MISSED OPPORTUNITY

In an insightful story connected to learned helplessness from author and podcaster Tim Ferriss, Tim speaks of the time he was giving a talk to a group of university students and set the group a challenge. All the students had to do was prove they had made contact, via a signature, letter or email, with either actress

Jennifer Lopez, ex-president Bill Clinton or author J.D. Salinger. The prize for doing so was an impressive $25,000 and a trip around the world!

Did anyone do it? The surprising answer was no, they didn't. The following year Tim went to the same university to give the same talk. In this talk, in addition to setting the challenge again, he told his students what had happened the previous year – that none of the students had won the extraordinary prize. So, what happened on this occasion? Well perhaps predictably an impressive six students managed to achieve the objective. Sometimes we have to work our way around the learned helplessness mindset. The first set of students no doubt believed what Mr Ferris was asking of them was impossible. So why even try?! In many ways this brief example has overtones of the incredible Roger Bannister's 4-minute breakthrough discussed earlier in the book. As soon as Bannister proved that something that had previously been thought impossible was possible, others achieved it also. How many of us don't even consider taking on a challenge, believing it to be inherently impossible to achieve?

SUMMARY

In this chapter we looked at trauma. Trauma is something we are all likely to experience in one form or another in our lives, but what events we take on as trauma will vary between individuals. If trauma is experienced in childhood, it changes the people we then become as adults. Unless we reprocess this trauma from childhood as adults, the painful emotions that have withstood time won't be worked through or dispersed.

Trauma is saved in our brains as snapshots of the sensory experience, rather than the whole story itself. We may remember certain sounds or smells from the traumatic event, but not the whole timeline of when it occurred.

STAGE FOUR

MASTERY

CHAPTER TWENTY-SEVEN

WHAT ARE THE CHANCES?

I wouldn't have seen it if I hadn't believed it.
– MARSHALL MCLUHAN

Take a look at the old photograph below. What do you see?

Did you see the lady with a wide-brimmed white hat and a gentleman staring straight into the camera lens? Oh, and did you see the large face of a bearded man, with wavy hair, eyes closed and looking to the left?

Alternatively, you may have seen what is actually there in this photo: a small child sitting on the lap of the gentleman, no doubt the child's father. The child dressed in white, wearing a white bonnet. To the right of the child, some undergrowth.

So why do the majority of us see the bearded man with closed eyes and a head the size of a tumble dryer before we see the young child on the man's lap? After all, when in your life have you seen a man with a head that large? The answer is simple, and it's something we can thank our hunter-gatherer ancestors for.

Imagine for a moment that you are one of your distant ancestors. Would it be better to be constantly hypervigilant to potential threat, such as a hungry wild animal? Or would it be better to have a more relaxed, chilled-out vibe – a 'Well, I could get run over by hairy mammoth tomorrow' type of attitude? Clearly the Palaeolithic ancestors that survived were the ones with the 'better safe than sorry' attitude, and it is thanks to them surviving and reproducing that you and I are alive today. That hypervigilant group was constantly on the lookout for threat – observing anything that looked like a shape and, in particular, a face, be that of an animal or another human. It's no surprise then that anyone alive today has that predisposition, and we have our ancestors to thank for it.

This hardwired propensity is also the same reason we see patterns everywhere, in clouds, in the froth of a cup of coffee, in a slice of toast or in the bark of a tree. In 2004, Diane Duyser of Florida was making a cheese sandwich when she saw what she thought looked like the face of the Virgin Mary on the slightly burnt bread. That cheese sandwich went on to be sold for an unbelievable $28,000 on eBay, in a listing that attracted 1.7 million hits.

Perhaps all of us at some stage have seen a clown's face in the dirt on our car, or the face of an animal in our wallpaper or in the trunk of a tree. This common phenomenon is a form of what is known as apophenia. It involves seeing a meaningful pattern within randomness, and it is a common occurrence throughout modern culture. There are fundamentally four subcategories of apophenia:

The first is pareidolia. Pareidolia is a type of apophenia that occurs specifically with visual stimuli. People with this tendency most often see human faces in inanimate objects, similar to the examples mentioned above.

The second is known as the gambler's fallacy. Individuals who gamble regularly often fall prey to the gambler's fallacy. They may perceive patterns or meaning in random numbers, often interpreting the pattern as an indication of an oncoming win. The gambler's fallacy is the mistaken belief that if an event happens more frequently than normal during a given period, it will happen less frequently in the future, or vice versa. Similarly, individuals who are lucky when they first gamble assume, clearly incorrectly, that this is a sign they will be lucky for the rest of their lives. It is believed that this makes such people more likely to become addicted to gambling – something we considered in Chapter 23 when we examined fate, luck and chance. Indeed, every roll of a dice or flip of a fair coin is an independent event that follows a random process.

The most famous example of the gambler's fallacy occurred in the early 20th century, at the Monte Carlo Casino. In August 1913, the roulette ball stopped on black an incredible 26 times in a row, causing gamblers to lose millions betting against what they thought to be a hot streak that could not possibly be sustained. What are the chances?! This is why the gambler's fallacy is also commonly known as the Monte Carlo fallacy after this seemingly implausible event.

A similar event happened when Apple released the shuffle feature on its hugely popular range of iPods. Users began to notice that songs from the same album or artist were often grouped by chance, and this felt like it wasn't random – forgetting that, with true randomness, events like this will happen. The number of complaints Apple received led Steve Jobs to alter the device's programming and begin offering what became known as Smart Shuffle. This alteration allowed users to adjust the likelihood of hearing similar songs in a row. Jobs went on to say that, 'We're making it less random, to make it feel more random'.

The next example is the clustering illusion. A clustering illusion occurs when looking at large amounts of data – humans tend to see patterns or trends in data even when it is entirely random. For example, most people would consider the following sequence 'OXXXOXXXOXXOOOXOOXXOO' (Gilovich, 1993) to be non-random. In reality, it has many of the properties that one would expect in a real random data stream, such as the same frequency of the two events, and the fact that the number of the same symbols directly adjacent is the same for each of the two symbols. In sequences like this, people seem to expect to see a greater number of alternations than one would predict statistically.

In another fascinating example, the answers of the SAT (Scholastic Aptitude Test), the multiple-choice standardised test in the United States, are specifically chosen not to contain any long runs. Experience has shown the test designers that students believe these runs are unlikely to occur. As a result, a student may feel pressured into choosing a wrong answer just to break a run.

Finally, there is confirmation bias, something that we have already discussed extensively in this book. As a reminder, confirmation bias is a psychological phenomenon by which we test a hypothesis under the assumption that it's true. This form of apophenia can lead us to look for things that confirm our beliefs and enthusiastically explain away information that disproves it. As philosopher Marshall McLuhan aptly states, 'I wouldn't have seen it if I hadn't believed it'.

GREASED LIGHTNING

Have you ever had anyone tell you that 'things happen for a reason', by which they mean that there are mysterious, unrecognised causes underlying extraordinary coincidences? Or that they were thinking of someone just before the phone rang and, lo and behold, it was that very person on the other end of the call? Or that they had experienced a dream about a specific event and then that event actually happened in real life? The truth that underlies all of these coincidences is the mathematics of chance, but looked at from a rather unusual perspective – what David J. Hand refers to as the 'the improbability principle' in his book of the same name. According to Hand there are five strands (or 'laws') contributing to the improbability principle: the law of inevitability, the law of truly large numbers, the law of selection, the law of the probability lever and the law of near enough.

So, what is the improbability principle? According to Hand, 'Extremely improbable events are commonplace'. It is only when an event catches our attention or captures our imagination that we sit up and take note, such as with the bizarre coincidence surrounding Dennis the Menace. On 12 March 1951, two separate comic strips entitled 'Dennis the Menace' went on sale, one in the UK, one in the US. The UK Dennis, which first appeared in the 452th edition of the beloved *Beano*, was created by David Law. Its US counterpart was created by cartoonist Hank Ketcham and distributed by Post-Hall Syndicate as a syndicated comic strip for newspapers.

Hand summarises this as 'Someone, somewhere, at some time won a lottery twice' and he provides several examples of this. One of these is the story of army major Walter Summerford, who was struck by a lightning bolt on a battlefield in Belgium in 1918 and paralysed from the waist down. Summerford then retired to Vancouver and slowly rehabilitated back to the point where he could walk again. Six years later, while fishing in 1924, lightning struck him again! This time the right side of his body was paralysed, and Summerford began another long, slow period of rehabilitation. Then, some 10 years after that, you will never guess what happened! Yes, you've got it: Summerford was struck once again by lightning while walking in a park in 1934. This time he was left completely paralysed and sadly never recovered, dying 2 years later in 1936. To add salt to a very shocked wound, shortly after his burial, Summerford's gravesite was struck by lightning!

Using the law of near enough, we often look for coincidences, and when we do, we can easily find them. For example, the assassinations of President Lincoln and President Kennedy famously inspire a lot of 'near enough' coincidences. The internet is chock-full of websites dedicated to these coincidences. Here are just a few of them: 'Oswald fired the shot from a library and fled to a theatre, and Booth fired the shot in a theatre and fled to a library'. Presumably someone eventually noticed that the Texas Book Depository wasn't a library, but a kind of warehouse for textbooks. Also, Abraham Lincoln was elected to Congress in 1846 and John F. Kennedy was elected to Congress in 1946. Lincoln was elected president in 1860 and Kennedy was elected president in 1960. Both wives lost a child while living in the White House. Both presidents were shot on a Friday. Both presidents were shot in the head. Lincoln's secretary was named Kennedy. Kennedy's secretary was named Lincoln, and the list goes on.

I FOUGHT THE LAW

The law of truly large numbers states that with a large enough number of samples, any outrageous (i.e. unlikely in any single sample) thing is likely to be observed. Similarly, Littlewood's law (named after maths professor John Littlewood) states that a person can expect to experience events with odds of one in a million (defined by the law as a 'miracle') at the rate of about one per month. Yes, you read that right: we can all expect a miracle about once a month!

Littlewood defines a miracle as an exceptional event of special significance occurring at a frequency of one in a million. He assumes that during the hours in which a human is awake and alert, a human will see or hear one 'event' per second, which may be either exceptional or unexceptional. Additionally, Littlewood supposes that a human is alert for about 8 hours per day. As a result, a human will in 35 days have experienced under these suppositions about one million events. Accepting this definition of a miracle, one can expect to observe one miraculous event for every 35 days on average – and, therefore, according to this reasoning, seemingly miraculous events are actually commonplace. How many of these do we actually take note of? And when we do, do we apply more meaning to them than there actually is?

References

IT'S MY PARTY

If you were in a room of people, how many people do you think would need to be in the room with you to guarantee someone else shared the same birthday as you?

This puzzle is known as probability theory, the birthday problem or birthday paradox and concerns the probability that, in a set of randomly chosen people, a pair of them will have the same birthday. In a group of 23 people, the probability of a shared birthday is just 50%, while a group of 70 has a massive 99.9% chance of a shared birthday. (Fairly obviously the probability reaches 100% when the number of people reaches 367, since there are only 366 possible birthdays, including February 29.) It's enough to ruin your birthday, isn't it?!

BALLROOM BLITZ

From June to October 1944, the Germans launched 9521 buzz bombs from the coasts of France and the Netherlands, of which a not insubstantial 2419 reached their targets in London. Londoners were understandably concerned as to the accuracy of these V-1 and V-2 death contraptions, which earned the nickname 'doodlebugs'. Were these death machines falling haphazardly over the city, or were they hitting their intended targets? Or had the Germans finally discovered a way to make an accurately targeting self-guided bomb? Fascinatingly, in 1944, a V-2 reached an altitude of 175 km (109 miles), making it the first rocket to reach space! What's more amazing is this event happened on 20 June, which happens to be my birthday! Not the year, of course, just the day – what are the chances! (See Chapter 23 for more on fate, luck and chance.)

From September of 1940, the British government had been meticulous in collecting and collating information relating to damage sustained during bombing raids – what was known as the Bomb Census. These data tracked the place and time of nearly every bomb that was dropped on London during World War II. With these data, they could statistically analyse whether the bombs were falling randomly over cities such as London,

325

Liverpool or Birmingham, or whether they were targeted. Due to the fact that very few bombs had dropped over the areas of Finsbury and Clerkenwell, north and east of the River Thames, many began to speculate that German spies were residing in these areas. Much suspicion befell those living in these areas. That would explain why those area was being protected from the devastation the rest of the city was enduring from the Nazis. Of course, this is a fairly obvious conclusion to make. Just imagine, for a moment, that you are working for British intelligence, and you're tasked with solving this problem. Someone hands you a piece of paper with a cluster of points on it, and your job is to figure out if the pattern is random or targeted.

The truth though was very different: the German onslaught was little more than a point and shoot attack. All the Germans were doing was pointing the bombs in the right general direction and hoping they had put in enough fuel. As psychologist Thomas Gilovich has shown us previously, when we are faced with difficult problems and data, most of us jump to completely the wrong conclusion.

At its core, the time spent in this book on the above ideas revolves around the concept of control. Simply stated, the more we buy into external factors influencing our lives, the more likely we are to feel powerless and have a desire for control in our own lives. If we recognise that the events that feel somewhat miraculous are just events that are due to probability, then perhaps we can dedicate more time making our own true miracles and create the life we want for ourselves and those we love.

ATTITUDE ADJUSTMENT

Sometimes being an expert in a particular area can create an unconscious bias when it comes to looking for a solution to a particular problem. Amazingly, it can hinder us and prevent us from finding a better, more simplified solution to a task.

This problem-solving effect was observed in 1942 by American psychologist Abraham Luchins. In a now famous problem-solving experiment, Luchins asked participants to use jugs of water to measure specific quantities of water. He first gave them five introductory water-jug problems that could be solved easily. Next, he gave them a superficially similar problem that required a new solution. Participants believed that the new problems were impossible to solve. Yet another group of individuals, who had not seen the introductory problems, solved them easily. What is fascinating about this experiment is that Luchins discovered that prior knowledge actually prevented people from noticing a new, more effective solution to a given problem. Luchins called this effect the Einstellung effect, the German word for 'setting'.

The Einstellung effect refers to the negative effect that experience can have on our problem-solving abilities. In essence, the more we solve a problem one way, the more we cling to that way of doing things, believing it to be the only way to do it. Indeed, the more we cling to one preferred way of doing a task, the more we close ourselves to other options – even to the point of giving up when our preferred option doesn't work.

The Einstellung effect is essentially a problem of expertise. Being an expert at something can actually be a disadvantage. It can make you less likely to come up with effective solutions to problems.

How many of us fall foul of the Einstellung effect in our own lives, believing we have exhausted all avenues when trying to resolve a problem? As we will discover in the final chapter of this book where we discuss Alexander the Great and the Gordian knot, sometimes the solution to a complex problem can be much simpler than we originally believed. Again, as humans we are hardwired to look for patterns in things, and in doing so our hunter-gatherer ancestors survived and reproduced, but in modern life the threats that our ancestors faced are no longer present. Therefore, when it comes to problem solving, the search for patterns can hinder and limit us in discovering new and more effective alternatives to problem solving.

So, the next time you see a face in your cup of coffee, feel a sense of gratitude to your hypervigilant Palaeolithic ancestors. Because they noticed these faces, shapes and patterns, you are alive today. But note that when it comes to problem solving, the belief that there are patterns in everything can blind us to finding more effective and simplistic alternatives. Indeed, the search for patterns in challenges can be a double-edged sword, leading us down a path where answers are much harder to come by. As statistician W. Edwards Deming writes, 'In God we trust, all others must bring data'.

SUMMARY

Chapter 27 looked at the patterns that we notice every day in life. As humans, we are hardwired to notice patterns in things – whether this be the shape of an animal in the clouds, or a significance in the winning numbers of the lottery. It is our way of looking out for threat as our ancestors did. However, always looking out for these patterns can lead us to be closed off to other, sometimes more obvious, solutions to a problem we are trying to solve.

These patterns of coincidence we notice frequently can simply be explained by mathematics and chance – however we can sometimes apply more meaning and significance to them depending on what we want them to mean. After all, it is thought that we all experience what is defined as a miracle once a month – but how often do you think you have experienced a life-altering event like this? The probability doesn't change for you, but you have just noticed one more than another.

References

CHAPTER TWENTY-EIGHT

DON'T WORRY, BE HAPPY

He who has a why to live for can bear almost any how.
– FRIEDRICH NIETZSCHE

Many years ago, a very wise peasant lived in a small village in China. This villager had a son who was his pride and joy. He was also the very proud owner of a rather majestic white stallion – a horse that was admired by many. One day, out of the blue, his horse escaped and disappeared. The other villagers came to him and one by one said, 'You are such an unlucky man. It is such bad luck that your horse escaped.'

The peasant simply responded, 'Maybe it's bad, maybe it's good, who knows?'

The following day the splendid stallion returned bringing with it a dozen wild horses. The neighbours visited him again and congratulated him on his good fortune. Again, he just said, 'Maybe it's good, maybe it's bad, who knows?'

The next day his son was attempting to train one of the wild horses that the wise peasant had acquired, when he fell down and broke his leg. Once again, the other villagers came to him with their commiserations saying, 'It's a terrible thing that has happened to your son.'

Again, he calmly replied, 'Maybe it's good, maybe it's bad, who knows?'

A few days passed, and his poor son was limping around the village with his broken leg when the emperor's army arrived at the village declaring that a war was beginning. They set about enrolling all the fit, young men of the village of fighting age.

However, they left the peasant's son due to his broken leg. Once again, the villagers proclaimed to the wise peasant how extremely fortunate he was that his son was spared. Once again, the wise old peasant calmly replied to them, 'Maybe it's good, maybe it's bad, who knows?'

ALWAYS LOOK ON THE BRIGHT SIDE OF LIFE

The classic 1979 Eric Idle song suggests 'Always Look on the Bright Side of Life'. The reality is, however, it's not always that simple. Particularly in the post-Covid world, where there has been a level of uncertainty far greater than any generation has experienced for decades. The perfect paradox of this song is that it's from the film *Monty Python's Life of Brian*. A film that, at its core, is about someone who furiously claims not to be the person (i.e. the Messiah) others believe him to be. The more he insists he is not the 'chosen one', the more his followers believe him to be just that – much like the confirmation biases we looked at earlier in this book. If we need to believe something, we will only look for evidence for its basis. Again, similar to the tragic tale of Captain Alfred Dreyfus we examined previously, the more innocent he appeared, the more his pursuers believed him guilty – the rationale being that only a spy would be that clean of any damning evidence against him.

Keeping a positive outlook and avoiding too much 'doomscrolling' of the media is perhaps far more necessary and recommended than ever before. 'Be informed but not inundated' is perhaps the best approach to take when it comes to the news. Think of news channels such as CNN as 'Constant Negative News', and NBC as 'No Body Cares'. Of course, people tell us not to be unhappy, but nobody tells us how not to be unhappy. With very few exceptions, often down to individual teachers rather than school curriculums, children are taught to be strong and successful, but teachers rarely prepare children to deal with the emotions of failure, anxiety and stress. Rarely are we taught how to develop resilience, and manage our thinking and our stress reactions.

References

In terms of living longer, the 1988 hit song 'Don't Worry, Be Happy' in many ways is the best model to aim for when it comes to longevity. To manage and reduce anxiety, we need to live in the moment more, rather than continually anticipating the uncertainty of the future. The huge rise in the popularity of mindfulness is perhaps testament to this new shift in mindset, showing that we need, perhaps more than ever, to learn how to think about and process our experiences differently. We need to accept our experiences, including painful emotions, rather than reacting to them with aversion and avoidance. Accepting that we will all have challenges in our lives perhaps focuses us to live very much more in the moment. When we become more aware of the present moment, we begin to experience afresh things that we have been taking for granted. In essence mindfulness is the basic human ability to be fully present, aware of where we are and what we're doing, and not overly reactive or overwhelmed by what's going on around us. Or in the words of the Cherokee proverb, 'Don't let yesterday use up too much of today'. Being mindful it seems affords us the ability to recover quickly from stressful situations. It is perhaps the ability to reduce and manage stress and have a positive outlook that is the key to a long disease-free life – as we will examine shortly.

One the important aspects to keep in mind is the link between longevity and having a positive mental attitude (PMA). This was first hinted at in 1937 by self-help author, Napoleon Hill. PMA is a philosophy that states that having an optimistic disposition in every situation in one's life can attract positive changes as well as increasing the likelihood of reaching your desired goals. An individual with a PMA is continually striving to attain a state of mind that permanently seeks ways to triumph in challenging times, as well as endeavouring to find favourable outcomes to situations regardless of the circumstances. This concept is the opposite of negativity, defeatism and hopelessness. It is the philosophy of finding amazing joy even in the smallest of things. It is about living life without hesitation or regret.

Negative thinking, however, does perhaps have its place. According to Barbara Fredrickson, negative thinking and negative emotions allow us to sharpen our focus, keep us safe from dangers and allow us to avoid threats – things that are vital for our survival. Perhaps, though, such defensive ways of thinking are much less required in modern times than they were for our hunter-gatherer ancestors.

Researchers continue to explore the effects of positive thinking and optimism on health. Benefits may include an increased life span, much lower rates of depression, lower levels of anxiety and distress, better cardiovascular health and a reduced risk of death from cardiovascular disease. In addition, we may find we have a much greater resistance to the common cold. Finally, having a PMA means we are far more able to cope during hardship and times of stress. Basically, it helps builds the resilience we examined earlier in this book.

Numerous studies over the past 20 years have shown us the strong correlation between PMA and the likelihood of living a long and, perhaps more importantly, disease-free life. One of the most remarkable studies is that David Snowdon and his team. Launched at the University of Minnesota but later moved to the University of Kentucky in 1986, the 'Nun Study' was a longitudinal study originally created to investigate the onset of ageing and Alzheimer's disease. Snowdon and his team produced one of the most powerful and dynamic studies on the impact of positive emotions and thoughts in living history.

Danner, Snowdon and Friesen decided to look at the life of nuns joining the disciplined life of the convent, as it was an almost perfect example of homogeneous individuals who had similar, regular meals, lived in similar surroundings, did not have children and did not smoke or drink to excess. In other words, the conditions for their lives were quite similar, something that would have been almost impossible to research in a regular group of people.

The study involved some 678 Catholic nuns from the School Sisters of Notre Dame, ranging in age from 75 to 106. Snowdon's team members were granted access to the medical and personal records of the sisters. They focused their attention on analysing the two-page autobiographies each nun had been asked to write when they joined the convent. With an average age of 22 when written these autobiographies were penned between the 1930s and 1940s. The researchers evaluated the text in terms of how positive, negative or neutral the words and sentences in the nuns' autobiographies were, giving the researchers a window into how positive or negative the outlook of the nun had been at that time in their history.

After the text analysis had been done, approximately 60 years after they had been written, and with the average age of the nuns between 75 and 94 years old, Snowdon's team set about tracking down the nuns. Sadly, 42% of them had passed away. However, what they uncovered next was astonishing. The nuns who had expressed more positive emotions in their autobiographies had, on average, lived a decade longer than their less positive peers. By the average age of 80, 60% of the least positive nuns had died. That's not a misprint! An unbelievable 60% of the less optimistic nuns had passed away.

This landmark study highlighted the following:

1. For every 1% increase in the number of positive sentences the nuns wrote, there was a 1.4% decrease in mortality rate.
2. The nuns who had written the most positive text, on average, lived 10 years longer.
3. By age 80, the most positive group had only lost 25% of its population, while the least positive group had lost around 60% of its members. The nuns with the most positive outlook had an 80% chance of getting to age 85, while the least positive nuns only had a 54% chance of reaching 85.
4. An estimated 54% of the happier, more positive nuns reached 94, while only 15% of the least positive nuns reached that age.
5. By age 90, the positive sisters survived 65%, of the time while the least positive sisters only survived 30%.

In 2011, Snowdon published his findings in the beautiful and inspiring book *Aging with Grace: What the Nun Study Teaches Us About Leading Longer, Healthier, and More Meaningful Lives.*

FOREVER YOUNG

Picture, if you will, a classic 1950s setting. Notice the furniture and the pastel shades of the post-war décor. Picture the stylish cars of the period. Notice the news on the 1950s box-style television. The music playing is Elvis Presley and Hank Williams. The sports news on the radio and the movies playing are all from the 1950s. The photos and pictures scattered around are also of the time. It is as if you are back in the 1950s again, or 1959 to be exact. Only you're not: you are in fact in a converted monastery in New Hampshire in 1979. Now introduce eight men in their late seventies into this setting. The only possessions they have with them are their clothes and photos of themselves from that period. For all intents and purposes, the men are back in the 1950s again. There are no mirrors and nothing to prompt the participants in this study that they are in fact not back in that golden period in post-war history. These eight men have been asked to live in this setting for a week, and to really 'believe' they are back in 1959 – talking, behaving and moving as if they are back there again.

This is the premise for what Harvard psychologist Ellen Langer termed her 'counterclockwise study'. Langer has spent decades testing the hypothesis that 'you are only as old as you feel'. In relation to this she has come to some interesting conclusions about the relationship between mental processes and bodily ageing. Langer believes that 'Wherever you're putting the mind, you're necessarily putting the body'.

So, what had happened by the end of the study? Well, as Langer later remarked herself, 'The results were extraordinary, almost too good to be true'. Langer found that the participants were suppler, showed greater manual dexterity and in fact sat taller! Perhaps the most extraordinary finding was that some of the participants' eyesight even improved, as did their hearing. Indeed, all eight participants even looked younger to outside observers who saw photos of them before and after the experiment.

Langer went on to note that the participants outperformed a control group that had resided at the monastery earlier. This group was not asked to imagine themselves back into the skin of their younger selves, though they were encouraged to reminisce about the 1950s.

Given the seemingly unbelievable conclusions, small sample size and the unorthodox nature of the experiment, Langer decided not to publish at the time. She decided instead to work on similar studies looking at how the mind affects the body. It wasn't until some 30 years later that she was contacted by the BBC, who discussed with her the possibility of staging a televised recreation of the monastery experiment. The result was the brilliant 2010 show *The Young Ones*. Using six, ageing former celebrities, the show transported them back to 1975 by similar means. The results were once again remarkable. The stars emerged after a week noticeably rejuvenated, as was the case in Langer's groundbreaking 1979 New Hampshire experiment.

By creating temporary illusions such the 1950s time machine, Langer has found that perception has a significant effect on ageing. Langer's research has shown that if we perceive ourselves to be younger, healthier, more capable and more vibrant, then despite societal conventions about how we should look and act at our chronological age, our cells and tissues get the message and act accordingly.

These experiments, and several others Langer conducted over the years, strongly suggest that chronological age is not a linear clock pushing us inevitably towards decline. It is rather a collection of variables, only some of which we have control over. Perhaps there is some truth in the age-old expression 'You're only as old as you feel' after all.

Similarly, if we are surrounded by people who have certain expectations of us, then we tend to meet those expectations, be they positive or negative. In fact, it is now believed that the beliefs and expectations we have may impact our physical health at least as much as diet and healthcare can.

Other research has had similar findings to Langer's research. In one study for instance, 650 people were surveyed about their attitudes on ageing. Twenty years later, those with a positive attitude had lived 7 years longer on average than those with a negative attitude. By comparison, researchers have estimated that we only extend our lives by 4 years if we lower our blood pressure and reduce our cholesterol! As we have discussed previously in this book, 'what the mind believes, the mind achieves' is perhaps truer than ever.

HERE COMES THE SUN

The effects of gratitude and thankfulness on our health are measurable, according to researchers and gratitude experts Robert Emmons and Michael McCullough from the University of California-Davis and the University of Miami. Together they have demonstrated that people feel better physically and mentally when they have an attitude of gratitude in their lives. Their study 'Counting blessings versus burdens: An experimental investigation of gratitude and subjective well-being in daily life' was first published in the *Journal of Personality and Social Psychology*. In it they claim that gratitude makes us appreciate the value of things, however little or big they are, and not take them for granted. They believe that gratitude helps us be more active and focus on positive facts, so that the joys we get from life are multiplied.

In one of the studies, participants were divided into three groups and asked to do the following:

Group one was asked to write down five things they were grateful for that had happened in the last week, for each of the 10 weeks of the study.

Group two was asked to write down five daily hassles from the previous week.

Group three was asked to list five events that had occurred in the last week, but not told to focus on positive or negative aspects.

Before the experiment commenced, participants had been asked to keep daily journals to chronicle their moods, physical health and general attitudes. This information was then used to provide a comparison for after the experimental intervention. After the 10 weeks, the participants who were in the gratitude group reported feeling a noteworthy 25% happier! They were more optimistic about the future, they felt better about their lives and they even did an impressive hour and a half more exercise per week than those in the other groups.

The benefits of practising an attitude of gratitude are that people who practise regularly have, on a physical level, a stronger immune system, less pain and lowered blood pressure. Not only that but they tend to exercise more and take care of their health, as well as sleep more and feel more relaxed when they wake up.

On a psychological level, gratitude can build more positive feelings. It can make you feel more awake, alive and active – feel more joy and pleasure and experience more optimism and happiness in life.

On a social level it can make you more helpful, generous and compassionate; more forgiving and less socially anxious. It can also help you feel less isolated and lonely.

Of course, there are many ways of expressing gratitude, including keeping a journal. It has been proven that when we express our gratitude on paper as opposed to just verbal expressions, the beneficial effects can be far greater.

THANK YOU FOR THE MUSIC

In a pioneering study by the University of Pennsylvania's Dr Martin Seligman, participants were asked to write a gratitude letter to someone they were grateful to but had never thanked before. The participants immediately reported a huge increase in their happiness. This effect was much greater than for any other intervention in the study, with the benefits lasting more than

1 month. Who would you write your letter to? Do you have one person or a handful of people you would personally like to thank?

Sometimes we feel grateful for what we have when we look at what others do not have or when we realise that they are worse off than us. But this is not gratitude: it is just a comparison and judgement on others. Indeed, psychologists are at pains to point out that gratitude does not mean the belief that we are somehow better than others.

Gratitude not only encourages us to become aware of the gifts we have received, but to give in return as well. For this reason, sociologist Georg Simmel, 1950, called it 'moral memory'. One of the main characteristics of gifts is that they should be given and reciprocated. An interesting example of this gift-giving cycle is the *Kula*, the ceremonial exchange of gifts by the inhabitants of the Trobriand Islands near New Guinea. *Kula* is a method of exchange on the part of the communities inhabiting a wide ring of islands, which form a closed circuit. Gifts are passed from one island to another. It takes between 2 and 10 years for each gifted item in the *Kula* to make a full round of the islands. This practice shows that it is not the gifts that count, but the exchange itself. The important thing is that the *Kula* gifts are kept in motion. If a man were to keep a gift too long, then he could potentially develop a bad reputation. Somebody who owns something is expected to share it; to pass it on.

Ultimately, gratitude is a life attitude and a point of view. American politician Frank Clark sums it up entirely when he says, 'If a fellow isn't thankful for what he's got, he isn't likely to be thankful for what he's going to get'. Equally applicable are the words of poet Khalil Gibran when he writes, 'Be thankful for the good and the bad things in your life. They have both taught you something.'

When you use the powerful, twice-daily 'Circuit Breakers' that we discussed earlier in this book, a gratitude journal can be the perfect way to break the pattern of your thinking. Perhaps take time each day to use the meditation technique known as Naikan. The Naikan technique involves reflecting on three questions:

'What have I received from _?', 'What have I given to _?' and 'What troubles and difficulty have I caused__?'

Naikan therapy was developed by Yoshimoto Ishin, a Japanese Buddhist, in the 1940s. Whilst on the surface these questions may appear simple, or perhaps even mundane, they are far more than that. The questions challenge us to see reality as it is. The Japanese word Naikan means looking inside or seeing oneself with the mind's eye. The practice of Naikan encourages us to step back and reflect on the life we are living, and how it impacts others we come into contact with. In our modern world Naikan has perhaps never been more desirable.

In the book *Naikan: Gratitude, Grace, and the Japanese Art of Self-reflection* (2002), author Gregg Krech describes Naikan as being a structured form of self-reflection that encourages and helps us to understand not only ourselves and our relationships with others, but the very fundamental nature of human existence.

As Alfred Nobel was compelled to do, If we picture ourselves near the end of our life and look back at how we have lived (as if playing back a movie), what would we see? Would we see someone who has taken more than they have given, harming others perhaps intentionally or unintentionally or through lack of consideration?

Let's dive a little deeper into the three questions:

Question 1: What have I received from ___?

With this question we start by considering what we have received from a specific person, object or a given time. To do this effectively, we must slow down long enough to see what we typically miss. For example, the shop assistant who smiled at us, the person who served us the hot cup of coffee or the person who washed the coffee cup that we drank from. Perhaps even the person who picked the coffee that we enjoyed. Indeed, the very act of listing all that we have received *promotes gratitude*.

Question 2: What have I given to ___?

Yoshimoto's teaching suggests we examine our *life balance*. Like a bank account, there are both deposits and withdrawals each day. Ask yourself what you have given and received recently. Perhaps also ask yourself the question: 'Am I taking more from the world than I am giving?' Often, we can fail to spot and feel gratitude for a lot of the work of others, such as the work of doctors, nurses, teachers, cleaners, builders and delivery drivers. Their contribution to the richness of our lives often goes unnoticed.

Question 3: What troubles and difficulties have I caused ___?
Often, we rarely notice, or even unconsciously choose to ignore, the harm or inconvenience we may cause others. Take time to ask yourself: 'When have I upset someone?' Maybe you have caused difficulties to someone either directly or indirectly? For example, parking inconsiderately may not appear to harm anyone directly, yet seeing it can be upsetting and annoying to others, and ultimately may inconvenience someone in need of a space, particularly if that person is in a hurry.

We all must take responsibility and be accountable for our behaviour. As Krech (2002) writes, 'if we are not willing to see and accept those events in which we have been the source of others' suffering, then we cannot truly know ourselves or the grace by which we live'.

Reflecting on the three questions requires practice, but it can help us reframe issues. For example, below we consider some obvious differences between Naikan therapy and traditional psychotherapy:

Traditional psychotherapy	Naikan therapy
Focuses on feelings.	Focuses on facts.
Revisits your hurts from the past.	Revisits how you have been supported in the past.

Your problems are blamed on others.	You take responsibility for your problems and those you cause others.
The purpose is to increase the client's self-esteem.	The purpose is for the client to increase their appreciation for life, and in doing so improve their self-esteem and self-identity.
Concentrates on how we may have been wronged by others.	Focuses on how others have provided support to us.
Focuses on feelings.	Focuses on the realism of relationships.

Whilst Naikan can be seen as a form of meditation, with its key objective being the focus on gratitude, it is also a type of therapy, the effects of which can have profound effect on the adopter of the processes it recommends. It grounds us in the moment and encourages us to live mindfully. As the Indian playwright and dramatist Kālidāsa writes, 'Yesterday is but a dream, tomorrow is only a vision. But today well lived makes every yesterday a dream of happiness, and every tomorrow a vision of hope.'

SUMMARY

Chapter 28 looked further into confirmation bias – if we want to, or need to, believe something, we will always look for the evidence that supports this belief. This can take place in both positive and negative thinking. Whilst negative thinking has its place – it keeps us safe from threats and danger – positive thinking can increase our life span, reduce the chances of us developing depression and build our resilience to difficult situations. Whilst our confirmation bias can tune us into the evidence we find to support our beliefs, the things we believe about the situation can change what then happens. The second half of the chapter encouraged us to find an 'attitude of gratitude', to become more positive, optimistic and generous. This can be developed by the Naikan theory, which reflects on what you have received, what you have given and what you have caused in a day.

CHAPTER TWENTY-NINE

THE ELUSIVE BUTTERFLY

*Thoughts become perception; perception becomes reality.
Alter your thoughts, alter your reality.*
– WILLIAM JAMES

Take a brief moment to consider the following. If you could rerun your life from the beginning, would it turn out the same as it is now? What tiny changes would you need to make to make it different? Are our lives more a result of happenstance or repeatable processes? What seemingly small and insignificant events in our past led to where we are today? What tiny changes would you have to make in the past to create the life you want for yourself now?

Of course, we can't travel back in time to make those changes, but we can consider the tiny changes we can begin to make today that will have a profound effect on our lives several years from now. These tiny changes are often paralleled with a phenomenon known as chaos theory, or more commonly as the butterfly effect. The term butterfly effect is closely associated with the work of meteorologist Edward Lorenz, the father of the chaos theory.

In his early years at MIT in the 1950s, it was Lorenz's task to examine long-range weather forecasting. One day whilst running what seemed to be the same calculation through a computer twice, the computer inadvertently appeared to come up with vastly different results. When he tried to ascertain what had happened, he noticed a slight decimal point change. Less than 0.0001 in fact. This small amount wound up leading to significant error. Unsurprisingly, weather is hard to forecast, because small changes like this can have a big impact on the weather.

That error became a seminal scientific paper, presented in 1972, concerning the butterfly effect. Lorenz suggested that a small change can make much bigger changes happen; one small incident can have a big impact on the future. Could a butterfly flapping its wings in Brazil set off a tornado in Texas? The theory has come to be known as 'sensitive dependence on initial conditions'.

On the surface it may seem a preposterous suggestion, or perhaps even poetic that a single minor perturbation such as the flapping of a butterfly's wings could have the power to set off a string of escalating events – events that could lead to the formation of a weather event in another part of the world. But the butterfly represents an unknowable quantity. A butterfly wing, perhaps not. But wind turbines or solar panels spread over a large enough area? Well, possibly.

When you consider your own life, what seemingly small events have happened that had a major effect on your future? History is scattered with such events.

Take for example traffic. A single car slamming on the brakes to avoid an object in the road at an inopportune moment could, conceivably, set off a chain of events that could contribute to a major hours-long traffic jam. Thousands of people could be late for work, and meetings or trips cancelled as a result of this event. Indeed, at this present moment in history, who could have conceived that a virus believed to originate in a market in China could cause so many major consequences for the majority of the planet – like a domino effect, one seemingly small event affecting another and so on.

Another perhaps familiar example is in Benjamin Franklin's 1758 essay *The Way to Wealth*. Franklin penned:

> *For want of a Nail the Shoe was lost; for want of a Shoe the Horse was lost; and for want of a Horse the Rider was lost; being*

overtaken and slain by the Enemy, all for want of Care about a Horse-shoe Nail.

IF I COULD TURN BACK TIME

If what we think about and talk about is what we bring about, perhaps we should take the time to be more careful of our thoughts. As the butterfly effect beautifully highlights, these thoughts are like seeds that in time can bring forth either great things or terrible tragedies.

As the Law of Concentration states, whatever you consciously and persistently direct your thoughts upon will grow and expand in your life. In other words, the more you think and reflect upon something, the larger the impact it will have on your daily choices, behaviours and actions. You have a choice either to concentrate upon what it is you want to appear in your life, your goals and the things that bring you the most joy and feelings of gratitude and abundance, or instead, you can choose to focus on your fears, failures and mistakes.

NOTHING'S GONNA STOP US NOW

When we set goals for ourselves, we can often fall foul of a bias we examined earlier in this book, survivorship bias. We tend to focus on the individuals who end up winning at something – essentially the survivors. In doing so we mistakenly assume that the winners had more ambitious goals than others in their winning endeavour. Unsurprisingly, it's every Olympian's desire to win a gold medal, every entrepreneur wishes their business to be a huge success and every candidate wants to get the job they desire. It's better perhaps to find happiness in the journey rather than the destination. After all, how many of us have achieved a goal or reached a destination only to find it wasn't as fulfilling as we had imagined? Instead let's work on visualising the steps to a goal, rather than the goal itself. In doing so we remove the conflict that can occur when we don't reach our objectives. We are no longer disappointed and see ourselves as failures.

APRIL SHOWERS

Have you ever noticed that you seem to get your best and most creative ideas when you are in the shower or when you first lay down to go to sleep, or is that just me?

So, you're mindlessly scrubbing away and – bam! – a great idea pops into your head.

Perhaps you've finally solved that problem that has been bugging you at work. Or maybe you've had an 'aha' moment and have come to realise something you hadn't realised before, like a brief moment of enlightenment. So why does this happen? What does lathering yourself up have to do with this creative frenzy? What is it about the shower that makes the 'perfect storm' of conditions for your creativity, enticing out your inner genius? The Persian poet Rumi held the answer to this in the 13th century when he penned, 'The quieter you become, the more you are able to hear'.

Research has shown that you are more likely to have a creative epiphany when you are doing something monotonous, like exercising, fishing or showering, since these routines require little conscious thought. Essentially you switch on the autopilot for a period, and, in doing so, you free up your subconscious to work on something else. You mind is free to wander and be creative with its natural problem-solving abilities.

This kind of daydreaming relaxes the prefrontal cortex – your brain's command centre – the part of your brain that is responsible for cognitive activities linked to decision making, goals and behaviour. It also switches off the rest of your brain's default mode network (DMN) clearing the pathways that connect different regions of your brain. Essentially with your cortex loosened up and your DMN switched off you are free to be more creative and explore possibilities. That is why the ideas you have in the shower are so different from the ideas you have at work. In the shower, often with your eyes closed, you instantaneously remove all of the mental roadblocks to creativity.

Strange as it may seem, your brain is not most active when you're focused on a task. Rather, research shows it's far more active when you let go of the leash and allow it to wander. Harvard associate Shelly Carson discovered that highly creative people share one amazing trait – they are easily distracted. The beauty of a nice warm (or cold!) shower is that it distracts you. It forces you to defocus for a short while. Your magnificent, creative brain is free to travel. Your DMN is activated, and you are free to allow zany and madcap ideas to bounce around for a brief period.

When it comes to working on a problem, never be afraid to take a break from it. Your amazing subconscious brain continues to work on it without you realising. Indeed, NASA aerospace engineer John Houbolt, the man credited with leading the team behind the lunar orbit rendezvous mission, was always having ideas in his downtime. He would report scribbling his ideas down on shopping bags, envelopes and even, on one occasion, along the side of his bathtub. Ideas can strike us at any time, often when we are not even consciously considering the problem we are looking to resolve. Friedrich Nietzsche sums it up perfectly when he states, 'All truly great thoughts are conceived while walking'.

AIN'T NO STOPPING US NOW

Indeed, sometimes we just don't know what we just don't know, and it's this unknowing that can free us from fear. Incredibly the average age of the flight controllers in mission control when the Americans first landed a man on the lunar surface was a staggeringly young 26 years of age. While it seems strange that such huge responsibility would be given to such a young group of individuals, not long out of university, their youth was for the most part regarded as a significant asset. As Apollo flight director Gerry Griffin stated, 'It wasn't that they didn't understand the risks, they just weren't afraid'. Sometimes not having the belief you can't do something is a distinct advantage. Perhaps if the team working on the Apollo mission had been significantly older, they might have thought going to the Moon an impossibility. Of course, if you believe that the Americans never landed on the Moon in July 1969, and it was all a complete hoax, then you may need to read Chapter 5 of this book again.

THE IMPOSSIBLE DREAM

Albert Einstein was known to have what he called 'thought experiments' (German: Gedankenexperiment). These so-called 'thought experiments' were a hallmark of his career. Einstein would relax and place himself into an Alpha/Theta brain wave state and allow his mind to wander, making full use of his imagination. At the age of 16, he imagined chasing after a beam of light. That particular thought experiment went on to play an important role in his development of the special theory of relativity.

As well as the creative benefits associated with freeing your subconscious mind for a brief period, during this time your brain may release the 'feel-good' neurotransmitter dopamine. This important neurochemical boosts mood, motivation and attention, and helps regulate movement, learning and emotional responses. This flush of dopamine can also boost your creative juices.

Alpha waves will also flow through your brain – the same waves that appear when you're meditating, having a massage or happily relaxing. Alphas accompany your brain's daydreamy default setting and may encourage the creative fireworks.

SUMMARY

This chapter examines the Butterfly Effect. How small initial changes can, over time, bring about massive transformations in any area. Shower thoughts, fact or fiction? Chapter 29 answers this for us by revealing that when we are doing our most mundane and autopiloted tasks, we are most receptive to creative thoughts. When we allow our minds to wander and take control, our brains become most active, and we can perhaps solve a great problem without even thinking about it.

CHAPTER THIRTY

IT'S ABOUT TIME!

Where is it, this present? It has melted in our grasp,
fled ere we could touch it, gone in the instant of becoming.
– WILLIAM JAMES

For all of us who have lived through the various lockdowns of 2020/21, you may have noticed that it's hard to pinpoint certain times in the past year. It may be that it all seems like something of a blur when you think back on that time, as if time is somehow distorted. Unless, of course, you have experienced loss, sickness or other trauma – then your perception of it is vastly different, I'm sure.

In this chapter, we are going to look at time and how to control time – how to make time appear as if it has slowed down. After all, who would not like more time? Unless of course you are experiencing the symptoms of depression, in which case it already feels like time has slowed down. Indeed, our emotions can also influence our perception of time. We seem to experience time as if it is somehow elastic. Some events seem to last forever whilst others are over in the blink of an eye. As Daniel Kahneman states in his TED Talk 'The riddle of experience vs. memory', 'There is a difference between being happy *in* your life and being happy *with* your life'. Fortunately, if you are experiencing depression at present, then what we will cover in this chapter will help you to overcome those debilitating symptoms as well.

Time appears to slow down when we are gripped by a situation that is life-threatening. In one study, participants with arachnophobia were asked to look at a spider for 45 seconds. Understandably, when they were asked to estimate the length of time they had been observing the arachnids for they greatly overestimated the elapsed time. The same pattern was observed in novice skydivers, who estimated the duration of their peers' falls as seeming short, whereas their own, from the same altitude, were deemed significantly longer.

A similar experience occurs when we go on holiday, in what has come to be known as 'the holiday paradox'. Imagine you are going on a well-deserved holiday and there is a long, frustrating wait at the airport before your departure. Eventually, you arrive at your destination and have days packed from morning till night with fun, adventure and new experiences. It feels as if the delay at the airport lasted a lifetime, whereas the fun-packed days are hurtling by in a flash. It appears that in the blink of an eye you are back at the airport again on your return journey. A month or so later, when you think back to your holiday, the delay at the airport will appear tiny, indeed unmemorable, whereas the fun-filled days that appeared to fly by are now remembered in a lot more detail as if they were a lot longer than they appeared at the time.

The Holiday Paradox is caused by the fact that we view time in our minds in two very diverse ways: prospectively and retrospectively. So, for example, if you spend your whole holiday on the same sunbed day after day, just relaxing and letting time pass, you'll have a harder time remembering it because there's nothing memorable happening during that time, unless you have a disagreement over a particular sunbed of course. This means, that even if it *seemed* like a long time while you were experiencing it, when you look back, it'll seem much shorter, even though you were probably having a lovely time having a well-deserved rest. Similarly, as you may remember from when we looked at the peak–end rule earlier in this book, we often remember a weekend break in more detail than a week's relaxing holiday, as we tend to cram our weekend breaks with a lot more memorable experience.

Time seems to speed up as we get older – a phenomenon on which competing theories have attempted to shed light. One, known as the 'proportionality theory', focuses solely on the mathematics of ageing. It suggests that a year feels faster when you're 40 than when you're 8 because it only constitutes one fortieth of your life rather than a whole eighth. Similarly to the holiday paradox, almost every day when we are young is filled with new experiences. The summers felt like they lasted forever and were always sunny, which is not such a surprise if you are fortunate enough to have grown up in California or Florida, but an amazing memory illusion if you have grown up in the UK.

An example of how experiencing novelty makes us believe time is appearing longer than it actually is in reality is a study called 'the oddball effect'. Imagine being shown the same image of a cute kitten over and over, each image lasting for about 1 second. Then, after about 10 or so viewings of the same kitten image, you are shown an image of a spider or something that really grabs your attention. This new image will appear to be on the screen for longer than the kitten images, even though it was onscreen for the same length of time. This perceptual phenomenon utilises novelty to create the illusion that the image has been there longer. The brain gets used to things very quickly. When something new is introduced, it literally sits up and listens, or sees, as in this example.

The phenomenon of inattentional blindness, which we examined earlier in this book, and the oddball effect seem, on the surface, to have little or no relationship to each other; however, they do in fact share an important commonality: they both occur in the presence of unexpected events.

I DON'T WANT TO MISS A THING

We tend to rely on memory rather than knowledge to date events happening within our lifetime but, as our memory distorts our perception of time, it also affects our sense of when an event took place.

When it comes to recalling a long-ago event, psychologists have found that it's common to think that it happened more recently than it actually did. But if the event happened within the past 3 years, we often think that it happened longer ago than it really did. This effect is known as telescoping. Think of it as looking backwards or forwards through a telescope where images are distorted depending on the orientation.

The Covid-19 lockdown is perhaps a perfect example of telescoping. Due to the mental haze many of us have experienced over the past year it may be quite a challenge to pinpoint events that have occurred over the past year or so. Frontline healthcare workers, on the other hand, reported how the heightened anxiety and attentiveness of working during the pandemic had the effect of vastly distorting their perception of time, making their waking day feel extremely long and incredibly stressful.

Similarly, scientists in Japan have shown that the distorted sense of time we all experienced may have been caused, in part, by brain cells getting tired. It appears that time in the brain doesn't follow the steady ticking of the world's most precise clocks. Instead, as we have all experienced at some stage in our lives, time seems to fly by at one moment and practically stand still at others.

2020 will not be forgotten as the year of the pandemic any time soon, but there is a high probability that we will misplace exactly when some events occurred.

As you find yourself looking back on this year, be aware of the illusion of time.

Our perception of time can sometimes be skewed, causing us to lose a sense of perspective about events not only from our past but from history. For example, did you know that Marilyn Monroe and Her Majesty Queen Elizabeth II were born in the same year, 1926, as each other? As were Anne Frank and Martin Luther King Jr, who were both born in 1929.

When we look back on major events, we can seem to lose perspective as to the passing of time. For example, when you think back to events such as the release of the film *Jurassic Park*, it may surprise you to discover that it was almost 30 years ago (1993).

Also, the release of the classic movie *The Lion King* was closer in time to the Moon landings than it is to us today. Similarly, it may amaze you to recall that the London Olympics was back in 2012!. In the same vein, are you easily able to pinpoint how far back in time it was that the Chernobyl disaster happened (1986)?

The way we perceive events from the distant past can also tell us a lot about how we view history. For example, Cleopatra (70 BCE) lived closer to the invention of Snapchat (2011) than she lived to the construction of the Great Pyramid at Giza (2550 BCE). And as the pyramids were being built woolly mammoths still roamed the earth. Similarly, the Stegosaurus was older to the Tyrannosaurus rex than the T. rex is to us living today!

Continuing in this vein, Charlie Chaplin was born in the same year as Hitler. In addition, he could have seen the film *Star Wars* on its release before he died in 1977 – Chaplin that is, not Hitler! Also in that year, in France you could still have been guillotined, as it had not yet been outlawed. Startlingly, pensions for soldiers who fought in the American Civil War were still being paid out in 2003. Perhaps even more shockingly, prisoners were arriving at Auschwitz just days after the McDonald's brothers opened their first restaurant in 1940.

What we see in the heavens is not exempt from the mysteries of time. Because light takes time to reach us, everything we see is in the past. The sunlight you enjoy coming in through your window is 8 minutes and 20 seconds old. In the night sky, the light from Proxima Centauri, our nearest star, is 4 years old by the time we get to see it.

Finally, if your brain hasn't begun to hurt yet, just ponder on the fact that it was a mere 66 years after the Wright brothers invented human flight that mankind landed on the Moon. And if that hasn't done it, think about the fact that actors Macaulay Culkin and Ryan Gosling were both born in the same year (1980) and the fact that if Anne Frank were alive today, she would be younger than the Queen.

SOMEWHERE A CLOCK IS TICKING

When it comes to time, physicists believe there's no such thing as 'now'. Space and time are fluid, affected by gravity and your speed. Einstein put it like this: 'For us physicists, the distinction between past, present and future is only an illusion, however persistent'.

Think about your perception of time. It's entirely possible that you can find a way to slow down your perception of time and therefore enjoy your life and live it to its fullest potential. We can't live longer, but we can slow our perception of time down.

In an episode of *Star Trek* penned by creator Gene Roddenberry entitled 'The Menagerie', Roddenberry first coined the phrase reality distortion field (RDF). The term was later used by Bud Tribble at Apple Computers in 1981 to describe company co-founder Steve Jobs' charisma and his effect on the developers working on the Macintosh project. Bud Tribble once said of Jobs, 'Steve has a reality distortion field ... in his presence, reality is malleable. He can convince anyone of practically anything.'

In chapter 3 of Steve Jobs' biography, biographer Walter Isaacson states that around 1972 (while Jobs was attending Reed College) Robert Friedland 'taught Steve the Reality Distortion Field'. The RDF was said by Andy Hertzfeld to be Steve Jobs' ability to convince himself, and others around him, to believe almost anything – utilising a mix of charisma, charm, bravado, overstatement, marketing, appeasement and sheer doggedness.

Whilst it is perhaps a romantic concept to believe that Jobs somehow manipulated time, his RDF was more about convincing those who worked for him that something they thought unobtainable in a given time frame was most certainly achievable. The concept of the RDF was said to distort his co-workers' sense of proportion and scales of difficulties to make them believe that whatever impossible task he had at hand was possible – something Jobs was clearly a master at.

MAGIC MOMENTS

In research carried out by Robin Kramer and his colleagues at the University of Kent, Kramer hypothesised that, given mindfulness' emphasis on moment-to-moment awareness, mindfulness meditation would slow down time and produce the feeling that short periods of time lasted longer. Kramer and his colleagues trained participants to link different shapes to either a short or a long period of time. Shapes shown on a computer screen for 400 milliseconds represented a short duration, while shapes shown for 1600 milliseconds represented a longer duration. Next, all of the participants were presented with shapes held on the screen for a variety of durations and had to decide whether the duration was more similar to the short or the long periods of time.

Half of the participants then listened to a 10-minute mindfulness meditation exercise. The other half listened to the audiobook version of *The Hobbit* for 10 minutes. Immediately afterwards, the researchers again presented them with shapes for varying durations of time.

The results showed that the participants who meditated were more likely to report that durations of time were 'long' after they had meditated. In contrast, those who had listened to *The Hobbit* recording didn't report any difference in time duration. The researchers concluded that the mindfulness meditation session shifted the participants' experience of time, making it appear that it was passing more slowly. Remarkably, they saw this effect after just a single 10-minute meditation, even among participants who had no prior meditation experience.

WHAT A WONDERFUL WORLD

In this final part of the this book, I want to look at bending time to your advantage. Not in the way Steve Jobs achieved, but in a way to make the most of each day of our finite lives, in a manner, warping time to our advantage. I like to think of these moments as 'Time Distortion Moments' (TDM).

As we have discovered previously in this chapter, time seems to slow down when we experience something new and original (as in the oddball effect). The reason that for many of us the lockdown year seems blurred is that there were few, if any, markers within it. No holidays, no weekends away, no ceremonies or celebrations. Indeed, no memorable shopping excursions or shared times with friends and family. Unless of course you were a frontline or key worker, in which case the whole experience was vastly different. Similarly, if you experienced the loss of a loved one during this time the whole experience would be different again.

At the heart of TDM is a practice that makes every day memorable; that makes every day stand out from the rest.

When it comes to overcoming the debilitating effects of depression, adopting TDM will allow the sufferer to place moments in time. To make the days that seem never ending and indistinguishable from one day to the next, stand out. To break the pattern of viewing time as a linear experience with little or no change to that repetitious rhythm of unmomentous events. When I work with clients with depression, they rarely speak of 'stand-out' moments in their week. Rarely, if ever, do they talk about working on the book they are writing or the sporting challenge they are undertaking.

Take a brief moment to picture a parent taking their little boy for a trip to a favourite beach for what might be the first time. The little one hears the roar of the surf, the squawk of seagulls; he builds a sandcastle and plays for hours in the sand. The happy lad doesn't need much to entertain him other than a bucket and spade. Close by, other families are sitting under beach umbrellas and toddlers are screaming with joy as they play in the water. There are shells on the beach to collect and ice creams to be eaten.

To the young boy, a plethora of amazing and exhilarating new experiences are being experienced, perhaps for the first time. To the parent, by contrast, this is a familiar experience – just another trip to the beach. Indeed, they may spend a good portion of their day on their mobile or with their head in a book or magazine.

The difference between the parent and the boy's subjective experiences of the identical experience offers a fascinating clue to something psychologists have pondered over for years; namely, why our sense of the passing of time can vary so much. For the little boy, who no doubt falls asleep whilst journeying home in the car, this has been an extremely long and thrilling excitement-filled day. To the parent, the day has flown by, and nothing of note has happened at all, unless of course they received a parking ticket for staying for too long on the beach.

What if the parent, rather than having their head stuck in a distraction, had spent the time watching and playing with their child? Building sandcastles and playing chicken with him, avoiding the water as it rushes up the beach. Observing the look of joy as he completes his tenth sandcastle. What if they had observed what was happening around them? What if they had taken time to listen attentively to the sound of the water lapping on the shore or the varied calls of the seabirds. What if they had focused on the sensation of the warm sand on the soles of their feet, or properly smelt the fresh air? Would the day have flown by so quickly? Would they be thinking about what they had to do at work or at home that week? I doubt it.

Mindfulness is very much about being just that, mindful; living in the moment rather than being concerned about the future or the past. Outwardly this appears to be obvious, but as we have discussed before in this book, common sense is rarely, if ever, common practice.

Now imagine that as you were being born (assuming you could understand the deal being offered) you were presented with a simple choice. You could live to be a healthy 100 years of age, but, less the time taken for sleep, you would only be aware of around 30 years of them; or you could live to be a healthy 80 years of age, but this time, adjusting for sleep, you would be fully aware of a full 45 of those years. Which option would you take? Most of us would perhaps take the latter, thinking it to be a good 'less is more' deal. But how many of us are living the former, without even realising it? How much of our lives are we fully aware of; how many of our days blend into one unmemorable day? How many of those days have identifiable events that make them truly memorable? It's perhaps worth bearing in mind what psychologist David Eagleman states when he reminds us that 'The more detailed the memory, the longer the moment seems to last'.

STUCK IN A MOMENT YOU CAN'T GET OUT OF

If you are like the majority of us, the moment you step into your car you choose the type of entertainment you would like for the journey: music, podcast or audiobook. But what if you had silence – how would that feel? Would you be forced momentarily to 'live in your head' and listen to the voices there? Would you be able to really notice what you see out the window? To really look at the road and the thousands of stimuli we see as we drive but often filter out?

In the brilliant *Dictionary of Obscure Sorrows* by John Koenig he has created the word 'Zenosyne' to describe the sense that time keeps going faster. He goes on to say 'Life is short. And life is long. But not in that order.'

The Bully In Your Brain methodology is not just about being mindful in your day-to-day life; it is about attempting to create a new TDM each day. They should become part of who you are, and you should be constantly looking for ways to mark your days. They can take on various forms. Here are just a handful of suggestions:

- Walk and explore somewhere you have never walked before.
- Eat something you perhaps have never tried before.
- Drink something you have never drunk before (ideally non-alcoholic).
- Talk to someone you have not chatted with previously.
- Watch a YouTube video that inspires you.
- Read something that motivates and educates you.
- Really examine a plant or a tree you have never really looked at before.
- Have a nice, relaxing bath in the middle of your day.

References

- Try to learn a word in different languages.
- Wear clothes you would never normally wear.
- Invent a new game to play with your child/children.
- Eat your food mindfully.
- Visit a museum or gallery you would not usually visit.
- Visit a historic place and read about its history.
- Try fasting for the day (always consult with your doctor first).
- Swim in the sea.
- Walk in the rain.
- Learn a new skill each day.
- Blindfold yourself for 1 hour and listen to what you can hear around you.
- Meditate for an hour.
- Visit a Buddhist temple.
- Listen to music you would not normally listen to.
- Take time to talk with an old person and learn about their story.
- Try indoor (or outdoor) skydiving.
- Learn to paddleboard.
- Visit a planetarium.
- Write a journal.
- Take 10 minutes to reflect on everything you are grateful for.

The list is virtually endless, and I would love to hear your ideas at hello@bullyinyourbrain.co.uk. Together, let's make every day that we are alive on this incredible planet memorable, so when it does come time to look back, it will feel like we have lived several lifetimes.

TIME AFTER TIME

Now, ask yourself for a moment how do you perceive time? Do you feel in control of your future, or do you feel that your future is very much out of your control?

Let's imagine the following scenario. Your boss calls you to arrange an important meeting. He states that he will meet you at noon on Wednesday at a local coffee shop. But the night before your meeting, he messages you to say that he has to move the meeting forward by 2 hours. You chirpily say, 'Great! See you then!' Shortly after hanging up the call, you start to think to yourself, 'Did he mean he's moved the meeting to 10 am or 2 pm?' Too embarrassed to call back, you start to fret about the upcoming rendezvous.

Chances are, you chose one of those two times automatically without giving it too much thought. In other words, it was obvious to you what time he meant. You then call your friend and explain to them that your boss has moved the meeting forward 2 hours, to which they reply, 'Gosh, does he mean 10am or 2pm?' At that point, you suddenly realise the time you thought it might be is fully dependent on how you interpret what your boss meant. Was it moved 2 hours earlier or 2 hours later? You then go and ask other friends what they think and are astounded that about 50% of them think it's at 10am and 50% think it's at 2pm. You are now beginning to get stressed.

The next day, you arrive promptly at 10am, sit in the chosen coffee shop and wait. You wait and you wait, until 4 hours later when your boss breezes in. Finally, as you leave the meeting after being there for what seems like a whole day, you berate yourself once again for having wasted the majority of the day on your mobile. You also make a mental note to take the bull by the horns next time and call your boss to confirm the correct time. Once again, you begin to realise how much your inner dialogue seems to rule your life.

So, did you think the meeting was at 10am or 2pm? Interestingly, whichever time you opted for is indicative of how you view the movement of time in your life. If you perceive time as something you move towards then you may lean more towards what is recognised as an 'ego-moving perspective' of time. You may also talk about events like you are advancing towards them, saying things such as, 'I'm approaching the deadline'. Whereas if you tend to see time as if you are stationary and it is moving towards you, then you take a more of a 'time-moving perspective'.

Think of the two types of movement as if you are standing in a stream. If you imagine that you are still and the water is moving towards you then you are more focused on the 'time-moving perspective'. If, on the other hand, you are moving forwards in the water, then your perspective of time is more likely the 'ego-moving perspective'. These can of course fluctuate and are not fixed for anyone.

Take a moment now to think about how our emotional experiences might affect our perception of time. In a study conducted by researchers Lee and Ji (2013), they looked at how people's emotional experiences affect their time perspective. They asked participants to recall positive and negative memories, and then asked them ambiguous time-related questions.

They discovered that subjects who recalled pleasant memories were far more likely to adopt the ego-moving perspective of time (i.e. move towards time). Conversely, subjects who recalled unpleasant memories were more likely to adopt the time-moving perspective (i.e. allow time to move to them). They suggested that this is perhaps due to people preferring to move towards positive stimuli and away from negative stimuli, which also applies to events in our future.

This assumption correlates with the research of neuroscientists, who have long believed that all animals, including humans, are hardwired to seek pleasure and avoid pain. These studies suggest that our emotional experiences affect our view of time. For example, we state things such as we are 'looking forward to a wedding', when we are looking positively on a future event. Conversely, we announce things such as 'I have a job interview coming up' when the event doesn't bring to mind such levels of potential joy and fulfilment.

On a psychological level, when you're talking about the ego-moving perspective, it can feel like you have more of a sense of control over what you're doing in your life. In other words, you are moving forwards in time, and feeling more in control of your own destiny. If, however, you are static, and waiting for time to pass you then it can feel that you are less in control of your life (more about a desire for control later in this book).

Take time each day to consider how you feel about the movement of time. Do you move towards it or do you allow it to move to you?

In the meantime, happy Time Distortion Moments!

SUMMARY

The penultimate chapter of the book examined time and how we experience it. If we are experiencing something mundane and routine, our brain will quickly get used to it, and the time will seem to pass quickly. If, however, we do something that is novel to our brains, then our attention is piqued, and time appears to be longer.

The chapter looked at how we can perhaps slow down our perception of time. We cannot stop time from moving, but the way we can experience it can change. By introducing mindfulness practice into our routines, we become more aware of everything that happens in a day and give ourselves more markers with which to remember that day. If a day is run of the mill, with nothing out of the ordinary happening, chances are it will be easily forgotten. If we however spend the day celebrating a birthday, or watching our favourite team win a sporting event, we will remember it for a lot longer. So, the secret is to fill our days with these unforgettable moments, so that we don't feel as if our lives are just whizzing by us. I have coined these moments 'Time Distortion Moments' – bending time to our own advantage.

References

CHAPTER THIRTY-ONE

DON'T STOP BELIEVIN'

You can do as much as you think you can,
But you'll never accomplish more;
If you're afraid of yourself, young man,
There's little for you in store.
For failure comes from the inside first,
It's there, if we only knew it,
And you can win, though you face the worst,
If you feel that you're going to do it.
– EDGAR A. GUEST

For the 1900 Paris World's Fair, a German chocolate company made the magnificent decision to create a range of beautifully detailed postcards depicting life 100 years from now. For a short time, the Theodore Hildebrand and Son chocolate company placed these colourful cards depicting life in the year 2000 into the boxes of their scrumptious sweets. In total 12 such cards were created, predicting how a range of activities would be upgraded for the 21st century. These futuristic predictions depicted men and women flying around in their own personal flying machines, buildings that were on rails so they could easily be moved around from city to city, X-ray machines that the police utilised to catch would-be criminals in the act, glass-roofed leisure submarines that facilitated tourists to view marine life, as well as canoe shoes that made it possible for people and animals to walk effortlessly on water. Amongst my personal favourites are cities sheltered in glass to protect their inhabitants from rain and the 'good weather' machines that ensured permanently favourable weather all year round.

Theodore Hildebrand & Son Chocolate Company

The most thought-provoking aspect of these amazing and meticulously crafted images is the fact that despite the incredible forward thinking and creativity that must have gone into the postcards, the fashion had not changed at all. In the future we can walk on water, but we still wear the same styles and fashions that existed 100 years prior. Had they depicted a man on the Moon, then that man would almost certainly have worn a fishbowl helmet and probably he would be sporting a black frock coat with grey striped trousers. In other words, on some levels so much had changed, but on others, things had remained just as they were. It makes me consider how often the way we think and in particular our limiting beliefs are similar to these futuristic chocolatier's postcards. Externally, so much has changed, and we have moved forwards, but on another level our old, comfortable ways of thinking have remained the same. Unless we change our thinking, there will always be something holding us back.

In this book my intention was to give you, the reader, a new perspective on your thoughts and your beliefs. Particularly your limiting beliefs, or as I prefer to call them, those 'auto-limiting thoughts'. To guide and assist you in beginning to think about and question the beliefs you have. In simple terms, to make the unconscious conscious. I believe that the majority of the thoughts and behaviours we have every day are underpinned by the beliefs we have – the majority of which were formed by the time we were 7 years old. But rather than saying the answer to a problem is the number 4, my intention is to ask you instead what 2 + 2 is? In other words, to allow you, the reader, to question your own thoughts and beliefs, rather than me didactically telling you how to challenge and change them. I believe that 'true' self-insight is perhaps one of the most powerful tools we have to make effective and lasting change in our lives.

SLOW BOAT TO CHINA

When it comes to long-lasting change in our lives, I think there are few better examples than that of the incredible Chinese bamboo tree.

When you sow the seed of the Chinese bamboo tree, you are required to water and nurture it regularly. For the first year nothing happens. Literally nothing. You continue to water it and by the end of the second year you will once again find that nothing has appeared. It fails to emerge even by the end of the third year, but of course you must continue to irrigate and fertilise it. By now you may be starting to get the picture and won't be too surprised to find out that by the end of the fourth year there is still nothing to be seen.

Now at this point you could consider giving up, wishing you had planted something else instead – thinking to yourself that you've put so much time, effort and energy in but have got nothing back. Not even a glimmer of a bamboo tree. It hasn't even broken the ground yet!

Then suddenly in the fifth year, something extraordinary happens – something that seems almost miraculous! Within 1 week it grows a whopping 90 feet! It's almost as if you can see the tree growing before your very eyes. It has been recorded that the tree can actually grow 122 cm (48 inches) in a 24-hour period! Not only that but it can sometimes reach a maximum growth rate of 99 cm (39 inches) per hour for short periods of time.

It seems almost inconceivable that a plant that lies dormant for years can suddenly explode with growth, but it happens virtually without fail with Chinese bamboo trees.

If the average person chose to grow any other tree, without doubt they would see results within just one season. Those trees then would continue to grow, but usually at a very slow rate. The grower of the Chinese bamboo needs patience, but the exponential growth you get in the end more than makes up for it.

But here's the question: did the Chinese bamboo tree grow in 1 week or 5 years and 1 week? Had the person growing the Chinese bamboo tree given up on watering and fertilising it when it was not showing up, then it almost certainly would never have broken ground.

If you saw somebody taking the time to nurture something, watering it, caring for it, but getting nothing back for 5 years, would you think they were crazy? Or would you consider that they are very patient, goal-driven and hugely motivated?

In many ways, accomplishing success in life can be very much like the incredible Chinese bamboo. More often than not we put a lot of time, effort and energy into the initial stages of a particular goal, only to give up quickly if we don't see the results we expected – in this way never knowing if, similar to the Chinese bamboo, it was just a matter of time and patience before the ground broke and the thing we hoped for exploded beyond all expectations.

By staying focused and working towards your goal, remarkable growth can take place in a staggering manner within a short period of time – just like the Chinese bamboo tree.

THE TIES THAT BIND

One day, a poor peasant called Gordius arrived with his wife on an ox cart in the public square of Phrygia. As good fortune would have it for Gordius, an oracle had previously educated the populace that their future king would come into town riding such a wagon. Seeing Gordius, therefore, the people immediately made him king. In gratitude, Gordius dedicated his ox cart to Zeus, tying it up with a highly intricate knot, which came to be known as the Gordian knot. Another great oracle foretold that the person who untied the knot would rule all of Asia.

Alexander the Great cutting the Gordian knot

Many tried to untie the complex knot but failed, and it wasn't until the year 333 BCE, when Alexander the Great arrived, that a solution was found. Alexander had set his mind upon conquering the world, so he was well equipped to deal with insurmountable challenges. The knot therefore was of great interest to him. After a careful examination he felt sure that he would not be able to untie it, so instantly he drew his sword and sliced through the knot. Although Alexander's method seemed to go against the spirit of the challenge, it probably would have been unwise to disagree with a man who had a desire to rule the world and, in particular, one holding a sword. His method clearly flew in the face of the rules, which were supposedly about undoing the knot by manipulating it successfully.

Alexander was no dummy. He was, after all, a former student of Aristotle, and thus would have been no stranger to logical puzzles. Most likely he resorted to the sword because he could see that the knot could not be untied simply by working the rope. Some believe that the knot must have been constructed by first splicing the two ends of a length of rope to form a circular loop, which was then 'tied up' – wrapped around itself in some way – to disguise the fact that it was not really knotted.

However, before Alexander came along, many fine minds had been stumped by the Gordian knot problem, and yet no one had claimed the puzzle was unsolvable. Surely, then, it must have appeared that, in principle, the knot could be untied. Nevertheless, Alexander demonstrated that sometimes in order to solve a problem we need to approach it from a completely fresh perspective. Either that or just carry a sword with you at all times for good measure.

For many of us it can feel like our thinking is similar to the Gordian knot. We have limiting beliefs that we believe are rigged and fixed and are unmovable. Sometimes, however, when we consider them from a unique perspective, we may find a simple, more effective solution to overcoming them.

NO REGRETS

We all perhaps have regrets in our life. Missed opportunities, romantic interests not pursued, jobs or ambitions we haven't pursued, seeking safety rather than taking risks. According to Tom Gilovich of Cornell University, our most enduring regrets are the ones that stem from our failure to live up to our ideal selves. Gilovich has found that people are troubled more by regrets about failing to fulfil their hopes, goals and aspirations than by regrets about failing to fulfil their duties, obligations and responsibilities. Gilovich goes on to say, 'When we evaluate our lives, we think about whether we're heading toward our ideal selves, becoming the person we'd like to be. Those are the regrets that are going to stick with you, because they are what you look at through the windshield (windscreen) of life.'

In his earlier work Gilovich found people tend to regret the things they hadn't done rather than the things they had. 'In the short term, people regret their actions more than inactions. But in the long term, the inaction regrets stick around longer'. Building on those ideas, Gilovich hypothesised that people's most enduring regrets in life tend to come from discrepancies between their actual and ideal selves. He goes on to state that often we assume that we first need inspiration before we can strive to achieve our ideals. But the good news is that there is a significant amount of research which shows this is not the case. Gilovich goes on to say, 'As the Nike slogan says: "Just do it." Don't wait around for inspiration, just plunge in. Waiting around for inspiration is an excuse. Inspiration arises from engaging in the activity.'

Intriguingly, Gilovich believes that people often fail to achieve their ideal goals because they're worried about how it will look to others. For example, a person might want to learn how to write a novel but feel they could never let others see how bad their writing may be. Once again this is a perfect example of the social anxiety that we examined in Chapter 21 – that all-consuming fear of being judged and scrutinised by others. Gilovich goes on to state that 'People are more charitable than we think and also don't notice us nearly as much as we think, if that's what holding you back – the fear of what other people will think and notice – then think a little more about just doing it'. As American cartoonist Bill Watterson says, 'To invent your own life's meaning is not easy, but it's still allowed, and I think you'll be happier for the trouble'.

KNOCKING ON HEAVEN'S DOOR

Whether you view yourself as religious or not, just for a few moments picture the following scenario. Imagine that you have died peacefully but unexpectedly in your sleep. You arrive in heaven, and God greets you lovingly at the gleaming, pearly gates. As part of your judgement God pulls out a document that features the accomplishments and challenges that have occurred over the course of your life. He starts at birth and finishes with the day of your death. Next, God lays out to you the life you would have had if you had not succumbed to being comfortable, had more 'grit' and an undeterred 'growth mindset'. The things you could have achieved if you hadn't' feared so much the judgement of others. He discloses to you where in your life you could have had more focus and when you could have worked harder rather than giving up. And also where you could have provided more value to others, and accomplished more, despite the odds. After all, every person ever born has exactly the same 24 hours each day to live and work in. In essence, he shows you what your full potential could have been. You stand in awe of the things you were meant to accomplish in your life, but also astonished and saddened by the missed opportunities and experiences you could have enjoyed. Hell, then, is perhaps not being able to return to achieve all of the things you could have achieved.

I was first introduced to the above scenario by the incredible ex-Navy Seal, ultramarathon runner and motivational speaker, David Goggins. Personally, I think about this scenario often, and I regularly share it with my clients in our practice. Sometimes we all need to be reminded that our time here is limited, and that we should all spend it sagely. As we go through our lives the days can often seem to merge, and we can lose our perception of time. Good reason then to try and enjoy as many 'Time Distortion Moments' in our lives as we can possible can (see Chapter 30). At least then we can achieve the illusion of time slowing down for us.

In *The Dictionary of Obscure Sorrows* author John Koenig has created a thought-provoking compendium of invented words. Each original definition aims to fill a hole in the language we use; to give a name to emotions we all might experience but don't yet have a word for. For example, the awareness of how few days in our lives are memorable he calls 'Oleka'.

INCREDIBLE

Use what we have discussed in this book to focus on exactly what it is that you want in life; never be ashamed to dream big – to have a purpose bigger than yourself. To once again quote from Viktor Frankl, 'Everything can be taken from a man but one thing: the last of the human freedoms – to choose one's attitude in any given set of circumstances, to choose one's own way'.

Also, never be afraid to think out of the box. On this subject I am reminded of how Pixar boss Steve Jobs became concerned that they had 'peaked' after the huge successes that Pixar had enjoyed with *Toy Story*, *Finding Nemo* and *A Bug's Life*. Jobs was worried that their successes could make them complacent. Rather than lean on the team of established top performers to come up with something new, he recruited outside talent in the hope they would bring something unique and fresh. He said 'Bring me the Black Sheep. I want artists and creatives that are frustrated. I want the ones that have another way of doing things that nobody is listening to. I want the ones that are laughed at.' These 'Black Sheep' were bought into Pixar and encouraged to try 'crazy ideas'. This team of outliers and misfits ended up creating the massively successful movie *The Incredibles*. *The Incredibles* beat all previous Pixar films – grossing over $600 million – and won the Oscar for Best Animated Feature.

Never be afraid to dare to dream big! As entrepreneur and motivational speaker Jim Rohn once famously said, 'If you don't design your own life plan, chances are you'll fall into someone else's plan. And guess what they have planned for you? Not much.'

WHO LET THE DOGS OUT?

So, harking back to a question I posed in Chapter 3: which British animal is more dangerous, dogs or cows? Well, perhaps surprisingly, according to figures from the Health and Safety Executive (HSE), 74 people have been killed by cows in the past 15 years whilst, according to figures provided by the NHS, dogs have been responsible for just 17 deaths in the past 8 years! Still man's best friend then … just!

In the first chapter of this book, we examined how those annoying 'jingles' can get stuck in your head. Often triggered by emotions, associations or just by hearing the melody somewhere, these recurring tunes involuntarily pop up and stick in your mind. Incredibly it is believed that up to 98% of the Western population has experienced these 'earworms', with 92% of people experiencing an earworm at least once a week! So how do we remove these repeated loops of mental musical monotony? How do we stop obsessing and hearing in our head a particularly 'catchy song' or 'jolly jingle'?

Psychologically, earworms are like a 'cognitive itch' that eventually needs to be scratched. It feels like the more you try to suppress the song, the more it seems to ramp up its' annoyingness. In many ways a similar thing is happening to what we examined in Chapter 15 when we considered Coué's law.

Psychologists from the University of Reading have long been looking for ways to turn off those unwelcome thoughts, and now a study suggests a fresh approach: chew some gum. Indeed, psychologist Philip Beaman and his colleagues discovered that college students exposed to a catchy song, who then went on to chew gum, reported fewer earworms than those who didn't have the oral distractor. The act of chewing gum it seems, as with silently reading, talking or even singing to yourself, engages the tongue, teeth and other parts of the anatomy used to produce speech – the subvocal articulators. It is believed that otherwise using these subvocalisations lessens the brain's ability to form verbal or musical memories. So, hey presto, no more bothersome psychological itches.

There are other strategies for eliminating earworms. British music psychologist Victoria Williamson believes 'distract and engage' is the best approach; for example, chanting a mantra, reciting a poem, listening to a different song or even playing a musical instrument (which is not great news if you don't have one and you can't play anyway!). Williamson believes that, 'If you fill it up with something else that occupies the same circuitry, there's not enough left to make the earworm'.

In a similar vein, researchers at the University of Cambridge designed what they believed was the perfect exercise to eliminate earworms: essentially mentally generating random numbers, at about one a second, without ever repeating a number. Ira Hyman, a professor of psychology at Western Washington University, also believes that focusing on a specific mental task, such as thinking through your schedule for the week, can defeat a repetitive melody. However, if the task is either too easy or too hard, your mind tends to fall back on the earworm. The task must take up just the right amount of cognitive load – what is known as the Goldilocks effect. Not too hard, and not too easy either. To be honest, this method seems a bit too much like hard work, particularly when you can just chew some gum!

The other common approach, and my personal favourite, is to engage the earworm. Instead of trying not to think about it – and in doing so evoking Coué's law – you either deliberately listen to the entire song, start to finish, several times in a row; or, as I do, just try and play the last bit of the song over and over in your head. Frustratingly though, most earworms are fragments of songs, which very likely contributes to their stubborn longevity; it seems that incomplete memories last longer than complete ones, a common phenomenon known as the Zeigarnik effect. In simple terms, the Zeigarnik effect is the idea that it's human nature to finish what we start and, if we don't finish something, we experience some cognitive dissonance. It was first observed by psychologist Bluma Zeigarnik, who observed that waiters in a café could recall the orders they had not yet delivered better than those they had distributed. Because as humans we continually pursue cognitive ease, not finishing something puts us in a state of tension that makes us pay more attention to the task we want to finish. The consequence is that we remember uncompleted tasks more than the completed tasks. In other words, we have little motivation to recall things we've finished whereas we have a strong investment and motivation in unfinished things, and this keeps them in the forefront of our minds.

So why have I dedicated so much space to earworms in the last chapter of a book about belief systems, and what is their relevance? Well, it's about action, or more specifically, about taking positive action. Yes, we can endure an earworm, like we can endure a negative belief. Unlike earworms beliefs don't usually disappear on their own, never to appear again. They need to be challenged, and it can take time, effort and energy to do so.

An earworm, like a belief, can outstay its welcome and make us feel frustrated, anxious and even, on occasion, depressed. The key takeaway, however, is this: if we give them our attention then we can change them. The problem is recognising them. It is my sincerest hope that this book has helped you in starting to do just that.

WE DIDN'T START THE FIRE

At the age of 67, Thomas Edison returned home early one evening from his work for dinner with his family. Just as he had finished eating, a man came rushing into his house with imperative news. A major fire had broken out at Edison's research and production campus a few miles away in West Orange, New Jersey.

Despite fire engines rushing to the blaze from eight nearby towns they could not contain the blaze. Fuelled by the chemicals in the various buildings, green and yellow flames shot up six and seven storeys, destroying what Edison had spent his life building.

Edison quickly made his way to the fire, where hundreds of onlookers and employees were gathered. Finding his son standing mesmerised at the scene, Edison asked him to 'Go get your mother and all her friends. They'll never see a fire like this again.' Seeing the panic on his young son's face, he calmly said, 'Don't worry, it's all right. We've just got rid of a lot of rubbish.'

The 'rubbish' that Edison referred to was years of priceless records, prototypes and research, all of which were turned to ash. In addition, the buildings, which were supposed to be fireproof, had been insured for only a fraction of their worth. Thinking they were immune to such disasters; Edison and his investors were covered for about a third of the damage.

Remarkably, Edison did not react with tears, despair and anger. Instead, he got to work. He told a reporter the next day that he wasn't too old to make a fresh start: 'I've been through a lot of things like this. It prevents a man from being afflicted with ennui' (a feeling of weariness and dissatisfaction). Remarkably, the fire that destroyed his life's work ended up energising Edison.

Thanks in part to a loan from his good friend Henry Ford, within 3 weeks of the fire, Edison's factory was partly back up and running. Within a month, his team were working two shifts a day producing new products the likes of which the world had never seen. Despite a loss of almost $1 million – more than $23 million in today's money – Edison would sustain enough energy to make nearly $10 million in revenue that year ($200+ million today). He took an unimaginable disaster and turned it into the remarkable final act of his incredible life.

So, what gave Edison this incredible outlook and perspective on the problems that he faced? Really what set Edison apart from other inventors was his tolerance for the difficulties he faced. He had an incredible appetite and willingness to tackle head on the kinds of problems most of us face at some time in our lives. He was an advocate of what is known as Stoicism.

Stoicism is an ancient school of philosophy of life founded around 300 BCE by Zeno of Citium. Zeno had been a merchant and had lost everything he had in a shipwreck. It was this adversity that drove him to become the founder of one of history's greatest philosophies. The name Stoic comes from the Greek word for porch – *stoa*. Zeno's followers met frequently to discuss their philosophy on the streets of Athens under a colonnade decorated with mythical and historical battle scenes, on the north side of the Agora in Athens, called Stoa Poikile. Anyone was welcome to listen and debate ideas, creating the very first group of Stoics.

Zeno of Citium.

The Stoic philosophy is one of practicality and focuses on the question 'How can we find a path to happiness, flourishing and prosperity?', which the Stoics called eudaimonia. Stoicism was a philosophy for the everyday men and women of the world, not just for the educated and the affluent. The path to eudaimonia is found in accepting the moment as it presents itself, by not allowing oneself to be controlled by the desire for pleasure or by the fear of pain, by using one's mind to understand the world and to do one's part in nature's plan, and by working together and treating others fairly and justly. Simply put, Stoicism was designed to help people live their best possible lives. It's a philosophy of life that maximises positive emotions, reduces negative emotions and helps individuals to hone their virtues of character. At any moment, in any situation and at any stage of life, Stoicism provides a framework for living well. It reminds people of what is truly important in life.

Stoicism is perhaps best summed up in the words of philosopher Friedrich Nietzsche when he writes the powerful words, 'amor fati' – a Latin phrase that can be translated as 'love of fate' or 'love of one's fate'. Amor fati is used to describe an attitude in which one sees everything that happens in one's life, including suffering and loss, as good or, at the very least, necessary. Indeed, when life seems to be throwing us a curveball, and our instinct is to declare 'Why me?' or 'Why is life so unfair?', amor fati can provide some solace to us.

As Nietzsche himself writes, 'My formula for greatness in a human being is amor fati: that one wants nothing to be different, not forward, not backward, not in all eternity. Not merely bear what is necessary, still less conceal it ... but love it.'

Along the same lines as amor fati is the Latin 'memento mori', which translated into English is 'remember you must die'. The point of this seemingly morbid reminder isn't to promote fear, but in fact to inspire, motivate and perhaps remind us of the one certainty we all will one day face. A reminder perhaps to worry less, and to live life more fully. Indeed, the idea of memento mori has been central to art, philosophy, literature, architecture and more throughout history. As Socrates says in Plato's Phaedo, 'The one aim of those who practise philosophy in the proper manner is to practise for dying and death'.

GOING UNDERGROUND

The Allegory of the Cave

Sometime around 380 BCE in his seventh book of *The Republic* Plato wrote of an imaginary group of prisoners who have been in chains since they were children. These prisoners are in an underground cave and have never seen the light of day; their hands, feet and necks are chained so that they are unable to move. All they can see in front of them for their entire lives is the back wall of the cave. Behind the prisoners are a fire and a walkway. Objects are projected onto the back wall of the cave for the prisoners to see. To pass the time the prisoners come up with names for the objects they observe. Understandably, they are interpreting their world as they see it. Hence, it is almost as though the prisoners are watching a puppet show for their entire lives. They believe what they are seeing is real because this is all they have ever experienced. Reality for them is this puppet show on the wall of a cave, created by shadows of objects and figures. Of course, if you had never seen the real objects before, you would believe that the shadows of objects were 'real'.

One day, one of the prisoners manages to break free of his chains. He immediately turns around and looks at the fire. The light of the fire hurts his eyes and makes him immediately want to turn back and seek sanctuary in the place that was familiar to him. Understandably, the prisoner is anxious about the things he is observing for the first time. After some time passes, his eyes adjust to the firelight. Reluctantly at first, and with great difficulty, he is forced to advance out of the cave and into the bright sunlight, the brightness of which is painful to him at first.

The first thing he finds the easiest to look at is the shadows, followed by the reflections of men and objects in the water. Finally, the prisoner is able to look at the Sun itself, which he soon comes to realise is the source of the reflections. He begins to see the truth of everything and sees that the Sun is the source of life. Feeling sorry for his fellow prisoners, who are still trapped in the cave, he makes his way back to them to explain what he has witnessed.

When he returns to the cave to explain the truth about the reality he has witnessed, he is met with hostility. His fellow prisoners feel that he is dangerous because he has returned and tried to change everyone's beliefs. The prisoners do not want to be free because they are comfortable with how they see their world. Finally, they threaten to kill him if he attempts to set them free.

This story is known as the 'Allegory of the Cave'. In this allegory Plato distinguishes between people who mistake sensory knowledge for the truth, and people who really do see the truth. Of course, as the prisoner becomes used to his new surroundings, he realises that his former view of reality was wrong.

The shadows in this story perhaps represent the perceptions of those who believe that observed evidence ensures knowledge. If you believe that what you see should be taken as truth, then potentially you are merely seeing a shadow of the truth. Similarly, the escaped prisoner represents the truth-seeker, who seeks knowledge outside of the cave and outside of the senses. The Sun possibly represents the pinnacle of truth and knowledge.

How many of us believe we experience the world as it actually is, rather than how we believe it to be? How many of us are comparable with the prisoners in Plato's cave witnessing what they believe to be reality? Similarly, how many of us, when confronted with an alternative potential reality, recoil from it believing it to be unbelievable, inconceivable or even possibly dangerous?

Indeed, are any of us in full control of what we think and what we believe? We all believe we are. In many ways our thinking is similar to one of those small, colourful, toy steering wheels that we purchase for our children – the ones that attach to the rear of the front seats of your car. As we drive along, the toddler in the back is happy steering away, fully believing that they are in total control of the vehicle. We too believe we have full conscious control over our thoughts and behaviours, but despite what we believe, as we have discussed previously, this is rarely the case.

What I hope you manage to take away from this book is the possibility that our beliefs underpin how we see the world. But is what we are witnessing how it is, or how our beliefs make us think it is. Are we seeing the world as the prisoners saw it on the cave wall, or are we brave enough to step out into the Sun and see how the world really can be for us?

HEROES

In 1949, American mythological researcher and author Joseph Campbell wrote his seminal work *The Hero with a Thousand Faces*. In his lifelong research Campbell had discovered many common patterns running through hero myths and stories from around the world. Years of research had led Campbell to discover that there are several basic stages that almost every hero quest goes through, regardless of what culture the myth is from. He called familiar structure 'the monomyth' – now more commonly referred to as 'the hero's journey'.

According to Campbell, 'A hero is someone who has given his or her life to something bigger than oneself'. Indeed, anyone can become a hero, either on purpose or even by accident, but the journey to becoming a hero involves a painful evolution that is a prerequisite to the greatness that can be achieved. Campbell defines 12 steps on that journey. Classic movies such as *Star Wars*, *Harry Potter*, *Lord of the Rings*, *The Matrix*, *Spiderman* and *The Lion King* all follow this hero's journey.

The 12 steps, as Campbell defined them, start with a call to adventure, followed by a challenge or quest that presents itself to an average person in an average world. Initially, the person is afraid and refuses that call. But with guidance from a mentor or from a piece of text, they overcome their fears, cross the threshold and commit to the journey. On this journey, the protagonist is tested, meets allies and enemies, and prepares for an ordeal – a challenge that will truly test their mettle. This ordeal forces them to face their worst fears. And when they survive this, the ordinary person is a hero and is rewarded, usually with knowledge or great insight.

The reward, however, is not the end of the story. Next, the hero must return to the ordinary world where the journey started. Transformed by their experience the hero shares with others what they've learnt on their epic journey.

The 12 steps of the hero's journey are:

1. The ordinary world;

2. The call of adventure;
3. Refusal of the call;
4. Meeting the mentor;
5. Crossing the first threshold;
6. Tests, allies, enemies;
7. Approach to the innermost cave;
8. The ordeal;
9. Reward (seizing the sword);
10. The road back;
11. Resurrection;
12. Return with the elixir.

The point I wish to make here, in examining Campbell's 'monomyth' structure, is that with any true story the hero is challenged repeatedly. For Edison, it was the fire at his factory. His stoic attitude helped him respond to the challenge he and his workers faced and allowed him to overcome this adversity and flourish. For Zeno of Citium it was the loss of his merchant's vessel that inspired him to create the new philosophy of Stoicism. As Campbell himself writes, 'If the path before you is clear, you're probably on someone else's'.

Perhaps we should all take to heart those two most powerful and grounding of quotes, 'amor fati' and 'memento mori', to remind ourselves that we will all face overwhelming adversity in our lives, and that if we constantly challenge our belief systems then we can overcome just about any challenge life pitches at us. After all, as 'memento mori' reminds us, in the end none of us is getting out alive!

Perhaps it's time to completely rewrite the beliefs that have not served you and begin to write yourself a new life story. In the words of Edward de Bono, 'If you never change your mind, why have one?'

SUMMARY

In this chapter we examine motivation and effort. Often, we can work away at something continuously and not see any results, until one day, when we may see immense growth in just a short period of time. This perhaps acts as a reminder to keep plugging away and never give up on something. It can be frustrating in those times when there seem to be constant hurdles, but often we need to look at a problem from a different angle and perspective in order to find a solution we couldn't previously find.

The chapter also explored the regrets that, as people, we all have about different things. The regrets that last the longest however are not the ones where we don't do the things, we are duty bound to do, but where we fail to live up to the ideals we have for ourselves. Most of the time we fail to do these things because we're worried about how other people will perceive us. This leads us to the question: 'Where would we be now if we had always met our full potential?'

As in any story, the hero is always challenged, and sometimes overcoming these challenges can feel impossible. But by channelling the phrases 'amor fati' – the love of one's fate – and 'memento mori' – remember you must die – you can learn to enjoy the ups and downs of life with the certainty that whoever we are, we are all certain to come to the same end point.

CHAPTER THIRTY-TWO

THE MOST IMPORTANT QUESTION

*"Every human life contains a potential.
It that potential is not fulfilled, that life was wasted."*
– CARL GUSTAV JUNG

Imagine if I told you that there is one profoundly simple question that you can ask yourself, your answer to which, I believe, could determine not only what sort of year you have but, possibly, what kind of life you can ultimately create for yourself. Don't believe me? Ok, well let's try it. This profoundly poignant question comes from theoretical physicist Albert Einstein. Einstein stated that *"The most important decision we make is whether we believe we live in a friendly or hostile universe."*

I told you it was simple, didn't I? So, what did you answer? Do you feel that the universe or indeed the world is for or against you? Of course, Einstein thinks in terms of the universe, but those of us not blessed with his genius, can reflect in terms of our own personal world view.

As I mentioned, Albert Einstein believed this question to be the single most important question any of us will ever ask ourselves. Einstein himself believed that for every example of the world being unfriendly, you can find an equally compelling example of it being friendly. It's very much about our perception.

Personally, I believe you can change this belief in a single moment. I believe, as Einstein did, that if you see the world as friendly, then you will attract a more friendly world into your life.

Not in any mystical way, but in what will be reflected back at you by how you consider others.

But here's the rub. As we have examined previously in this book, we are hardwired to see the negative before the positive. Similarly, in mediums such as the news, we are more likely to believe something negative than something positive. In addition to this, we are far more likely to believe something, if we have heard it before, even if we are not consciously aware that we have heard it before. So yes, the odds are stacked against us.

Let's think about our own experiences. Picture a day at work for example. You may have a tremendous and productive day at work, but an offhand comment from another colleague stays with you for hours, if not days! Should your partner ask you about your day, your reply most likely will be biased to your negative experience with your colleague, not the majority of your day.

Similarly, as humans, we are far more likely to recall traumatic experiences than positive ones. Our brains are wired towards the negative, not the positive. We're naturally drawn to it.

As we have examined previously in this book, avoiding pain is a stronger motivator than seeking pleasure. For example, how easy is it for us to recollect insults instead of positive praise?

Indeed, we all tend to react more strongly to negative stimuli. As a throwback from our hunter gatherer ancestors, we all have hardwired into us this largely redundant negative cognitive bias.

In an intriguing study conducted by psychologist John Cacioppo at the University of Chicago, participants were shown pictures of either positive, negative, or neutral images. The researchers then observed the participants electrical activity in their brains. Unsurprisingly, it was the negative images that produced a much stronger response in the cerebral cortex than did the positive or in fact even the neutral images.

Take a moment to reflect on that. Indeed, your entire life is being lived by your brain. The brain that never touches light, where one-third of its capacity is allocated to vision. In essence, reality is far more subjective than we suppose. But when it comes to making a significant change in your life, here is the thing - as humans we won't invest energy into things that we believe won't yield a result. Or put another way, we are far more likely to focus on a potentially negative outcome for something and we are less likely to place any effort into something if we believe the outcome won't be what we desire.

Indeed, our conscious mind is very much like a newspaper. It delivers headlines but rarely show us what's going on behind the scenes, those subconscious programmes that are running constantly outside of our awareness. We do however regularly make decisions consciously and then begin to automate them and follow them unconsciously.

Amazingly, often the simpler something seems, the more neural circuitry there usually is behind it. As we have examined throughout this book, to make a true change in your life, you first need to make something that was previously unconscious, conscious. As Carl Jung states perfectly "In each of us there is another who we do not know."

CAN'T TAKE MY EYES OFF YOU

Psychologist Dr. Thomas K. Landauer has estimated that the average person has one Gigabyte (GB) of stored knowledge in their brain. When you think about the average memory stick you can purchase on Amazon is around 32 or 64 GB, it becomes apparent why we need to easily adopt the beliefs of others. To go through our lives each day and question just about everything would not only be impossible, but quite honestly exhausting!

Your entire life is being lived by your brain. When you look out into the world and see something, light rays are directed to the back of your eye, onto the retina. When light lands on your retina, it sends electrochemical impulses through your optic nerve to your brain. Your brain then translates that image into something that you can understand. But how often do you consider your blind spot? The spot where your optic nerve connects to your retina has no light-sensitive cells, so you can't see anything there.

You don't notice it because your other eye makes up for it. Each eye sends data your brain independently, and your brain fills in what is missing. Simply put, what one eye doesn't see, your other eye does.

So, do we have blind spots in our belief systems? Do we rely on the beliefs of others to make sense of our world? I believe we do. Many of us go through our days and indeed our lives without questioning what we see and experience, believing what we see to be 'real'. At its core, this book is about not just questioning what we see, but what we believe. How many of us adopt the beliefs and belief systems of others without ever questioning their reality or indeed truth? But do we know our minds? Indeed, do we not speak our minds because in fact we don't always know our minds. As E. M. Forster remarked: "How do I know what I think until I hear what I say?"

THIS IS ME!

If we wish to bring about a significant and lasting change in our life then I believe we need to focus on shifting our self-identity, who we believe we are.

Often, we can get bogged down. For example, focusing on what I call the 'Activity'; such as losing weight, stopping smoking, creating a business, or quite simply eliminating distractions in our lives. We go about these 'activities' by, for example, starting a new diet, or setting a day to finally quit smoking, or perhaps we buy the latest book on how to get started in business.

What can often happen is, that after a few weeks, we can 'fall off the wagon', often blaming the failure on the timing of other external, uncontrollable events in our life, or indeed in the world. When however, we focus on our 'Self Identity' or what I also like to think of as the 'Why', then real, and long-lasting change can and will most definitely occur.

For example, if right now you are a parent, at no stage since your child was born have you ever forgotten that you were a parent. You are the world to your child, and at no stage is that role disremembered. In essence it has become your new 'self-identity', it is who you are.

Similarly, if you have made the decision to be a vegan or a vegetarian, then I would wager a bet that at no time have you ever returned home from a trip to the supermarket having accidentality purchased some meat produce. Of course not! Why? It is because that is who you are. That is not only how you think of yourself, but how you wish to be viewed by others. Nothing and no one can change this sacred belief you have about yourself, to the extent you never ever need to think about it. It's as if it is part of your programming.

The same can be true if you view yourself as somebody who is religious, or perhaps has strong political beliefs, it is extremely unlikely that another person or agency can easily change your fixed beliefs in these areas.

Recently, I worked with a terrific young client who said to me that he goes out and drinks heavily every weekend because that is what everyone does. It wasn't until he stood back and examined his beliefs around this activity that he began to question its irrationality. I recall him affirming to me that 'it's just what you do at the weekend, absolutely everyone does it'. Often the stories we tell ourselves about why we do something are underpinned by the tremendous need to believe that very thing. In this instance if I believe that 'everyone does it', then I reduce any possible cognitive dissonance. By believing that if everyone does it, then I am only doing the thing that everyone already does.

It is those 'stories' that we tell ourselves that can make all the difference between concentrating solely on the 'Pursuit' and the potential transformation in our 'Self-Identity, the 'Why'. As I have discussed previously in this book, and in the words of author Robert Trivers, the more we believe our own lies, the more sincerely, and hence effectively, we can mislead others. In simple terms, often we can deceive ourselves in order to deceive others.

We don't necessarily do this consciously, but we all do it. That is why, as in the diagram below, we must be extremely mindful of the 'stories' we tell ourselves about who we are and why we want to accomplish something. It is far easier for someone who wants to lose weight and get fit, to think of themselves as 'slim, fit and healthy', even before they actually are, because everything they do will then be filtered through the 'is this what someone who is slim, fit and healthy would eat' paradigm. Similarly, is this activity something a 'slim, fit, healthy' person would partake of?

In January of 2022 I had the pleasure of meeting and watching a presentation by, English Footballer Francis Benali. During his incredible and motivational speech, Benali shared how, when he first joined the football team that he became associated with, he was amazed at how brilliant some of the other players were. He stated that they had a 'God Given' natural talent, something he felt he didn't have to the same degree. To balance this, he spoke about how he made the conscious decision to not drink alcohol, not to smoke and to eat well for his entire footballing career. He stated that other players indulged in these potentially negative pastimes far more regularly than perhaps they should have. From that moment onwards, Benali made that decision - that became his self-identity, and he never questioned it. That is who he was and to this day still is. In the same vein, someone who has the self-identity of a slim, fit, healthy person is rarely, if ever, tempted to stray from this identity, as another way of thinking would not be aligned with who they are.

THE SELF IDENTITY FLOW

THE PURSUIT
Lose Weight, Stop Smoking, Get Fit, Write a Novel, Start a Business, Procrastinate Less etc

THE STORY
The Story We Tell Ourselves And Others About Who We Are And What We Want

SELF-IDENTITY
The Why

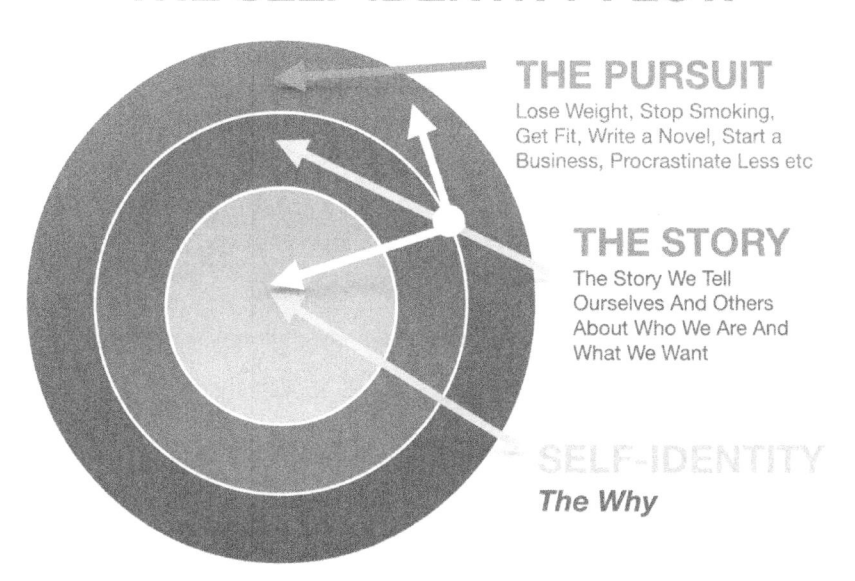

As I have mentioned previously in this book, in the words of writer and motivational speaker Jack Canfield, when it comes to motivation to make a change '99% is a Bitch: 100% is a Breeze'.

Let's dig deeper into what I call the 'Self Identity Flow'. When we are in the 'flow' life can be much easier. We don't have to use our cognitive processing power to think too much, we just do it. We are in cognitive ease. Similarly, when we are focusing on a particular activity that we are passionate about, we can easily lose track of the time - hours can appear like minutes. Sports professionals and Olympians search for this often elusive 'flow' to achieve maximum success in their chosen field. The state of 'flow' is when everything appears aligned and when all progress seems effortless.

Self-identity flow occurs when you are totally aligned with what you want to achieve, and the changes you wish to make, until they are part of who you are. For example, there is little effort in being a Vegetarian or Vegan other than dining choices at home or in a restaurant. We may wish to take it further and support causes that care for the welfare of animals, and we may wish to inspire others. But one thing is certain, we are rigid in our identity. It is extremely unlikely another human could make us alter our view about this.

Our Self-Concept is the image we have of ourselves in our mind. It is how we see ourselves and how we wish to be viewed by those around us. There is total alignment with our beliefs and our world view. Again, all behaviours are belief driven. As American author Scott Turow writes; "Who are we but the stories we tell ourselves, about ourselves, and believe?"

Over the past twenty or so years, I have worked with clients who have experienced the most horrendous abuse as children, yet as adults have the most incredible and positive outlook on life. Similarly, others who have had the most idyllic childhoods but are suffering from the most debilitating depression and anxiety.

From one client who recently purchased an incredibly expensive sports car yet found the purchase only made him more unhappy with his life, to others who have needed to come to me to help them to quit smoking despite being given just a few years to live by their doctor.

Some who appeared to have the world at their feet, but had incredibly low self-esteem, to others who couldn't help but see the negative in just about everything, not just in their own life but in the world as a whole.

As people of this incredible planet, we are all full of peculiar habits and individual neurosis. Not only do we have no idea how others think, but often, we have little idea how we ourselves think, and make sense of the world around us. Our own personal 'blind spots' if you will. Perhaps then the true purpose of therapy is to begin to truly know ourselves better, and in doing so allow ourselves to move forward to a fresher, more insightful perspective. As author Sandra Cooze writes *"The most rewarding journey you can ever embark on is the journey to your Self".*

My sincerest wish is that what we have examined in this book will springboard you to the life you want and deserve. To focus on changing your self-identity, to becoming the person you wish to be. Free from anxiety and stress and living more in the moment. Enjoying the little things as well as your big successes in life.

I began this book with a quote from psychologist and philosopher William James, so it only seems fitting to end it with his poignant and stirring words. I hope they resonate with you and inspire you to carve out the life you desire for yourself.

> *"The great use of life is to spend it*
> *for something that will outlast it."*
> *— William James*

James Holmes

Spring 2022

Chapter 30 Summary

In the final chapter of the book, we look at whether or not you see the world as a friendly or a hostile place and how this can be changed by the way that we think. The chapter goes on to explore how our brains are hard-wired to have a stronger response to negativity – whether this be in the news, or in our own day-to-day lives.

The second half of the chapter discusses our self-identity, and how this can impact on us when we are looking to change a habit. Our behaviour will align with who, or what, we believe we are – so by changing the beliefs we hold about ourselves and our identity, we can more easily change our behaviours.

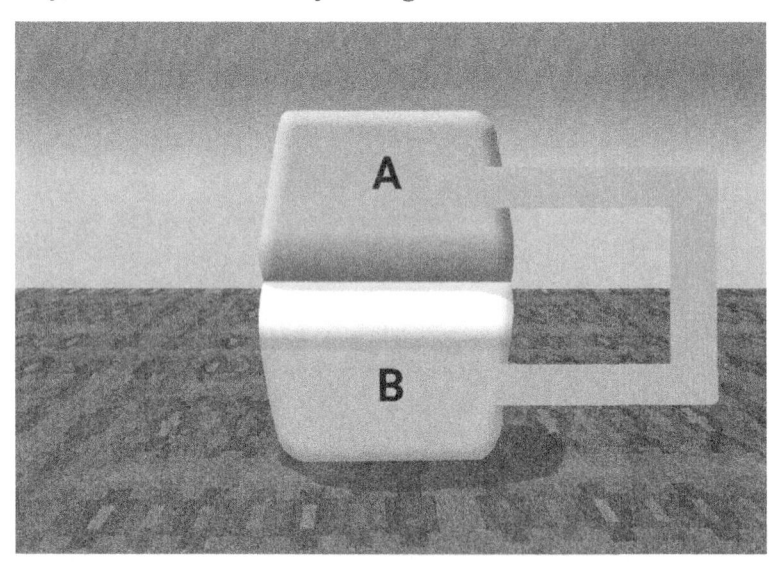

FIGURE A.

REFERENCES

Auden, W. H. & Jacobs, A. (2011). *The Age of Anxiety: A Baroque Eclogue*. Princeton University Press.

BBC (2016). *The Doctor Who Gave Up On Drugs* (No. 1).

Bechara, A., Damasio, H., Tranel, D. & Damasio, A. R. (2005). The Iowa Gambling Task and the somatic marker hypothesis: Some questions and answers. *Trends in Cognitive Sciences, 9*(4), 159–162.

Benedetti, F., Colloca, L., Torre, E., Lanotte, M., Melcarne, A., Pesare, M., Bergamasco, B. & Lopiano, L. (2004). Placebo-responsive Parkinson patients show decreased activity in single neurons of subthalamic nucleus. *Nature Neuroscience, 7*(6), 587–588. https://doi.org/10.1038/nn1250

Birley Rowbotham, S. (2018). *Zetetic Astronomy*. Adansonia.

Bottoms, H. C., Eslick, A. N. & Marsh, E. J. (2010). Memory and the Moses illusion: Failures to detect contradictions with stored knowledge yield negative memorial consequences. *Memory, 18*(6), 670–678. https://doi.org/10.1080/09658211.2010.501558

Bowen, W. (2013). *A Complaint Free World: How to Stop Complaining and Start Enjoying the Life You Always Wanted*. Three Rivers Press.

Bstan-vdzin-rgya-mtsho & Cutler, H. C. (1999). *The Art of Happiness: A Handbook for Living*. Coronet.

Campbell, J. (2008). *The Hero with a Thousand Faces* (3rd ed). New World Library.

Chiappori, P.-A., Levitt, S. & Groseclose, T. (2002). Testing mixed-strategy equilibria when players are heterogeneous: The case of penalty kicks in soccer. *American Economic Review, 92*(4), 1138–1151. https://doi.org/10.1257/00028280260344678

Christensen, C. M., Allworth J., & Dillon, K. (2012). *How Will You Measure Your Life?*. Harper Business.

Coué, E. (2011). *Self Mastery Through Conscious Autosuggestion*. Stokowski Press.

Diener, E. (Ed.) (2009). *The Science of Well-being*. Springer.

Diener, E. & Seligman, M. E. P. (2002). Very happy people. *Psychological Science, 13*(1), 81–84. https://doi.org/10.1111/1467-9280.00415

Epley, N. (2015). *Mindwise: How We Misunderstand What Others Think, Believe, Feel, and Want*. Penguin.

Farias, M. & Wikholm, C. (2019). *The Buddha Pill: Can Meditation Change You?* Watkins Publishing.

Frankl, V. E. (2004). *Man's Search for Meaning: The Classic Tribute to Hope from the Holocaust*. Rider.

Gilovich, T., Medvec, V. H. & Savitsky, K. (2000). The spotlight effect in social judgement: An egocentric bias in estimates of the salience of one's own actions and appearance. *Journal of Personality and Social Psychology, 78*(2), 211–222.

Greenwell, R. (2019). *How To Wear A Crown: A Practical Guide to Knowing Your Worth*. KDP Self-Publishing.

Hand, D. J. (2015). *The Improbability Principle: Why Coincidences, Miracles and Rare Events Happen All the Time*. Corgi Books.

Harris, S. (2010). *The Moral Landscape: How Science Can Determine Human Values*. Free Press.

Heath, C. & Heath, D. (2010). *Switch: How to Change Things When Change Is Hard*. Broadway Books.

Hebb, D. O. (2012). *The Organization of Behavior: A Neuropsychological Theory*. Routledge.

Herrman, H., Kieling, C., McGorry, P., Horton, R., Sargent, J. & Patel, V. (2019). Reducing the global burden of depression: A Lancet–World Psychiatric Association Commission. *The Lancet, 393*(10189), e42–e43. https://doi.org/10.1016/S0140-6736(18)32408-5

Hof, W. (2020). *The Wim Hof method*. Rider.

Hone, L. (2020). *3 Secrets of Resilient People*. TED.

International Food Information Council (2012). *2012 Food and Health Safety Survey*.

Isaacson, W. & Jobs, S. (2015). *Steve Jobs*. Abacus.

Kahneman, D. (2012). *Thinking, Fast and Slow*. Penguin.

Katopol, P. (2017). Maybe best practices aren't: How survivorship bias skews information gathering and decision-making. *Library Leadership & Management, 32*(1). https://doi.org/10.5860/llm.v32i1.7287

Keller, J., Kwasnicka, D., Klaiber, P., Sichert, L., Lally, P. & Fleig, L. (2021). Habit formation following routine-based versus time-based cue planning: A randomized controlled trial. *British Journal of Health Psychology, 26*(3), 807–824. https://doi.org/10.1111/bjhp.12504

Koenig, J. (2021). *The Dictionary of Obscure Sorrows*. Simon & Schuster.

Konner, M. (1990). *Why the Reckless Survive – And Other Secrets of Human Nature*. Viking.

Krech, G. (2002). *Naikan: Gratitude, Grace, and the Japanese Art of Self-reflection*. Stone Bridge Press.

Latham, G. P. & Locke, E. A. (1979). Goal setting – A motivational technique that works. *Organizational Dynamics, 8*(2), 68–80. https://doi.org/10.1016/0090-2616(79)90032-9

Lee, H. (2016). *To Kill a Mockingbird*. Cornelsen Verlag.

Lyubomirsky, S. (2010). *Hedonic Adaptation to Positive and Negative Experiences*. Oxford University Press. https://doi.org/10.1093/oxfordhb/9780195375343.013.0011

Mack, A. (2003). Inattentional blindness: Looking without seeing. *Current Directions in Psychological Science, 12*(5), 180–184. https://doi.org/10.1111/1467-8721.01256

Maltz, M. (2015). *Psycho-Cybernetics: Updated and Expanded*. Perigee Books.

Maslow, A. H. (2013). *A Theory of Human Motivation*. Wilder Publications

Millard, J. (2009). Performing beauty: Dove's 'Real Beauty' campaign. *Symbolic Interaction, 32*(2), 146–168. https://doi.org/10.1525/si.2009.32.2.146

Nightingale, E. (2013). *The Strangest Secret in the World*. Merchant Books.

Pinker, S. (2018). *Is The World Getting Better or Worse? A Look at the Numbers*. TED.

Rokeach, M. (1964). *The Three Christs of Ypsilanti*. Knopf.

Sanders, R. (1987). The Pareto Principle: Its use and abuse. *Journal of Services Marketing, 1*(2), 37–40. https://doi.org/10.1108/eb024706

Schlosser, M., Sparby, T., Vörös, S., Jones, R. & Marchant, N. L. (2019). Unpleasant meditation-related experiences in regular meditators: Prevalence, predictors, and conceptual considerations. *PLoS ONE, 14*(5), e0216643. https://doi.org/10.1371/journal.pone.0216643

Sharma, R. S. (2015). *The Monk Who Sold His Ferrari: A Spiritual Fable About Fulfilling Your Dreams and Reaching Your Destiny*. Thorsons.

References

Skinner, B. F. (1948). 'Superstition' in the pigeon. *Journal of Experimental Psychology, 38*(2), 168–172. https://doi.org/10.1037/h0055873

Slung, M. (1986). *Mother Knows Best—A Timeless Collection of Maternal Wisdom*. Century.

Trivers, R. (2014). *Deceit and Self-Deception: Fooling Yourself the Better to Fool Others*. Penguin.

Tversky, A. & Kahneman, D. (1991). Loss aversion in riskless choice: A reference-dependent model. *The Quarterly Journal of Economics, 106*(4), 1039–1061. https://doi.org/10.2307/2937956

Wegner, D. M. (1994). Ironic processes of mental control. *Psychological Review, 101*(1), 34–52.

Wurtzel, E. (1995). *Prozac Nation: Young and Depressed in America*. Riverhead Books.

Zerega, W. D., Tseng, M. S. & Greever, K. B. (1976). Stability and concurrent validity of the Rotter Internal-External Locus of Control Scale. *Educational and Psychological Measurement, 36*(2), 473–475. https://doi.org/10.1177/001316447603600230

Printed in Great Britain
by Amazon